SEEDS OF
MAGNOLIA

Dorthy Pulliam Hake
take care and best wishes
Bill Miller
September 27 2014

BILL MILLER

ISBN: 1494938308
ISBN-13: 9781494938307
Library of Congress Control Number: 2014900453
CreateSpace Independent Publishing Platform
North Charleston, South Carolina

DEDICATION

Ruby Miller and I are not much when we are apart, but
together we can take on the day. Whenever I run into
that infamous brick wall, she tells me that I can
climb over, or knock a hole in it and keep
on going ... then I do it to show
her that she was right.

Chase Dyle, Kiev Graham, and Rhonda Miller are the
seeds that we planted. Almost every day, I let them see
me
with a book in my hand, albeit sometimes
a facade, to keep the light shining
that they see in me.

Acknowledgments

Rebecca Davis, Professor of English
Grambling State University
Grambling, Louisiana

Katie Miller, Professor of English
Tennessee State University
Nashville, Tennessee

Some people impact our lives more than others.
Sometimes they do it, and we're not even aware of what
they are doing until years later. In my life, Rebecca
Davis and
Katie Miller were two of those people.
They were outstanding educators.
Both are now deceased, but
they are two people
that I will remember.

ONE

Austin Miller was single. He had been scratching and clawing for a long time, trying to get out of the hole that sometimes made him wonder if it had become his home forever. He had heard about the light at the end of the tunnel, but it had never shone in his eyes. Yet, he could see a shadow every now and then, one that had to have been cast by a ray of brightness from somewhere— he just needed to keep moving in the right direction.

Although modest, he had purchased his first home. He had bought Elizabeth to be his housekeeper. She had been dragged along from North Carolina to Tennessee with the Taylors. She had been their housekeeper, and since she had done it before, she could hit the ground running with no training required.

Elizabeth had absolutely no idea as to what life might be like with Austin Miller—he could stick her in the cotton fields from sun up until sundown if he wanted to— but she was sure that she would rather be his slave than to be owned by the Taylors. The Taylors had sold most of her family prior to moving to Tennessee. She had been separated from her mother, her siblings and almost all of her other relatives. Therefore, she hated the Taylors. Elizabeth had been hoping for a chance to get away from the Taylor plantation. On the other hand, Mrs. Taylor had been as anxious to get rid of Elizabeth as Elizabeth had been to get away from her. Mrs. Taylor wanted to get rid of Elizabeth, because Elizabeth had a daughter named Sophia, and Sophia's father was Mrs. Taylor's husband. Therefore, when she sold Elizabeth and Sophia, she was glad to see both of them hit the road, and her attitude was goodbye and good riddance.

Elizabeth didn't expect things to be any different just because Austin Miller held the papers on her and her daughter—going from one slave owner to another was not a step up. She felt like all slave owners were about the same. They got whatever they could get from you, and when they didn't need you anymore, they got rid of you. Still, she was glad just to get away from where she had been.

When Mrs. Taylor told Elizabeth that she and Sophia had been sold, it didn't come as a surprise. Mr. Taylor had died, and Mrs. Taylor had decided to clean house. The first thing on her list was to get rid of those two constant reminders of her husband's infidelity.

The few things that Elizabeth and Sophia called theirs had been stuffed in a sack. They waited on the porch for their new owner to show up and take possession—sold like a cord of wood, the only difference being that they could climb aboard rather than having to be tossed on. When Mr. Miller arrived, he and Mrs. Taylor stood on the porch and talked. While they talked, Elizabeth had placed their things in the buggy, and she and Sophia had climbed aboard. They had taken the back seat, and they sat there waiting. Aside from the fact that they had been sold, they knew nothing else. Elizabeth didn't know if she would be his housekeeper, or if she would work in the fields, and she didn't try to anticipate.

Mrs. Taylor and Mr. Miller had already confirmed their business transaction at his office in town. Mr. Miller had the understanding that he had purchased Elizabeth. When he saw Elizabeth and a child sitting in his buggy, he told Mrs. Taylor that he had only bought Elizabeth. Mrs. Taylor told him that the child belonged to Elizabeth, and that she had sold both to him. Still, that had not been his understanding, because a child had never been mentioned as being part of the deal.

The problem for Mr. Miller was that he didn't need or want Sophia, because he didn't want a child on the loose running around the house creating a ruckus. On the other hand, Mrs. Taylor didn't want her either—if left up to her, she may have turned her loose and let her run wild. Sitting in the buggy, Elizabeth could hear them arguing, and she could hear enough of their conversation to know why.

She prayed that she wouldn't have to leave her daughter behind to become the property of someone else. After some haggling, Mrs. Taylor must have negotiated a deal that Mr. Miller couldn't refuse, maybe a discount or something like that. Whatever the case, he ended up with Elizabeth, and her daughter.

Sophia sat very close to Elizabeth—almost under her—because she was afraid. During the trip, Mr. Miller didn't say anything, and neither did Elizabeth or Sophia. They didn't talk, probably because they had nothing to talk about. Elizabeth had no idea as to where they were going, and no idea as to what it would be like. Yet, it didn't really matter, because wherever they were going she would still be a slave.

When Mr. Miller had arrived at his home, he climbed down from the buggy. Elizabeth and Sophia were still in their seats, sitting there looking around at the place that would be their new home. Mr. Miller still hadn't spoken—he hadn't said a single word since leaving Mrs. Taylor's place. Standing near the buggy, he had looked up at Elizabeth and then nodded his head, suggesting that they could climb down. After Elizabeth had gotten down, she then reached up to help Sophia.

Mr. Miller had gotten their sack of belongings from the buggy. He carried the sack, and Elizabeth had grabbed what was left. She walked along behind him with Sophia holding on to her dress. When they were inside, Mr. Miller showed Elizabeth and Sophia to their room, while at the same time, explaining his expectations of her. Only then did he tell her that his name was Austin Miller.

Mr. Miller had told Elizabeth that he needed someone to take care of things around the house—a housekeeper. He explained that he was not married, and that there would only be three people in the house, he along with Elizabeth and Sophia. He had told her what he did to earn a living, and that he sometimes worked late at his office in town; sometimes he worked late at home; and he didn't like being bothered—no doubt referring to Sophia, not wanting to be disturbed by a noisy kid running around.

A couple of months had passed, and Elizabeth had become familiar with the daily routine, and what was expected of her. She had learned that Mr. Miller was an early riser, and that he cared more for a cup of coffee than he did for bacon and eggs. Yet, she cooked breakfast every morning, but she wondered why. She had realized that he was right when he explained things to her on the first day that she arrived. He did work all day in town, and it was hard to guess when he might return home at the end of the day. Sometimes, he worked at home and well into the night.

She had also noticed that he didn't talk a lot, and he let her take care of things around the house in her own way. It had become obvious to her that he didn't pay much attention to the way that she did things, perhaps because he was too busy doing his own thing. Therefore, she had assumed that whatever she did, and whatever her methods, it must have been alright with him.

Mr. Miller's law office was located within walking distance of his home. As a businessman and politician, out of town trips were rather common. Whenever he was away, only Sophia and Elizabeth were left in the house. Still, Elizabeth went about her daily activities as usual while Sophia entertained herself.

Taking care of Mr. Miller's house was not a job that kept her very busy. She could cook and clean house, and still had lots of time to spend outside with Sophia. Whenever Sophia was outside, Elizabeth usually sat on the porch, or out in the yard on the bench.

Eventually, Elizabeth had gotten to the point where she didn't mind working for Mr. Miller. If she had to be a slave, she felt like she would rather be his slave than anyone else's. She had decided that he was a big improvement compared to where she had been. She didn't know many slave owners, but she knew very well how some treated their slaves. Since being owned by Austin Miller, she felt like life for her and Sophia had gotten to be a little better.

Elizabeth had cleaned up and wiped down everything that she could reach. She had walked through the house looking to see what was next, but there was literally nothing else to do. It was a strange feeling for her, because never before had she ever had idle time—she felt awkward. She had gone outside, found a seat in the backyard, and sat down while keeping an eye on Sophia. She felt so awkward that she wondered what Mr. Miller would do if he had walked up and saw his slave sitting in the shade out back.

After a while, three girls about the same age as Sophia had wandered into the yard. They walked over to Elizabeth, and asked if they could play with her—referring to Sophia. Elizabeth had been talking to the girls when three women walked around the corner of the house. She had been surprised when the girls walked up, but she was more surprised when she saw the women. She stood up as they walked over to where she had been seated.

One of the women explained that they had been sitting in the yard talking when they noticed that their children had wandered off. One of the women had started reprimanding the girls for leaving without letting them know. When one of the girls said that they had just come over to play, Elizabeth offered to keep an eye on them if they wanted to let them stay for a while.

The women knew that Mr. Miller was not married, and they knew that Elizabeth had been his housekeeper for several months. They had seen Sophia several times in the yard, and they had assumed that she might be one of Mr. Miller's relatives. Since they were there, one of them asked about Mr. Miller's relationship to Sophia. Elizabeth told them that Sophia was her daughter, and that she was not related to Mr. Miller. Only then did they realize that Sophia was a slave just like Elizabeth.

Sophia and the other three girls had gone out into the yard, and started playing together. Their parents introduced themselves to Elizabeth, and then they connected each girl with the proper mother. They had decided to let their children stay and play with Sophia for a while.

That day when they wandered into the backyard was the beginning of a relationship that would last a long time. It would become a relationship that would mend some fences, tear some down, and on others, remove some barbs. Traditional social values would eventually evolve into a mini-social order completely different from that of the surrounding populace. It would happen in the most unlikely of places.

Several days had passed, and Mr. Miller had been in his study sifting through some papers as usual. When he peered outside from the window, he was surprised when he saw four girls playing out back. He walked out onto the porch. Elizabeth had noticed his curiosity, and she told him who they were. She hoped that he wouldn't be angry, since she had given them permission to come over. He told Elizabeth that he knew the girls, because he was well acquainted with their parents. Elizabeth realized that he didn't mind them being there after he had said that Sophia was probably glad to have some playmates.

After he had gone back inside, Elizabeth started thinking about Mr. Miller. She had thought that all slave owners were alike, but then she wondered if some might be different. The slave owner to whom she had belonged prior to Austin Miller had been very strict. He didn't stray much from the unwritten rules regarding the handling of slaves—the lash had been common, and it didn't collect dust because it had been hanging on the wall for so long and gone unused.

However, her new owner didn't seem to care that Sophia played with the girls from across the street, and nor did their parents. In time, Mr. Miller's backyard had become their playground. When circumstances permitted and more often than not, they could be found out back under the shelter of the big oak tree. Eventually, but only symbolically, the big oak would become theirs.

Elizabeth had set the edge of Mr. Miller's yard as the line fence for Sophia, and that was as far as she could roam. However, when their day at school had ended, the other girls crossed that imaginary line almost at will, and walked into their playpen. Sophia didn't know one hour from the next on a clock, but her instinct would tell her when to expect Amanda, Caroline and Emily.

Since Sophia was a slave, formal education was an absolute no-no. However, as time passed, she had learned to read and write just from being around the other girls. She had learned because they taught her while playing school—one girl would pretend to be the teacher and the others would be the students. They taught her the things that they had learned in school. Eventually, and through the simple processes of association, and emulation, Sophia had adopted the mannerisms, and dialect of the girls that she had played with, and she learned to use them fluently.

As with most children, they had not been separated by the established standards that had been set by society. Instead, they were just friends, someone to play with, and nothing else mattered. Appearances and attitudes had been such that they were completely unconscious of the racial and social inequities characteristic of traditional customs. Passersby seeing them playing in the yard, or romping up and down the street that had clearly been established as off limits, saw or heard nothing to indicate that one was a slave.

Elizabeth had said to Mr. Miller that the parents of Amanda, Caroline and Emily seemed to be good people. Her comment had been prompted by the fact that they didn't care about their daughters playing with Sophia. She had been a house servant since the time that she was old enough to work. She had learned early in life that white people didn't want their children to be around slave children, let alone socialize with them. Yet, there in plain view in Mr. Miller's yard, it had never seemed to matter.

Amanda, Caroline and Emily were usually out back with Sophia every afternoon. Elizabeth had been sitting out back keeping an eye on them. Mr. Miller had walked out onto the porch, and without speaking, he stood there with his eyes fixed on the children. After a while he walked back inside, still without saying anything. It was something that he had done several times before. Elizabeth always wondered what it was that he was looking at, and what he might be thinking.

Elizabeth had already considered that the day would come when Amanda, Caroline and Emily would abandon their relationship with Sophia for more conventional ties—go back to society's norms. If Sophia's friends didn't break off their relationship, she wondered how long it would be before their parents decided that it had become time. Yet from little tots to adolescence, they had stayed together. Instead of society's social wedge splitting them apart, they had become like sisters. No others in town could be like them, because their relationship was on the scale of one in a million, and their town was too small.

The time had come when Elizabeth and Mr. Miller both noticed that they had let go of the games that they used to play. Yet, they had been in the backyard as much as ever. It was still too soon for anyone else to agree with their personal assessment, but they had gotten to the age where they no longer considered themselves to be children. The games that they once played had been left behind for the amusement of those that would come along after them.

Since they had abandoned their former pastimes, they found other interests to while away their times spent together. Whenever Amanda, Caroline and Emily came over, they usually sat together under the big oak tree and talked. Sometimes, after her friends had gone home, Elizabeth would ask Sophia what they had talked about. Most of the time, she would get the same response. Sophia would tell her that they didn't talk about much, they had just been talking.

They had let go of what they thought were foolish things that occupied the minds of children. They had started to focus their attention on a subject that they deemed more relevant—boys. Whenever they were together, they could talk about boys, but dating, they had to keep that thought within their own circle. Before they could go on a date, they would have to go through the same process as a fine wine; they had to age a bit more before they would be ready. Yet, they had two things that they had been looking forward to, the town picnic, and the chance to flirt a little with the boys when no grown-ups were watching.

The picnic had become a community affair, and a common means of entertainment in an era that was literally oblivious, and therefore, void of technological diversions. Amanda, Caroline and Emily had been attending the picnic each year for as long as they could remember. That had sounded like a long time to them when they told Sophia, but their memories could only take them back about ten years or so. Still, they felt like it would be so different from the past. As teenagers, they would be able to stroll around on their own, and be less of a target for the watchful eyes of their parents. It would be a time when the boys could look at the girls, and each girl would wonder if she's the one that he had his eyes on.

Sophia knew that she wasn't going, and she had no expectations of going. It was an event for whites only. Still, it excited her about as much as it did Amanda, Caroline and Emily. Although they had shared a close bond from the very beginning, Sophia knew when to step back, and let them go their way without any questions. It had always been that way, and she knew why. Yet, she could hardly wait until they were together again, so that she could be filled in on what had happened.

The picnic had always been on Sunday afternoon, and Monday afternoon meant getting together at Mr. Miller's house to visit with Sophia. That would be the day when they would sit out back under the big oak tree, and relive the happenings of the day before. They would recall everything, and they didn't leave anything out—gossip or not, they didn't care.

The picnic had been born with the idea of it being a wholesome family oriented occasion, an event where children could romp around and have fun, and parents could sit and talk for hours on end. That had always been the intention, but invariably, someone had a jug of moonshine hidden somewhere, but only for the purpose of an occasional sip. On the other hand, there had always seemed to be someone that didn't consider himself to be a drinker, but just might find himself in need of a mid-afternoon pick me up—something to get rid of that sinking feeling.

Amanda, Caroline and Emily had been in Mr. Miller's backyard with Sophia—it was Monday, the day after the picnic. They all laughed when they talked about old man Jacobs. He had had a few too many sips from the jug—but it did belong to him—and he had to be literally thrown across his horse, because he couldn't steady himself well enough to climb up unassisted. Then, there had been the brawl between Billy Ray and Thurmond. Both were teenage boys, but unlike old man Jacobs, they were sober. Both boys had been competing for the attention of a girl named Hannah.

The brawl had started out as a petty quarrel, and it ended up being a petty fight. With clenched fists, Billy Ray and Thurmond mostly circled each other like two roosters, neither wanting to use his spurs against the other, and each hoping that the other would back away. While Billy Ray and Thurmond had each other occupied, another boy had Hannah occupied. She and her beau had been standing off to the side holding hands, and watching the makeshift scuffle. Hannah had no interest in either Billy Ray or Thurmond. Later during the afternoon, Emily had seen Billy Ray and Thurmond tossing horseshoes together. They had apparently forgotten about Hannah, probably because she had forgotten about them.

Sophia listened as they told her about the trivial goings-on, but what she really wanted to know about was what they had done. Sophia knew that Amanda, Caroline and Emily would all comb the crowd for the new boy that had moved to town. She had never seen him, but she had heard them talk about him. His family had purchased a house down the street, and the girls had seen him a few times, but it had always been from a distance. They had been hoping that he would attend the picnic, and he did.

Amanda, Caroline and Emily had walked around until they spotted him. Emily had already found out that his name was Caleb. They wanted to talk to him, but they had all been too shy to do anything other than keep him in sight, and stare at him whenever he wasn't looking. Caleb didn't know many people, and that made him pretty much a stranger. He had mostly been walking around alone, probably wanting to talk to someone just as much as they wanted to talk to him—especially the girls.

Amanda, Caroline and Emily were not the only girls that had found Caleb handsome, and wanting to get acquainted. However, the other girls had the same problem that they had. They were all too shy to walk up to him, and start a conversation. As they walked through the crowd, they could hear the other girls talking about how cute he was. They had come to the conclusion that if they didn't make a move soon, some other girl would, and they would come up lacking.

Amanda and Caroline had been walking a few steps ahead of Emily, and all three were walking directly toward Caleb. When they had met, Amanda and Caroline spoke to him, but they kept on walking. He had smiled at them, and said hello. Emily had been looking at Caleb when Amanda and Caroline spoke to him. Suddenly, she decided that it had to be now or never. She had to do something to get Caleb's attention.

Emily walked toward Caleb, and just when she was in front of him, she put on a stellar performance. She had pretended to stumble, and was going through the motion of falling, but she had everything timed perfectly. Just as she had hoped, Caleb extended his arms, and caught her before she could fall to the ground. Caleb stood there, holding her in his arms, while she enjoyed the moment. Emily looked up at him, and said that she may have sprained her ankle. Caleb had suggested that she sit on the ground, but she had told him no. Instead, she asked Caleb if he would help her over to the nearby bench, so that she could sit down for a spell.

Emily leaned against Caleb, and he still had his arm around her waist to provide assistance that she didn't need. He helped her over to the bench where she sat down. Caleb had knelt down in front of her to try and assess the extent of her injury. While holding her foot with one hand, he gently rubbed her ankle with the other. Emily had told him that she didn't think that it was anything serious. However, Caleb insisted that she not stand on it for a while, not until she had made sure that it was alright. While sitting there, Emily apologized to Caleb for falling into him, but he quickly assured her that it wasn't necessary. He said that he was glad that he just happened to be there to keep her from falling.

Emily and Caleb spent the rest of their time at the picnic together, a good portion of it sitting on the bench talking. Every once in a while, Caleb would kneel down, hold her foot in one hand, and gently rub her ankle, but it was only to see if there had been any swelling. Whenever he applied what she thought had been sufficient pressure on her ankle, she would let him know that it was still a bit too painful to walk on.

After a short while, Emily had become the envy of every girl that had been hoping to talk to Caleb. Amanda and Caroline had witnessed Emily's entire performance. Beginning with the time that she had stumbled, they knew that it had all been an act. However, Emily had played the part so well, and it played out just the way that she had intended. When they had finished telling the incident to Sophia, Emily stood up and danced around. She laughed, and said that the pain in her ankle had gone away, and then, they all laughed.

Slave children worked in some capacity when they were no more than ten years of age, or even sooner. There was no such thing as getting the work done, and then having some free time. Instead, when one job was finished, they moved on to another—and another was always waiting. All day and every day—except on Sunday—they had to at least go through the motion of being busy. That had always been the expectation, but it had never seemed to apply to Sophia. Mr. Miller had never seemed to mind that she spent so much time with her friends. She did help Elizabeth with the housekeeping chores, but there had never been a lot to do, and therefore, it didn't take long to get it done. After all, there were only three in the house to clean up after.

Amanda, Caroline and Emily had completed their education in the local school system. The time had come for them to go away for a few months to attend finishing school. While away at school, among other things, they would learn proper etiquette along with good cultural and social graces. They would be taught the things that an affluent southern belle should know.

Sophia had already thought about how boring it would be when they left. There would only be Elizabeth and Mr. Miller around for her to talk to. She wouldn't be able to talk about the same things with them that she could talk about with her friends.

Amanda, Caroline and Emily would all be attending the same school. They had been excited about the idea of being away from home for a while, and more excited about the fact that the three of them would be there together. Sophia had been wondering what it would be like if the four of them could go away, and attend school together. Although she wondered, she didn't talk about it—not to them. She knew for sure that she wouldn't be going anywhere, and thinking about it would only be a depressing waste of time.

Sophia and Elizabeth had made the move with their master from North Carolina to Tennessee, but that had been a long time ago. It had been so far back that any memories that Sophia had of North Carolina were all but gone. She had wondered what it might be like to visit other places. She wondered because, the edge of Austin Miller's yard had pretty much marked the extent of her travels, at least that was about all that she could remember clearly.

Sophia didn't even know what things looked like on the other side of town, because she had never been there to see for herself. She had once said to Elizabeth that if she decided to run away, she would probably end up right back where she started, because she wouldn't know which road to take to get out of town.

In addition to Amanda, Caroline and Emily, several other girls in town would also be going away to school. Their parents had planned a social affair for them—a going away party. Most of the girls had been pretty much like Sophia; they had never been anywhere except around town. Still, that was further than Sophia had been. They all felt like they would be leaving behind their make believe world of yesteryear, and stepping into the new world of here and now—about to become grownups.

Unexpected circumstances had made it necessary for Amanda's mother and father to be away from home for a couple of days. They didn't want to leave their daughter at home alone, and like her parents, Amanda had no desire to be left alone. Consequently, they had made arrangements with Mr. Miller for her to stay at his house while they were gone.

If Amanda needed a place to stay, Sophia was glad that it would be in Mr. Miller's house. Amanda had been satisfied as much as Sophia with the arrangement. Through the years, Sophia, Amanda, Caroline and Emily had all become close friends. As much as they cared for each other, it had become obvious to Elizabeth and Mr. Miller that the strongest bond had always been between Sophia and Amanda.

It had not been by chance that Amanda would be staying at Mr. Miller's house. As soon as she had found out that her parents had to be away from home, she told Sophia. Sophia and Amanda had talked about the possibility of her staying at Mr. Miller's house, and the idea sat well with both. Therefore, the only thing that Amanda had to do was to talk her parents into agreeing on what she and Sophia had already plotted for them to do.

Amanda's parents had left town during the morning. During the afternoon, Amanda had a piece of luggage, and she was on her way to Mr. Miller's house. A neighbor passing by had recognized her, and even though it wasn't far to walk, he gave her a ride in his buggy. Upon seeing the buggy arrive at Mr. Miller's house, Sophia knew who it was, and she had gone outside. Amanda had stepped down from the buggy, and she and Sophia grabbed each other. Seemingly unconscious of their surroundings, they walked together, talking and giggling, and both holding onto Amanda's single piece of luggage.

Mr. Miller and Elizabeth had been standing on the porch when Sophia and Amanda walked inside. They had brushed past them without a single word, and neither Mr. Miller nor Elizabeth said anything to them. Amanda had been busy whispering words that were barely audible to Sophia, and Sophia didn't want to miss anything. They had entered the house as if no one else was around—just the two of them.

Mr. Miller had looked at them very intently when they walked past. For a while, he seemed to be in a trance. He stood there with Elizabeth, but he didn't say anything. Elizabeth felt like he may have been looking, but unable to see, or looking and not wanting to see what he was looking at—she didn't know. However, to her it seemed like he may have been lost in his own thoughts. Perhaps questioning not just his own morality with regards to the social order of existence, but questioning that of his country's as well. In the end, it appeared that he had gotten things together again, and he had gone back inside.

Sophia and Amanda had spent most of the afternoon together in the privacy of Amanda's temporary room. Amanda had received some literature from the school, and she had it with her. They looked at the brochures, and tried to imagine what it might be like to be so far from home for such a long period of time. Amanda had told Sophia that the school was for girls only, and that the girls would not be allowed to leave the campus. They both had considered that to be a major drawback.

Eventually, they got around to unpacking Amanda's belongings. She had gotten a new dress to wear to the party. They had placed the dress on the bed so that they could have a better look at it. Then, Sophia asked Amanda to stand in front of the mirror. She held the dress up against Amanda to see what it might look like when she put it on. Standing there looking at the dress, they both had agreed that it was beautiful, and that it would be a perfect fit.

Later during the evening, Elizabeth had told Mr. Miller that supper was ready. On his way to the dining room, he stopped by Amanda's room, and tapped on the door. Sophia opened it, and Mr. Miller asked Amanda if she would please join him for supper. Amanda had been sitting on the side of the bed, but she got up immediately. After she had told Mr. Miller that she and Sophia were both hungry, she started moving toward the door. Suddenly she stopped, first to gaze at Sophia, and then at her host. The room had suddenly become quiet, because they had all heard Amanda's response to Mr. Miller's invitation.

Amanda had inadvertently made the mistake of assuming that the three of them would be dining together. Due to their relationship, she had forgotten about the fact that Sophia was a slave. Amanda knew very well that slaves did not dine at the table with their master. However, she had spoken without giving due consideration to the words that she had said, or their implication. In doing so, she knew right away that she had put her best friend on the spot, and she had created an embarrassing moment—something that she would never do intentionally.

Sophia had been trying to disguise Amanda's blunder. She had suddenly turned, and started fumbling around with the new dress that had been placed back on the bed. She tried to pretend that she was unaware of what had been said. Mr. Miller quickly assessed the situation, and he resolved the issue in the most unconventional of ways. He looked at Sophia, and very suggestively, he asked her if she had planned on joining Amanda for supper.

He had asked Sophia in such a way to make it seem like it was not uncommon, and that he had really been expecting her to dine with them. Sophia was slow to process his invitation, or his reason for asking her to dine with them. She just didn't get it, because being asked to dine at the table with white people—one of them being the slave owner that owned her—had been more than uncommon, it was an invitation that she had never had.

Finally, Sophia had put two and two together. Slowly, and reluctantly, she and Amanda had started making their way to the dining room with Mr. Miller following them. He waited until they had sat down—across from each other—and then he sat at the head of the table. Elizabeth had gone back outside after telling Mr. Miller that supper was ready. Consequently, she had no idea about what had taken place inside.

Sophia felt awkward, and she tried to hide her feelings. After all, she had been placed in a most unthinkable position. Still, she wanted to maintain her composure and ladylike posture in front of her friend, and her host as well. Mr. Miller had her doing something that she had never done before, and she didn't have time to prepare— she had never even thought about it.

Elizabeth still hadn't become aware of the to-do that had taken place inside. She had been busy creating some fresh floral arrangements for the house. Needing some help, she had gone inside to get Sophia. She had to walk past the dining room to go to where she thought Sophia might be. Not paying much attention, she had almost made it past the dining room when it dawned on her that three people were sitting at the table. She had stopped to take a second look, and she saw that one of the three was Sophia.

Like Sophia, it had taken a few seconds for Elizabeth to figure out what was going on. When she did, she placed her hands on her chest as if having a heart attack. She stared at the trio sitting at the table, and they sat there staring back at her—no one said a word. Elizabeth had taken a step backwards, and then she leaned backwards toward the wall, hoping that she was close enough for it to catch her before she could fall to the floor. For a short while, she had made a bigger scene than the three at the table had made. She shouted at Sophia, and asked her what in the world she thought that she was doing.

Mr. Miller could see that Elizabeth had gotten all worked up. He knew that Sophia had been confused, even before Elizabeth had walked in. Therefore, he decided that he should explain things. He assured Elizabeth that everything was alright. He said that he had asked Sophia to join him and Amanda for supper. Still, Elizabeth was as confounded as ever. She couldn't believe what she had seen, and she couldn't believe that Mr. Miller had asked Sophia to join them for supper. Never in her life had she seen what appeared to be such a brazen move by a slave owner, or such an act of insubordination by a slave. Elizabeth felt like Sophia and Mr. Miller had both crossed the line.

From Elizabeth's point of view, it had been something that should have never taken place. She knew the social position that slaves occupied, and Sophia was in the wrong place. She wondered if Mr. Miller had lost his mind, because what he had done seemed crazy to her. Elizabeth had left the dining room, and gone back outside—fumbling around with her flowers. Still stunned and confused over the sight that she had just witnessed, she had to sit down just to give herself some time to sort things out.

Mr. Miller could detect the thoughts that had to be going through everyone's mind. He could tell that there was an obvious tone of uneasiness with Sophia and Amanda. The tense feelings that they had before Elizabeth walked in had been amplified—big time. He tried to ease the tension by engaging Amanda in conversation. He questioned her about school, and how she felt about being away from home for a while.

Amanda knew that his attempt at conversation had been nothing more than an effort to smooth things over, and remove some of the wrinkles. Still, she responded to his queries as if they had been real. While they talked, Sophia had been unconsciously moving food around on her plate, while trying to show that she was interested. At the same time, she had been trying to disguise the nerve racking predicament that she had been placed in.

Sophia hadn't said anything. Nervously, she sat there, her eyes moving from left to right, looking at Amanda, and then at Mr. Miller. He had tried to get her involved in the conversation, probably hoping that it would help Amanda relax.

In the past, he had come to Sophia's rescue many times; but sitting at the table with him, she felt so down and out that she couldn't help him. She didn't know how. He had to sink or swim, because he was on his own. As long as they had been around each other, they had never talked much. It had been her choice—not his—but he didn't know why. If he had been expecting that to change, it wouldn't be while they were sitting at the table together.

Timidly, Sophia and Amanda looked at each other from across the table. The only thing that they wanted to do was to get up and leave, but that would be rude. Sophia was ill at ease, because she had been caught up in the midst of an uneasy setting, one that had been spawned by her best friend's unintentional slip of the tongue. Eventually, the three of them had finished eating—none too soon for Sophia and Amanda. Mr. Miller had gone to his study and Amanda to her room.

It hadn't ended for Sophia; she still had to deal with Elizabeth. She had been furious at the sight of her sitting at the table with Mr. Miller and Amanda. Sophia had peeped out back, trying to determine Elizabeth's frame of mind, but she couldn't tell. Elizabeth had gone back to work with her flowers. Sophia didn't want to, but she had gone outside, and stood near her mom. Since she didn't know what to say, she stood there watching. After a while, and just loud enough to be heard, she told Elizabeth that she was sorry.

Elizabeth didn't say anything, and she kept on working with her floral arrangements. Her silence had been so loud that Sophia wished that she would end it by saying something—anything—just get it over with. After a while, she did. When Elizabeth spoke, her voice didn't have the usual soft tone; instead, it was forceful. Sophia listened while Elizabeth told her off. When Elizabeth had almost finished raking her over the coals, she told her that she was a slave, and she should never forget it.

Sophia knew as well as Elizabeth that she was a slave. When Mr. Miller had invited her to have supper with him and Amanda, she didn't recognize it as being an invitation. Instead, she had recognized it as a request, or more so, a command from the person that owned her. She didn't consider that saying no thank you was an option, not for her.

Pursuant to his so called invitation, she had responded in the manner that she had interpreted as being an order in disguise. Sophia and Elizabeth had both sat down. Sophia had been hoping that she could explain things so that Elizabeth would understand, but Elizabeth didn't want to listen.

After a while, they found themselves sitting closer to each other, and Elizabeth had quieted down. Still daunted, Sophia tried again. She said that Mr. Miller had asked her to join them for dinner, and that she had been afraid to say no. Her feelings had been hurt, partly because Elizabeth wouldn't even listen to her explanation, and partly because of the harsh words that she had spoken. She had been looking directly at Elizabeth when she said that she had never forgotten that she was a slave. Then, Elizabeth knew that of all the things that she had said to her, reminding her that she was a slave had hurt her the most.

However, Elizabeth still felt like there had been times when Sophia really did forget that she was a slave. When she had given that thought its' due, she realized that she didn't know any other slave that could ever forget that they were a slave. If her daughter's life had been such that she could sometimes forget, then she deemed it a blessing—halleluiah.

Sophia felt like she had come to that fork in the road, and like always, her only choice was to go left or right, but either way would be the wrong way. When Elizabeth looked at her, she was sure that she had stepped on her a little too hard, especially after listening to her explain how things had happened, and how she had interpreted them. Then she wondered if maybe she should have just kept quiet from the beginning—everybody would have forgotten about it a lot sooner.

Elizabeth realized that Sophia, dining at the table with Mr. Miller and Amanda, had been far from ordinary. At the same time, Mr. Miller's invitation had also been far from ordinary. Elizabeth loved her daughter, and she knew that she had been hurt by her ill spoken words. After she had apologized, Sophia laid her head on Elizabeth's shoulder, and closed her eyes, but she was still awake. Elizabeth felt like Sophia had always been the only other person in her part of the world—she didn't want to ruin it.

Elizabeth was almost mindless, because she didn't want to think about anything. She focused on the nesting birds, and the beautiful flowers in the backyard. Everything seemed so peaceful and quiet. After a while, the quietness around them, and Elizabeth's love and compassion had settled their differences. Sophia sat up, and she had given her mom a kiss on the cheek, letting her know that all was well. It had been so quiet in the house that Sophia decided to do a walk-through. She had noticed Mr. Miller sitting at his desk, and consumed by a tall stack of papers—she didn't let him see her. Amanda had left the door to her room slightly ajar, and she was sound asleep.

Later, Elizabeth had walked pass the door to Mr. Miller's study. When he saw her, he spoke her name to get her attention. He knew that she had been angry with Sophia, because of what had happened in the dining room.

25

He said that Sophia and Amanda were good friends, and that he just decided to ask her to join them for supper. He said that it didn't hurt anything, and there had been no reason to be upset about it.

He admitted to seeing how awkward and tensed, they had been. Still, he thought that everything had worked out fine, and there had been no reason to be angry. He was still trying to smooth things over. He could sense that everybody in the house had been as nervous as could be, except maybe for himself.

The afternoon had turned into evening, but the transition seemed to be ever so slow. Sophia had decided that she should get Amanda up. She needed to try on her new dress, and make sure that it would fit properly, especially since she had never had it on. When Sophia got to her room, she found that Amanda had already gotten up, and was in the process of trying on the dress. Sophia helped her, and when Amanda finally had the dress on, she stood in front of the mirror. Again, both had decided that it was beautiful, and that it fit perfectly.

While talking to Sophia, Amanda had been looking at herself in the mirror. She kept on talking, but her eyes had shifted to Sophia's image in the mirror. She said that she was sorry for the way that she had answered Mr. Miller's question when he invited her to dine with him. She also said that she didn't mean to embarrass her. Although she had been, Sophia denied being embarrassed, and she told Amanda that she should forget about it. When Amanda asked about Elizabeth, Sophia said that she was okay.

Elizabeth had been back and forth around the house, and when she came to Amanda's room, she paused for a moment to listen. Then, she tapped on the door, and walked in without waiting for a response. That had always been Elizabeth's style, tap, open, and walk in, with no pauses. As she stood there holding the door, she told Amanda that she was beautiful in her new dress.

Elizabeth walked closer to have a better look. She saw that it was a perfect fit in the waist and shoulders, but she had noticed that it was just a tad too long. With Amanda still wearing the dress, Elizabeth checked to see how much of a hem would be needed to get the right length. When she had finished, Amanda took the dress off, and Elizabeth had taken it to her room. Meanwhile, Amanda had started doing some other things while giving Elizabeth enough time to hem the dress. Sophia had gone with Elizabeth.

When Elizabeth had finished altering the dress, Sophia took it back to Amanda. She had been standing in front of the mirror holding a brush, and complaining about how difficult it was to manage her hair. Sophia placed the dress on the bed. She took the hairbrush from Amanda, and told her to sit down so that she could do her hair. Once again, they had started chatting about what the evening might be like, and what to expect.

Sophia had made sure that the door to the room was closed before asking Amanda who was escorting Emily to the party. Amanda told her that she was going with Caleb. Amanda said that they had been sweet on each other ever since Emily had faked that sprained ankle. Sophia wondered if Emily had ever told him the truth about her stumbling.

When Amanda stopped talking, Sophia asked her if anything was wrong. She said that it would be so much fun if all four of them could go to the party together. Then Amanda started talking about how wrong it was for people to have slaves. Sophia listened, and she figured that Amanda's mind had probably gone back to the misunderstanding that had happened in the dining room. However, she didn't comment, she simply kept on brushing her hair.

After a while, their thoughts had gone back to something easier to talk about. Sophia knew that David would be Amanda's escort for the evening. She knew because David and Amanda had been nurturing a crush on each other for quite some time.

At last, the hour had come. It was time for Amanda to finish getting herself ready—David would be arriving pretty soon. She had put on the new dress, and they could see that Elizabeth had been right when she suggested altering the length. As Amanda waltzed around the room, she paused just long enough to say that she hope David would like it. Sophia told her that David would probably have his eyes on her rather than the dress.

Sophia pushed her in front of the mirror, and told her to have another look at herself. As Amanda stood in front of the mirror, Sophia said that he'll like the dress, and he'll like you too, because he'll be with one of the most beautiful girl's in the world. Sophia's rave review reinforced some of what Amanda had already been thinking, but not quite to the extent that Sophia had described.

They had been expecting David to arrive at any time. Amanda and Sophia were still fiddling around in the room. Amanda had been back and forth in front of the mirror, still wondering if she looked alright. Sophia had been nipping and tucking at her dress, while lecturing her on proper etiquette, and the dos and don'ts of her first date—one that she had never had, still she had lots of advice. Finally, they both had agreed, everything was perfect.

Elizabeth had walked into the room, and she had given Amanda a silk hankie. She looked at her in the dress, and then told her that she was beautiful. At the same time, Mr. Miller's voice rang out announcing the arrival of Amanda's escort. Sophia had told Amanda to wait in the room while she went out to meet David. They had already decided that they were going to make him wait, because they didn't want David to think that Amanda had been waiting for him. When Sophia was about to exit the room, she looked back and told Amanda that she would let her know when it was time to walk out.

Elizabeth had been listening to them scheming for several minutes. She asked Sophia what made her such an expert on courtship. Sophia had been on her way to the front door, and she never paused when she answered Elizabeth's question. She said that it's good to let him wait, even if it's for no reason other than just to make him wait.

Sophia and Mr. Miller stood on the front porch, and watched as the carriage came to a stop. Amanda had parted the drapes, so that she could secretly watch from the window. It was obvious that David was as nervous as Amanda. Yet, he had managed to step down from the carriage, and boldly make his way toward Mr. Miller and Sophia with sufficient confidence and pride. He had shaken hands with Mr. Miller, and then he acknowledged Sophia. Politely, Sophia curtsied, and then told him that she would tell Miss Amanda that he was here.

Sophia went back inside, and told Amanda that David was handsome. Amanda was ready to go outside, but Sophia had told her that it was too soon. Sophia went back to the porch to tell David that Miss Amanda would be out shortly. Elizabeth had been watching, and she thought that it was all so silly and unnecessary, but she hadn't said anything.

Again, Sophia had left David on the porch with Mr. Miller, and she had gone back inside. She told Amanda that Mr. Miller had been laying down the rules. He had told David that he expected him to be a perfect gentleman during the evening. Amanda said that he had probably put the fear of God in him, and then she laughed. Sophia said that he might be afraid to touch you. Amanda had been placed in Mr. Miller's custody, but they didn't want him to scare David too much, and spoil the evening.

Once more, Amanda asked Sophia if they had made him wait long enough ... not yet. Sophia told her to be patient, and let him wait just a little longer. While they were waiting, Elizabeth had seen enough of their antics. She accused both of them of being silly and ridiculous. She had told them to stop all of their foolishness, and she told Amanda to get outside.

Finally, Amanda had composed herself long enough to once again ask if she looked alright. Elizabeth tinkered around a bit with her dress, and at the same time she had been pushing her toward the front door. Mr. Miller held it open when he saw her approaching.

Sophia had been absolutely right when she said that Mr. Miller had been laying down the rules for David. Amanda had been placed in his care for a couple of days, and he would look after her as if she had been his own daughter. He had told David that he could dance with her, and he could hold her hand, but anything more than that would be too much.

Feeling a bit timid after Mr. Miller's somewhat stern lecture, David had assured him that he would be nothing less than a perfect gentleman. Mr. Miller knew that there would be chaperones present to keep things the way that they should be. Still, Amanda had been placed in his care, and he intended to give her back to her parents in the same condition that she was in when she had first arrived.

David helped Amanda into the carriage, and then he climbed aboard. After he had been seated, the driver summoned the horse's attention, and they were off. As she watched them ride away, Sophia wondered if she would ever be picked up by a handsome young man, and carried off for an evening of pampering, and social excitement—someday maybe, she thought.

David, riding away with Amanda had reminded Sophia of one of the tales that they used to read from the storybook when they were all kids—she had been swept up, and taken away by the handsome prince. Standing next to Mr. Miller, they both stared down the street. Even though the carriage had nearly gotten out of sight, they kept watching. Mr. Miller had said that he was going to sit on the porch for a while. Sophia heard him, but she didn't say anything. She had a smile on her face when she turned, and went back inside.

Sophia told Elizabeth that Mr. Miller had decided to sit outside for a while. Elizabeth poured a cup of coffee; she gave it to Sophia, and told her to take it to him. She knew that he would have several more cups before the evening had ended, and that he would sit out there for more than just a while. He would be sitting right there on the porch until David returned with Amanda. On her way to the porch with the cup of coffee, Sophia stopped by his study, and picked up a couple of newspapers from his desk.

When she was back on the porch, Sophia placed the cup of coffee on the small table that was nearby, and she had put the newspapers on his lap. Without saying anything, she had turned to go back inside. Just when she had reached for the door, Mr. Miller started talking, and she stopped. He said that you and Amanda seem to be really good friends—knowing all the time that they were best friends. Sophia paused for only a moment, and then said that she did like Amanda. As quickly as she had answered his question, she turned and walked away.

Numerous times, Mr. Miller had tried to engage Sophia in conversation, maybe just to get her to talk, and sometimes maybe to really see how she felt about things. However, his attempts had always been countered by Sophia's brief, but direct responses, followed by a quick retreat. She had always sought to avoid talking to him, but he didn't know why.

After a while, Sophia had gone back to Amanda's room to tidy things up. When she walked in, she found that it was already quite neat. Still, she slowly shuffled a few things around here and there, not that it was necessary, and then she sat down on the side of the bed. Later, she wondered what Amanda, Emily and Caroline might be doing.

When she had stopped wondering about Amanda, Caroline and Emily, Sophia though about what her mother had said when she saw her dining with Mr. Miller and Amanda. She had merely sat at the table with them, because Mr. Miller had asked her to. She knew that dining with them had been nontraditional, and she herself felt extremely uneasy. However, she had been sharply censured by her mother for doing so.

Sophia knew very well why Elizabeth had reacted the way that she did—she was out of her element. Elizabeth had never seen it before, and as a slave, it was never supposed to happen. Still, she wondered why or how it was possible for some people to see such unbelievable differences, and have such strong opinions of others based simply on the color of their skin. It seemed strange to Sophia, because it had never mattered to her, Amanda, Caroline and Emily.

While pondering her own situation, Sophia started thinking about the inequalities between white and black people. Then, she wondered what life might be like for the slaves that worked in the fields from daylight until dark. She couldn't relate directly to their problems, because most of what she knew about their labors was what she had been told by Elizabeth, or what she had overheard from listening to others talk. She had heard about the many atrocities that plagued blacks. Yet, she lacked personal experience, because most of her brief life had been sheltered by Elizabeth, and although a slave, in the not so bad confines of Mr. Miller's home.

Sophia thought about Amanda, Caroline and Emily a lot. They were the only people that she knew that were her own age. For years, they had played together, and one of them had become her very best friend. Mr. Miller owned her and Elizabeth, and he owned them in the same way that a person owned livestock. Yet, he had always treated them in such a way that at times, Sophia had to wonder if Elizabeth might have been right—maybe every now and then she did forget that she was a slave.

Sophia had let herself get bogged down with deep thinking. She had asked Elizabeth if she thought that the world was strange, or is it just the people that were strange. Elizabeth said that it made no difference if the world was strange, or if the people in it were strange. She said that it's a big mess no matter how you look at it.

Elizabeth hadn't responded to her question in the way that she had expected. Sophia said that she had just been thinking and wondering about things.

When Sophia had walked away, Elizabeth looked at her, and wondered what she might be like when she becomes an adult. She wondered, because it had been so apparent that Sophia's life style had been very different from that of any other slave she had ever known. She didn't know if that was good or bad.

Elizabeth knew how slaves had always been bought, and then sold when their owners no longer needed them. If for whatever reason, she and Sophia ended up with another slave owner, she questioned whether or not Sophia would survive in a world away from Austin Miller—no other slave owner would tolerate her off the cuff attitude, or her laid back happy-go-lucky life style.

Elizabeth and Mr. Miller both knew that Sophia's attitude about white and black relationships had always been different. Mr. Miller had never seemed to mind, and if he did, he never said anything about it. Sometimes when it seemed that she had gotten too far out of line, it had always been Elizabeth that brought her back to reality.

Sophia knew that she and Elizabeth lived in a nice home—it wasn't theirs, but it was nice. They wore good clothes, and they were treated with dignity—excluding the fact that they were slaves. At the same time, she also knew that she and Elizabeth were no different from the field hands. When everything was over and done, they too would have nothing to show for their labors, because their pockets would be empty as well.

When she thought about Amanda, Caroline and Emily, and even Mr. Miller, Sophia couldn't understand the social disorder of existence between human races, and how it had come to be. She couldn't understand what had happened that allowed one race of people to go to church on Sunday, worship God, and then act as lord and master over another. When the sermon ends, they say amen and walk away, assured that the gates of Heaven will be opened wide when they get there—expecting to shake hands with the Savior, and get a warm welcome ... "Well done, thou true and faithful servant."

The day had seemed to pass so quickly, but then the clock slowed down as if it had grown old and tired. The pace around the house had become like that of a snail. Elizabeth and Sophia sat and talked about this and that, and nothing in particular. Mr. Miller was still sitting on the porch. He had exhausted two newspapers, and the good part of a pot of coffee—Sophia had been refilling his cup. He had dozed off several times, only to be awakened by the sounds of the night, and wondering if David had been keeping his hands to himself. Yet, he had remained steadfast with his first decision. He would be sitting right there on the porch when he brought her home.

Mr. Miller had been caught somewhere between asleep and awake, when he heard the carriage coming down the street. Slowly he stood, and removed the watch from his pocket. It was a little after ten o'clock—a decent hour he considered. He had walked over and leaned against the column on the porch, all the time keeping an eye on the carriage, and trying to see the passengers.

When they had pulled in and stopped, David stepped down, and then he helped Amanda. Arm and arm, and like a lady and a gentleman, they made their way toward the house. Seeing Mr. Miller standing on the porch, David had been just as nervous then as he had been when he picked her up. He had already hoped that ten o'clock wouldn't be too late with Mr. Miller. To help him relax, Amanda had told him not to worry, but that had been easy enough for her to say—it didn't do much for David.

When they were within speaking distance, Mr. Miller asked if they had enjoyed the evening. Both responded at the same time with a spirited, "Yes sir." They had stood outside for a few minutes making small talk. Then David turned to Amanda. He had thanked her for a wonderful evening, bowed as he kissed her hand, and then he said goodnight. Mr. Miller had said that David seemed to be a nice young man. He then held the door for Amanda, and they went inside.

Elizabeth had been asleep, but Sophia was wide awake. She couldn't sleep, because her mind had been entertaining too many thoughts of what might be going on at the party. She had heard Amanda and Mr. Miller when they entered the house. She had stayed in her bedroom just a couple of minutes; enough time so that Mr. Miller could say goodnight to Amanda, and then go to bed. When she felt like it had been enough time for Mr. Miller to be gone to his room, she quietly started making her way toward Amanda's room.

She had rounded the corner when she saw Mr. Miller still talking to Amanda. It was too late for her to back up and hide, so she just stood there, and looked at him. Amanda was still standing in the doorway to her bedroom. Mr. Miller figured that they wanted to talk, so he told them that he would see them tomorrow. He had correctly assumed that Sophia had been waiting for Amanda to come back, and that he may as well let them have some time together before going to bed.

Sophia had followed Amanda into her bedroom and closed the door. They sat on the bed and spoke softly, being careful not to disturb Mr. Miller or Elizabeth. Sophia started questioning Amanda. She wanted to know if she had fun, did they dance, and what it was like being with David.

They had been talking for a long time when Sophia asked Amanda if David had kissed her. Just as Amanda was about to speak, there was a light tap on the door. When they heard the tap, the door had already been opened. It was Elizabeth. She told Sophia that it had gotten way past her bedtime, and that she could talk more tomorrow. Elizabeth and Sophia said goodnight to Amanda, and then closed the door.

The next morning, Elizabeth was up before dawn. When she had dressed, and left the room, she left the door wide open, so that any sounds that she made would disturb Sophia as much as possible. Later, the aroma of freshly brewed coffee had spread throughout the house, and it had gotten Mr. Miller's attention. Whenever he smelled the coffee, he knew that Elizabeth was in the kitchen, and it was time for him to crawl out of bed. However, he had been awakened before he could smell the coffee. He couldn't sleep because of the noises coming from the kitchen. Elizabeth had been dropping pots and pans just to disturb Sophia—letting her know that she should have gone to bed sooner.

Sophia had crawled out of bed. She knew that the noises had been deliberate, and she knew what they meant. After she had gotten dressed, she went to the back porch to wash her face and hands, so that she could come to life.

Mr. Miller had entered the dining room carrying one of the out of town newspapers that had been delivered on an almost regular schedule. Sometimes it would be one that he may or may not have already gone through. He had spoken to Elizabeth and Sophia, and then sat down for his first cup of coffee. Sophia had placed his food on the table in front of him, and without saying a word, he sat there reading. It had become a morning ritual, one that occurred like clockwork—day in and day out.

Very slowly, Amanda walked into the kitchen. She and Sophia both had planned on sleeping late, but she had gotten up early for the same reason that everybody else had gotten up—noises coming from the kitchen. Mr. Miller had asked Amanda to have a seat, and join him for breakfast. She declined his offer, and said that she was going to sit out back for a while and enjoy the morning.

Elizabeth told Mr. Miller that she didn't know why he had even bothered to ask Amanda to join him for breakfast. When he had asked why, she said, because he wasn't going to do anything but sit there and read, and drink coffee. She told him that if the food wouldn't spoil, she would just keep it until tomorrow morning, and give it to him again.

Elizabeth refilled his coffee cup. When it was full, she said that she had a good mind to just start making a pot of coffee every morning, and let that do. Mr. Miller went on with his morning ritual, acting as if he hadn't heard a single word, and maybe he hadn't.

Sophia had headed toward the back porch to talk with Amanda, but Elizabeth stopped her. Elizabeth knew that she was going out there just to talk. Sophia had turned around when Elizabeth spoke her name. She told her that she could get started straightening up the bedrooms, while she finished up in the kitchen. Sophia did as she was told, but she really wanted to go out back with Amanda.

Mr. Miller never paid any attention to Elizabeth or Sophia. He kept sitting at the table with his newspaper in hand, and every now and then, verbalizing his thoughts as he read. When he had finished, he told Elizabeth that he was leaving for his office, and that he would be there all day long. He didn't really have to tell her, because that was what he did every day, and she already knew it.

Elizabeth was still fussing about the fact that Mr. Miller didn't touch any of the food that she had put on his plate. Talking out loud to herself, she wondered what he would do if she got up every morning and made a pot of coffee, and then went back to bed. Sophia had heard her talking, and she knew that Mr. Miller had gone. When she walked into the kitchen, she looked around, but she didn't see anyone other than Elizabeth. She asked Elizabeth who it was that she had been talking to. She said that she hadn't been talking to anybody.

Elizabeth asked Sophia if she had finished with the bedrooms. Sophia said that Amanda had cleaned up her own room, but she hadn't finished with Mr. Miller's room. Elizabeth told her to get back at it, so that she could get through. Slowly, Sophia made her way toward Mr. Miller's bedroom. It wasn't long before she had things in order. When she had gone back to the kitchen, Elizabeth told her that she could sit down and eat breakfast. After she had put food on her plate, Sophia went outside to be with Amanda. She had been reliving the night when she was with David.

Sophia had sat down next to Amanda, and they had started talking, being careful not to be overheard by

39

Elizabeth. Unconsciously, Amanda had taken a slice of bacon from Sophia's plate, and then she told her everything, even how she felt when David had kissed her. She said that they kissed on the way to the party, and he had kissed her several times on the way home. She said that the last time had been when they were pulling in at Mr. Miller's house.

Sophia told Amanda that Mr. Miller had been sitting on the porch waiting for her to come home. She said that she didn't realize that he had been on the porch until they had stepped down from the carriage. Sophia asked her if she thought that he had seen them kissing. Amanda couldn't say for sure, but she hoped not.

Sophia had been listening to Amanda, and she tried to imagine what it would feel like to be kissed by a boy, because she had never been so lucky. Not only had she never been kissed, she had never had a boyfriend. Furthermore, she had never had the chance to have a boyfriend, and the possibility of having one seemed slim to her. In fact, it was pretty much impossible. The only time that she and Elizabeth had ever been away from Mr. Miller's house was on Sundays when they would go with him to church.

Elizabeth and Sophia had to sit in the back. A few other slaves had always sat back there with them, and there had been a couple of boys that had gotten Sophia's attention. Sometimes they made eyes at each other, but that was all. Sophia's opinion had been that they may as well have been a thousand miles apart, because the church, especially the white folk's church, was no place to start up a romance.

Amanda and Sophia had started thinking about something that they could do to help pass the time. They had the entire day together, and they wanted to do something other than just sit around the house. The problem was that they didn't have a lot of options. They couldn't even walk around the neighborhood without causing a stir.

Mr. Miller had returned home. It hadn't been long since he had left to go to his office. He told Elizabeth that he had come home to get some papers that he needed. Meanwhile, Amanda had come up with something for her and Sophia to do other than sit around the house. They could spend the day at her parent's house since it was just down the street. It had been an idea that pleased both of them, because they would be away from Elizabeth, and they could talk about whatever. Since Emily and Caroline lived nearby, they could invite them over, but first, they had to get themselves there.

Although they liked the idea of lounging around together at Amanda's house, they still had a hurdle to overcome. They had to get permission from Elizabeth. If she didn't' give them the okay, then they weren't going anywhere. Sophia knew that the probability of Elizabeth saying no was greater than the probability of her saying yes. They definitely couldn't tell her that Emily and Caroline might be joining them, because then, the answer would be no for sure.

Elizabeth didn't mind the four of them being together, but she wouldn't want the four of them being in Amanda's house while her parents were gone. Sophia and Amanda didn't feel like they would be hiding anything by not mentioning Emily and Caroline. They hadn't talked to them, and therefore, they didn't know for sure if they would be coming over anyway. However, that was all secondary.

Amanda and Sophia had gone inside to talk to Elizabeth. As soon as they had gone into the house, they heard Mr. Miller's voice. They hadn't expected to see him again until toward the end of the day. However, since he had come home, the odds had shifted considerably in their favor. Sophia knew that Mr. Miller had always been less strict than her mother. Although they had planned on asking Elizabeth for permission, Sophia knew that she would more than likely say no. Amanda had presumed just the opposite. She thought that they should wait until Mr. Miller had left, and then ask Elizabeth.

They had stayed out of sight while discussing whom to ask. Realizing that Mr. Miller was about to leave, Sophia had to stop explaining things. She told Amanda to hush, and go ask her mom for permission before Mr. Miller left. Sophia then pushed her into the room.

When Mr. Miller saw Amanda and Sophia, he asked them if they had anything planned for the day. Amanda was closest to him, but she didn't say anything, not until Sophia had poked her in the back with her thumb. Amanda had gotten the hint, and while asking the question, she was cognizant of her body language. She had chosen to stand more squarely in front of Elizabeth than Mr. Miller. In doing so, it would appear to Elizabeth that she was talking to her. They just needed to make sure that Mr. Miller was there to hear the question. They couldn't have Elizabeth thinking that they had bypassed her in order to get to Amanda's house. Yet, in a way that was exactly what they were doing.

After asking the question, Amanda had taken a short step backward—like making sure that she was out of Elizabeth's reach. Then she looked at Elizabeth, and then at Mr. Miller. Just when Mr. Miller was about to speak,

Elizabeth started talking. She had taken a step closer to Sophia. She hadn't referred to either of them by name, but they knew that she was talking to both of them.

Elizabeth wanted to know what it was that had led them to think that they were going to spend any time at somebody else's house. With Elizabeth staring her in the face, Sophia had taken it to mean that her mom was waiting to hear what she had to say. Still, she didn't say anything. Instead, Sophia looked at Mr. Miller, very intently, and he recognized her plea.

Mr. Miller had started to say something, but Elizabeth cut him off once more. She had accused Sophia and Amanda of sitting around all morning scheming in order to get out of the house. Her accusation had been correct, and Mr. Miller figured as much. Yet, Sophia's assessment of Mr. Miller had also been correct. He told Elizabeth that they were probably bored, and just needed something to do. Elizabeth said that she could give them plenty to do. Still, Mr. Miller said that it would be alright, and that he would take full responsibility should there be any questions.

Mr. Miller had left the house, and headed back to his office. That left Amanda and Sophia there with Elizabeth. Even though Mr. Miller had given them permission, they still weren't going anywhere unless Elizabeth said that they could. She questioned them as if they were in a courtroom. They had to explain why it was necessary for them to go to Amanda's house. Amanda told her that they didn't have anything special planned; they would probably just sit around and talk. With that response, they had to explain why they had to go to someone else's house to sit around and talk.

Amanda had been looking at Sophia, and Sophia knew that she was asking her to help. Sophia couldn't think of anything new to add to what had already been said, so she said it again. She told Elizabeth that they just wanted to be alone, so that they could talk about things. Elizabeth had had enough of their shenanigans. She left Amanda and Sophia standing near the front door wondering what had gone wrong.

Again, Sophia and Amanda found a seat on the back porch. When Mr. Miller had given them permission to go to Amanda's house, they thought that they were on their way, but Elizabeth had stepped in and foiled their plan. With their plan gone awry, they knew that the day would be just like Mr. Miller had said, boring.

After a while, Elizabeth found them sitting quietly out back—moping and not saying a word. Yet, she got a hug from both of them after she had said that the only reason that they were going anywhere was because Mr. Miller had come home. On their way to Amanda's house, Sophia told Amanda that if Mr. Miller hadn't been at home, her mom wouldn't have let them leave. She said that the best time to ask is when Mr. Miller is around, because he had always been more likely to say yes than her mom.

Sophia was a teenager, but she had seen the inside of only two houses that she could remember, the one that belonged to the Taylors, and Mr. Miller's house. When she entered Amanda's house, she looked around, and was amazed at the beautiful furnishings. She had the opinion that Mr. Miller's house was rather plain in comparison, but she felt that it was probably due to the fact that he didn't have a wife.

Sophia had been walking around eyeballing things, while Amanda had been trying to figure out a way to get Emily and Caroline to come over. She had considered that their moms might have the same attitude as Elizabeth. When they looked out the window toward Emily's house, they saw her sitting on the porch with her mom. Emily and Caroline and their parents all knew that Amanda was supposed to be at Mr. Miller's house while her parents were away.

Sophia and Amanda had sat down in the parlor, still trying to come up with a plan that would get Emily and Caroline over. They had gotten permission from Mr. Miller and Elizabeth for them to be there. Therefore, they had decided that they should just go outside and sit down. Eventually, Emily and Caroline would see them, and then they would come over on their own.

They liked the plan, because that way Caroline and Emily would come over without having to be invited. If anybody had anything to say about it, they would be in the clear. They could say that they had been sitting on the porch, and when Emily and Caroline saw them, they came over. They granted that a bit of conniving might have been involved, but none of it had been terribly bad. It didn't take long before all four of them were together at Amanda's house—there had been a few hurdles to overcome, but things had turned out just the way that they had intended.

They had spoken the truth when they told Elizabeth that they were going to sit around and talk at Amanda's house. There wasn't much else for them to do. They had the freedom to talk about anything and anybody, and they didn't have to bite their tongue, because there was no one around to listen.

They had gotten so carried away with being alone and having the house to themselves that they hadn't been paying attention to the time. The sun was shining, but it wouldn't be for long. Caroline and Emily didn't have anything to worry about. Their parents could see them whenever they looked in their direction. It was Sophia and Amanda that had to take it home, and they had to do it in a hurry—like two or three hours ago.

First of all, Sophia and Amanda knew that Elizabeth would have a fit if she found out that all four of them had spent the day together at Amanda's house. They had permission to be there, but they didn't have permission to be there with anyone else. Before they had left Amanda's house, Sophia reminded the others that the best way to handle things, especially for herself and for Amanda, would be to say nothing unless they had to.

Things didn't go right for them at all, and it started as soon as they had left Amanda's house. It had gotten so late in the day that Mr. Miller had locked the door to his office and was on his way home. He had seen Sophia and Amanda as they were leaving Amanda's house. He waited on them so that they could walk together. He had asked them if they enjoyed the day. When they said that they did, he made the remark that it's good to get together with your friends and talk about things every now and then.

Amanda and Sophia knew that they had to be in it up to their waist, and that the cat was out of the bag when he said that the four of them spending the day together must have been really nice. That meant that he had also seen Emily and Caroline on their way home. They had just left Amanda's house, and what they had vowed to keep secret had already made its' way to the street. It had made its' way to the street before they did. That was all that Mr. Miller ever had to say about their caper, but they were sure that Elizabeth would pick up where he had left off.

When they first went to Amanda's house, they hadn't planned on being there that long. They simply got carried away and lost track of time. When Sophia and Amanda walked into the house, Elizabeth wanted to know where they had been. Mr. Miller could see that Elizabeth had expected them to be back a lot sooner. He had gone to his study and closed the door, so that he wouldn't have to listen.

Sophia told Elizabeth that they had been over to Amanda's house. Elizabeth said that she already knew that. She wanted to know why they had been at Amanda's house all day. She knew better, but Sophia told Elizabeth that she and Amanda had assumed that she knew that they would be gone all day. Elizabeth had heard enough of their half-truths. She told them that if they tried to pull a stunt like that again she would walk the streets until she found them and then lead them home by the hair on their head.

After realizing that they couldn't pull the wool over Elizabeth's eyes, they decided to tell the truth. Sophia and Amanda apologized for being gone all day. They said that Caroline and Emily had seen them at Amanda's house, and that they came over to be with them. They didn't intend to be gone so long, but they said that they had so much fun being together that they didn't realize that it had gotten so late. Elizabeth told them that they should have said that at first instead of making up some dumb excuse, and expecting her to believe it.

When Amanda's parents returned, they stopped by to get their daughter. Elizabeth talked with them, because Mr. Miller had not made it home. She never mentioned the fact that Amanda had played host to Sophia, Emily and Caroline in their house while they were away. She figured that Amanda would get around to telling them when she was ready.

Sophia helped Amanda pack her bag. It had taken far longer than necessary to get the few things that she had brought with her. However, no one rushed them, because they knew why. Amanda was in no hurry to leave, and Sophia didn't want her to go. When she had finished packing, they walked out onto the porch. Amanda stopped and put her arms around Sophia while her parents and Elizabeth watched.

Amanda would be leaving for school in a few days, but she had told Sophia that she would see her again before she left. Amanda's mom apologized to Elizabeth for having put an extra burden on her. Elizabeth had to bite her tongue a bit when she said it, but she told them that she could hardly tell that Amanda had been in the house.

Amanda's parents had been considerate of the fact that Elizabeth had a hand in helping raise their daughter. They felt like she had spent almost as much time in Mr. Miller's house with Sophia as she had spent with them in their own house. Elizabeth had seen all of them grow up, or at least get to where they were. Even though she had to get on them once in a while, she still appreciated having them around. Most of all, she appreciated the fact that they had been friends with her daughter. Elizabeth was sure that Sophia's life had been made better, because of Amanda, Caroline and Emily.

Amanda kept her promise to Sophia. Before nightfall on the day prior to leaving, she, Caroline and Emily had stopped by Mr. Miller's house to say goodbye. They talked with Mr. Miller first, because they had seen him first—he was on the porch. They had all known him since they were little girls, and he had become like a relative, or more like a second father.

He had asked them if they were looking forward to going off to school. Caroline said that she had been really excited about it, but her feelings had changed. As the time for them to leave had gotten closer and closer, she had started having mixed emotions about leaving home. Mr. Miller told her that it was not unusual to have feelings like that; he felt the same way when he left home to attend college.

Sophia had heard them talking, and she went to find out who it was. She had not been surprised when she saw Amanda, Caroline and Emily. Mr. Miller knew that they hadn't come over to talk to him, so he left them alone.

Mr. Miller sat outside reading, but he could hear Sophia and her friends talking in the parlor. Elizabeth had walked out onto the porch to see if he needed anything. He had said no, but he interrupted her after she had turned to go back inside. He said that he had never seen four girls quite like them. Elizabeth agreed with him. Their relationship had been one that she had never seen before. When they first met, Elizabeth was sure that it would last for a while—being little tots—and then it would end as quickly as it had started. However, they had become teenagers and nothing had changed, except for the fact that they had become even closer.

Mr. Miller and Elizabeth were quiet for a while. She had been standing not far from where he was seated—holding onto the door. She was sure that he had something else to say—he acted like he did—so she waited. When she had decided that he was done talking, she went back inside.

Elizabeth knew Mr. Miller perhaps better than anyone. Often times it seemed to her that Sophia's relationship with Amanda, Caroline and Emily may have put
him in a position that made him feel somewhat uncomfortable. She had thought that he was sometimes uncomfortable from the standpoint that a slave girl—owned by
him—had become best friends with three white girls.
She felt like their relationship had been so unique that
it might have made him wonder about his role in the
scheme of things—he had certainly been involved, and
he had to have known that he had contributed to them
being the way that they were.

He owned Sophia, but he had let her live a life that had
not been very different from that of Amanda, Caroline
and Emily. The fact that she couldn't pack her bags and
leave had always been the biggest reminder that she was
a slave—it may have been her only reminder.

No attempts had ever been made to squash Sophia's
relationship with Amanda, Caroline and Emily, or to
keep it in the closet. Elizabeth's guess had been that
some had to have known, and if some did know, then
some had to disapprove. However, if there had ever
been any talk about it around town, it had never become a hot topic. Elizabeth considered that there had
to have been some talk simply because people love to
talk; it had probably been kept hidden because of the
people involved.

The people involved didn't be the girls, but rather,
their parents, and the slave owner. Elizabeth couldn't be
sure about the parents of Amanda, Caroline and Emily,
but if anyone had anything to say about how Austin
Miller managed things at his house, her opinion was that

there would have been hell to pay. He wouldn't sit quietly by and listen—people knew that he wouldn't.

Elizabeth went about doing whatever she was doing, and she was always doing something. She and Mr. Miller had pretty much ignored their house guests and let them have their privacy. They had all become young ladies, or at least they had thought so. Therefore, they needed some time together, and they didn't want to share what they had to say with anyone outside of their circle.

Sophia and her friends had been inside talking for a long time. Every now and then, Elizabeth and Mr. Miller could hear them laughing. It was far from amusing the day that it happened, but they laughed when Amanda told them that she and Sophia had thought that Elizabeth was going to give the two of them a good spanking for spending the entire day at her parents' house. They recalled lots of things that made them laugh. They had to, because they had all come to realize that leaving home—even just for a few months—and leaving one behind had become a bit depressing.

Mr. Miller had grown weary from sitting so long, but he stayed put. He didn't want to interrupt what had been going on in the parlor. Elizabeth had been doing the same thing. She had made it a point to occupy herself with something, so that she could stay clear of them. After a few more stories, and a little more laughter, they had to leave. Otherwise, they would have to ask if they could spend the night—it had gotten a little late. Staying any longer might wear out their welcome.

Elizabeth had heard them as they were leaving the parlor, and she followed them out onto the porch. When they were all on the porch, Mr. Miller stood and wished them well. Amanda, Caroline and Emily had all given him a hug, and then they did the same with Elizabeth. Sophia saw that Elizabeth had gotten a little emotional; she had wiped a tear from her eye.

TWO

Amanda, Caroline and Emily had been gone for about two weeks, and Sophia felt like that had been long enough for them to have written a letter. Although very capable of reading and writing, she had never written or received a letter in her entire life. She had never had anyone to write a letter to, and up until then, there had never been anyone that could write to her. Yet, she had to wait until she had received a letter from them, so that she would know their mailing address.

Amanda, Caroline and Emily had taught Sophia how to read and write. Mr. Miller had always known, because he had seen them. Many times, he had heard her reading the Bible to Elizabeth, and he had seen notes that she had written to herself. Although learning to read and write had always been taboo for slaves, with his seemingly laissez-faire attitude, it didn't matter to him.

After her friends had left, Elizabeth noticed that Sophia had started spending more time helping her with the chores around the house. Not only had she been helping more, she had been doing it without being told. Mr. Miller noticed that she had become withdrawn, and didn't have much interest in things anymore. They had always known that she had a unique personality, but her personality had nothing to do with it, she had become lonely and depressed.

Mr. Miller and Elizabeth both had recognized the fact that Sophia's change of attitude had been due entirely to the absence of Amanda, Caroline and Emily. That had to have been the problem, because nothing else had changed. Since the day that they had first met, they had never been separated for more than a few days at a time.

Mr. Miller's routine never varied much from one day to the next. Whenever he was at home, and when circumstances permitted, he usually sat on the porch to go through the mail. Sophia had been inside with Elizabeth when he called for her. When she walked out onto the porch, he asked her if everything was alright—hinting at the fact that he was aware that she had been missing her friends and had become depressed. Yet, she told him that everything was alright.

They talked briefly, but as usual, he had to do most of the talking while she listened. When there was a pause, Sophia assumed that whatever he had to say had been said. She had turned to go back inside, and Mr. Miller had gotten up from his seat. He then stopped her, and she stood in the doorway. He had extended his arm, and said that this is for you.

Sophia knew what it was, because it was what she had been expecting. Holding the door with one hand, Sophia used her other hand to literally snatch the letter from him. In her haste to get back inside, she and Elizabeth had met in the doorway. Sophia ricocheted off of her and onto Mr. Miller, as the door closed and slapped Elizabeth in the face. She didn't look back, never said excuse me, or anything. She just kept on walking.

She rushed through the house to the back porch, but she didn't stop there. While tearing open the envelope with her less than steady fingers, she sat down on the bench underneath their big oak tree—it was a good place to read. When she had torn the envelope open, she saw that the letter had three different handwritings, all on the same page, and she could recognize each.

It was the first letter that she had ever received, and it was a day that she wanted to remember. Thanks to Amanda, Caroline and Emily, she could read and write. Although they were miles apart, they could do the next best thing short of being face to face to keep in touch.

Sophia had received a letter about once every two weeks, and she always answered them immediately. Lying in bed at night, she would read her letters over and over, and she had always been very deliberate in choosing just the right words for her own compositions. She had to let Mr. Miller look at the first one that she had written just to make sure that she had addressed it correctly.

She didn't throw any of her letters away. Instead, she put them in a small box, and placed them on the shelf. She had told Elizabeth that she was going to keep them forever. Mr. Miller received a stack of mail almost every day. Sophia didn't, but she would wait anxiously as he sorted through his to see if there was anything for her.

Several months had passed since Amanda, Caroline and Emily had gone off to school. During that time, a lot of letters had been sent back and forth, and Sophia kept everyone that she had received.

The warm days of summer had ended and it had gotten well into the fall. The air had become crisp, and the fall colors seemed to be more magnificent than ever. Mr. Miller had just finished eating supper, and he had gone out onto the front porch to read the newspaper. Periodically, he interrupted his reading to observe the beautiful western sky. The sunlight filtered through the clouds, creating multi-colors just above the horizon. Elizabeth opened the door to ask if he needed anything. He had told her no, but he did ask her to look at the beautiful sunset. He said that God must have worked all day to create something like that.

The sun was about to sink below the horizon, when Mr. Miller noticed a buggy coming down the street, and then it pulled in at his house. When he had recognized the driver as being Amanda's father, he walked out to meet him. They hadn't spoken to each other in a while, so he figured that he must be stopping by to chat.

Amanda's father didn't get down from the buggy as they talked. He remained seated while Mr. Miller stood nearby, with one hand resting on the seat. They talked for several minutes, and then, Amanda's father drove away.

Mr. Miller slowly walked back onto the porch. He had reached to open the front door, but then, he stopped short. While staring off in the direction of the setting sun, he had walked over and leaned against one of the columns on the porch. Once again, he looked at the western sky, at that spot where a few lingering rays of sunlight still danced and then disappeared from view.

He stood on the porch for a long time, seemingly resigned to the spirit of life, and lost somewhere between the passage of daylight to darkness. Elizabeth had looked out every once in a while, just to see if he was still there. She knew that he could sometimes get lost in his thoughts, and when he did, he was out of touch with everything around him.

He had stayed on the porch—leaning against one column for a while, and then another. He stayed there until it had become pitch black outside. Only the chill of the night air made him go inside.

Elizabeth and Sophia were in the kitchen. He had stopped in the doorway, and looked at Sophia. She had been standing over near the stove with her back to him. He then looked at Elizabeth, staring hauntingly into her eyes—almost frightening. She stared back at him. Elizabeth could tell that he wanted to say something, but it seemed like he was unable to speak.

It had become obvious to Elizabeth that something was wrong, but her brain seemed useless as she tried to anticipate what it was that he was about to say. With a softer than usual tone of voice, he began to speak. He said that he had been outside talking with Amanda's father. There had been a fire at school, and five girls had been killed. At that moment, Sophia had turned around and she looked at him.

Elizabeth saw a part of his emotions that she had never seen before. He had always been well composed, and in complete control of his feelings, but not then. He had been looking directly at Sophia when he said that one of those girls was Amanda.

When he said it, Sophia dropped the bowl that she had been holding, and then she stood there looking at him and then at Elizabeth. The expression on her face seemed unchanged. Then she said that she was sorry that she had dropped the bowl, but she would clean it up. She had stooped down to pick up the shards from the floor, but Mr. Miller had taken her by the arm. He told her that it was alright, and that she could forget about the bowl. Elizabeth had placed her hand on Sophia's shoulder. The house had become eerily quiet.

Sophia stared at the fragments on the floor, and then very slowly, she walked between Mr. Miller and Elizabeth and went to her bedroom. Momentarily, Mr. Miller and Elizabeth didn't move or say anything. They had been shocked by Sophia's display of emotions, or the lack thereof. Shortly afterwards, they too had gone to her bedroom.

Sophia was standing at the far side of the bed, peering out the window. Mr. Miller had said that he was sorry. When she turned around, and looked at him, she was crying. Looking back at her, he didn't know what else he could say—he had already said more than he wanted to—and he didn't know what else he could do. He simply left the room.

Through the years, Amanda, Caroline and Emily had spent lots of time in Mr. Miller's home with Sophia. It had always seemed like there was where they belonged. Like a surrogate nanny, Elizabeth had cared for them from the beginning. She had tended bruises and scratches on all of them at one time or another, and she had threatened them with a spanking when need be. She had experienced her share of heartfelt hugs, but then she wished for one more.

Elizabeth knew well that the unconventional, free spirited attitude characteristic of Sophia, and the freedoms of life that were hers, had to be due to her relationship with Amanda, Caroline and Emily. Without their influence, Sophia would have been something different, and Elizabeth was in love with what they had helped her become.

Elizabeth could fix cuts and scratches, but Sophia had been hurt on the inside. She had an aching heart, and a troubled mind. It was something that she would have to fix herself.

After a while, Mr. Miller had left the house. When he returned, he had a small bottle of medicine, something that he had gotten from the doctor. Elizabeth had given Sophia a dose, and then she sat down in the room with her. She had lost track of time by just staring outside at the blackness of night. When she walked over to the bed, her daughter had fallen asleep.

Elizabeth had left the bedroom. She walked through the house to make sure that everything was the way that it should be. Mr. Miller had been sitting at the kitchen table. When Elizabeth saw him, she stopped. Both of them needed someone to talk to, and that someone had to be each other.

Elizabeth said that Amanda had been Sophia's best friend, but she felt like she had been her own daughter. He didn't have one, but Mr. Miller said that he knew exactly how he would feel if he had a daughter to lose. She had asked him if he needed her to do anything. He didn't, but he had decided that he needed a strong shot of something to help him fall asleep; otherwise, he would be up all night. When he had asked her if she cared for a small shot, she told him that he could have her part, because she didn't want any.

Elizabeth had sat down at the table with him. She listened to him talk while slowly sipping on his bourbon. He told her about sitting on the porch earlier, and staring at one of the most beautiful sunset's that he had ever seen. He had left the almost empty glass of bourbon on the table, and said that he was going to his study.

After he had gotten up from his chair, he said that God had let him see what may have been the best that he could offer, and then it seemed like he had punished him for looking at it. After telling Elizabeth to leave his glass on the table, he said that the worst part about it had been how quickly things had changed—first a magnificent view on the horizon, and minutes later, the heartrending news about Amanda. He had experienced the good and the bad—it was nothing new, he had seen them before—but it was just that they had been too close together.

She had done it many times, but she did it again. Elizabeth had let her mind ramble back to the day when she first met Amanda, Caroline and Emily, the day that they wandered over to Mr. Miller's house without telling their parents. She thought about how close the four of them had been, and then she wondered why someone so sweet and innocent had to leave so soon. Still, she knew that life came with no exceptions, no promises, and no guarantees.

Elizabeth was wide awake as she lay in bed. Her mind seemed to have a thousand thoughts, all scrambling for that one spot up front—each wanting to be the first recognized, and her not wanting to get acquainted with any. She had thought about Mr. Miller, and how compassionate he had been throughout the evening. Not only had he been concerned about Amanda and her parents, but he had been equally concerned about Sophia, and the impact that Amanda's death had on her. His behavior had been like that of a person that truly cared, and very much unlike that of anyone else that she had ever known—she didn't know how he could own slaves.

Elizabeth thought about the many years that she and Sophia had been the property of Austin Miller, and how he had always treated them with respect. He had never questioned the way that she had done things, and he had always been satisfied with whatever she had done. There had been times when she felt like the place belonged to her. However, she knew that she couldn't sell out, nor could she walk away—she was still his slave. When she had thought about him having slaves, it seemed like things had suddenly turned upside down, because in her mind, he didn't fit the role of slave owner.

He owned thousands of acres of farmland, and he owned lots of slaves to work in the fields. However, Elizabeth could not understand how a man could seemingly care so much about the welfare of her and Sophia, and at the same time, not just tolerate, but participate in a system that thrived on human injustice. It didn't make sense to her—she had found him to be so confusing.

Elizabeth slept late the next morning, because it had been so hard to fall asleep the night before. She was in the kitchen preparing breakfast, and trying to hurry the coffee pot along, so that Mr. Miller could have his first cup. When the coffee had finished brewing, she filled a cup and took it to him. He had been sitting on the porch shuffling through some papers. Mixed in with some of his legal documents, he had found a letter. It was from Amanda, and it had been addressed to Sophia. He reasoned that the letter had been on his desk for several days, and that it had been inadvertently overlooked.

He had gone inside and showed the letter to Elizabeth. She felt like it might be a good sign, something that might help Sophia feel better. He had given the letter to Elizabeth, but she gave it back to him. Since he was the one that had always given them to Sophia, Elizabeth wanted him to be the one to give her the last letter from Amanda.

Sophia had gotten out of bed, and gotten herself dressed. Still groggy from the night before, she made her way through the kitchen and to the back porch in search of Elizabeth. She had opened the door, but instead of finding Elizabeth, she found Mr. Miller. She stopped in the doorway and spoke to him, but only because he was looking at her.

She had turned to go back inside, but he spoke her name and asked her to sit down. She had paused, and then slowly, she walked over and sat down next to him. After he had asked her how she felt, she said that she had a headache. He said that it was probably due to the medicine that she had taken last night.

At that moment, Mr. Miller and Sophia both found themselves in somewhat of a rare setting. Sophia was a teenager, and she had been living in Mr. Miller's house most of her life. During that time, any talking between the two of them had been kept to a minimum. It had been like that, because Sophia had made it that way. However, the death of her friend had overshadowed her past behaviors—if only temporarily. It was the first time, but they were seated next to each other, and openly expressing their personal heartfelt emotions.

They talked about Amanda. Sophia couldn't understand why she had to die. Mr. Miller had considered the fact that Sophia was very young, and death was probably something that neither she nor any of her friends had ever thought about. He told her that sometimes things happened, and the reasons why could not always be explained or understood. Yet, he told her that she had to accept them as being God's will, and there's nothing that anyone can do to change them. He said that God had taken Amanda, but he had left her with lots of beautiful memories, and those memories were hers to keep forever.

Sophia held back her tears, but with a faltering voice, she said that Amanda had been her best friend. Mr. Miller said that she was your best friend, but now, she's with the angels, but part of her will always be with you. He wasn't sure, but he hoped that Sophia had been listening. He said that God had taken Amanda home, but before He took her away, He saw to it that she left something for her. He held Amanda's last letter in front of Sophia. He told her that the letter had been lost on his desk for several days, and that it was for her.

Sophia had taken the letter, and after seeing who it was from, she just held on to it. Mr. Miller had asked if she was going to open it, but she said that she was afraid. She didn't know if she wanted to read what Amanda had written. He understood her feelings, and told her that she could put it away, and read it whenever she was ready.

Mr. Miller told her about the funeral arrangements, and that Caroline and Emily had already returned home. Then, as if she hadn't heard a single word that he had said, Sophia asked again, "Why did she have to die?" He merely stated that he didn't know why. He did know that she had been experiencing a tremendous hurt, and it was a hurt that she had never felt before.

The very first time in her life that she had to grapple with death had been when death had taken away her best friend. Mr. Miller knew that she had been good friends with Caroline and Emily, but at the same time, he knew that the relationship between her and Amanda had always been special.

Mr. Miller had gone back inside, and Elizabeth had taken his place next to Sophia. Elizabeth had always been a very religious woman. She had told Sophia that her letter was God's way of letting Amanda talk to her one last time. Sophia had been a little baffled by what Elizabeth had said, but she knew that Elizabeth was usually right. Elizabeth had left Sophia on the porch alone, so that she could think about things. After a while, Sophia had gone inside, and she placed her letter in the small box with some of her other personal things.

Mr. Miller had consumed all of the coffee that he could hold, and he had found his leather satchel. He told Elizabeth that he was going to his office. Elizabeth had started on her chores. She had decided that Sophia might be better off if she just left her alone, and let her sort things out in her own way. She couldn't ask her to help with the chores, not with what she had been going through—there wasn't much to do anyway.

Sophia had gone out into the backyard, and she had picked a handful of fall's blossoms. She walked over, and stood under the big oak tree where she, Amanda, Caroline and Emily used to play. It seemed to her like everything had ended so suddenly. She looked at the wooden bench where they had once sat, then overlaid with a greenish hue of algae, because it hadn't been used in a while. Still, she sat on it, just because it had been theirs.

Unassumingly experiencing the sweet fragrance of the freshly picked flowers in her hand, Sophia thought about the good times that used to take place in the backyard. As she thought about what used to be, she realized that it would never be that way again. Her only possessions of yesteryears with her best friend would be limited to fond memories, and the handful of letters that she had saved. In comparison, the letters had been few, but the memories were many, and they were hers to keep. Once in a while, Elizabeth would peek out back just to see what she was doing.

Sophia had stayed in the backyard well into the morning just to be alone. From time to time, her thoughts had been interrupted, but only by the chirping of birds, and a pesky squirrel that at times seemed to be getting too close. She had heard voices coming from the house. When she turned around, she saw Elizabeth on the porch with Caroline and Emily. Sophia had started walking hurriedly in their direction. When they had met, the three of them stood together with their arms locked around each other—then each had become three times as strong. What had happened was more than either could bear alone, but together they could ride the tide and weather the storm.

They had walked over to their bench and sat down. They were together again, beneath the big oak tree that had sheltered them for so long. Then, however, it seemed like a time that had been far too short. As they talked, every now and then they let their thoughts go back to an earlier time in life. Whenever they did, they were always reminded of the one that was missing, Amanda.

Too quickly, their circle had been forever broken, and they realized that they had taken too much for granted— they had assumed more than Heaven would allow. For them, it was like death had crept in and stolen her when no one was looking. Elizabeth had been watching from the window. She knew that the three of them could do more for each other than everybody else combined—she left them alone.

Caroline told Sophia that the funeral would be the next day. Amanda had made lots of friends while away at school, and some had traveled down to bid her farewell. Eventually, they got around to telling Sophia about the tragic fire, and how Amanda had been trapped at the end of the hall with no way out. Sophia cried while they told her. After she had heard it, she wished that they hadn't told her anything at all, because she didn't want to know. She wanted to remember Amanda standing in front of the mirror, the two of them plotting to make David wait for her, and their scheme that had gone awry when they spent the day at Amanda's house—those had been the memories that she wanted to keep.

Toward the end of the day, Mr. Miller had returned home. After he had tossed his leather satchel on the desk, he found Elizabeth. He wanted to know how Sophia had been doing. After being told that Caroline and Emily had come over, he was pleased. That was what he had wanted to hear, because he had been hoping all day that they would stop by. He started talking about the funeral, assuming that Elizabeth and Sophia would be attending, but they had decided not to. Sophia didn't want to go, because she knew that she would have to sit at the back, and she didn't want to be that far from Amanda—not then.

Mr. Miller had a bag in his hand. He opened it so that Elizabeth could see the rose bush that was inside. He had purchased it in town, hoping that Sophia might want to plant it in memory of Amanda. Sophia had been out back working in the flowers. When she saw Mr. Miller approach, she stood up.

He told Sophia that it had gotten late, and that he could get someone else to take care of the flowers. Nevertheless, she insisted and said that she didn't mind. She had been doing something to help pass the time, and maybe help her forget some things that she would rather not remember. He held the bag with the rose bush inside. After he had showed it to her, he explained why he had purchased it. He told her that if she took good care of it, she would have it for a long time

Mr. Miller, Elizabeth and Sophia had all gotten up early on the day of the funeral. The early morning sunlight shining through the clouds created a brilliant work of art. Mr. Miller stood on the porch and took it all in. It reminded him of the splendor that he had witnessed the evening when Amanda's father had stopped by. His next thought had reminded him of how quickly things could go from good to bad. It had been unusually quiet around the house, but they all knew why. The only thing that Mr. Miller had for breakfast was coffee, but that was close to normal for him.

When Mr. Miller had left the house, Elizabeth and Sophia sat on the back porch for a while. They avoided talking about the funeral. Yet, each of them knew that the other had been thinking about nothing but the funeral. Still, they didn't talk about it. Finally, Elizabeth had left her alone.

Mr. Miller didn't return home until mid-afternoon. He didn't talk about the funeral, and he had gone directly to his study. Sophia had been outside pampering the rose bush that she had planted. Elizabeth watched her. She had stood over the rose bush, and looked at it for a long time. Elizabeth thought that it may have been just what she needed.

The afternoon passed slowly, and no one had done much until Elizabeth decided that it was time for her to get started on cooking supper. Sophia had gotten a fire going in the cook stove, and then she went to her room. Just before supper, Mr. Miller had been in the kitchen talking with Elizabeth, and then they heard a knock at the front door. Elizabeth had started toward the door, but Mr. Miller told her that he would see who it was.

When he opened the door, he saw that it was Amanda's parents. He invited them in, and they had sat down in the parlor. After they had talked for a while, Mr. Miller called for Sophia. When Sophia walked into the room, Amanda's parents had stood up. Elizabeth's curiosity had her watching—more conspicuously than she realized—from just outside the parlor. She had become curious as to why Mr. Miller had called for Sophia.

When Sophia saw Amanda's parents, she suddenly stopped. Standing just inside the parlor, she stared at Amanda's mother—neither of them had said anything. Just for a brief while, they stood there looking at each other. Moments later, Sophia had started crying, but she was still quiet. The only sign of her crying was the unbroken stream of tears that flowed so freely down her cheeks. Softly, she told Amanda's parents that she was sorry.

Amanda's parents had known Sophia since she was a little girl. They also knew that Amanda and Sophia had been best friends. Sophia hadn't moved. She was still standing near the entryway to the parlor. Amanda's mother had walked over to her, and she had put her arms around her. As she held her, she whispered words to Sophia that only the two of them could understand.

Then, Amanda's mother stepped back and turned toward her husband. When she held her hand out, he gave her a small ornamental box, and she passed it to Sophia. She told Sophia that Amanda had it special made in Memphis; she had planned on giving it to her as a Christmas gift.

Sophia opened the box, and inside was a pendant with Amanda and Sophia's name scribed on it. The words, "best friends," had been scribed on the reverse side. Sophia looked at the solemn faces in front of her. Then she told them about the letter that she had received from Amanda. She even told them that she hadn't read the letter yet, because she had been afraid. Unaware that she had done so, Elizabeth had moved closer, so that she wouldn't miss anything. Sophia had been the only one in the room with any visible tears, but Elizabeth could see that the others had been crying too—they just didn't let it show.

Sophia had moved over near Elizabeth, and she showed her the pendant. Elizabeth had been standing there listening all while Amanda's mother told Sophia about the pendant, but Sophia told the story to her mom as if she had never heard it. Conscious of the fact that her mother couldn't read, Sophia pointed to each word scribed on the pendant, as she read them to her.

Elizabeth and Sophia had left the parlor. Mr. Miller had walked outside with Amanda's parents. When they had left, he went back inside. Sophia was in the bedroom, still admiring the gift from her best friend. Mr. Miller had a message for Elizabeth from Amanda's mom. She wanted Elizabeth to know that if she was moving away and never to return, then she would kidnap Sophia and tell everybody that she was her daughter.

THREE

The house where Austin Miller lived had been good enough, but it had gotten to the point where it was a little less than what he wanted. Back when he had first bought it, he got it because it was reasonably priced, and therefore, it was what he could afford. Since money was no longer a barrier, he had decided that it was time for an upgrade.

He had spent lots of hours during the winter developing construction plans. He relied on his experience from years past when he had worked as a carpenter's apprentice. What he had in mind wasn't just a house, it would be a mansion. He had already purchased a lot on the north edge of town. He had slaves that were skilled in woodwork and masonry, and he was almost ready to start building—not him, but his slaves. He would supervise things just to make sure that they got it right. Before putting things into action, there was one other slave that he had been wanting as part of his construction crew.

The other slave that he had in mind was named Alfred. Alfred had made the trek from North Carolina with the Taylor family—the same Taylors that had once owned Elizabeth and Sophia. When Mr. Miller purchased Elizabeth and Sophia, Alfred had already been sold. However, at that time, he didn't need him anyway.

Mr. Miller had seen some of Alfred's work, and he had been impressed with what he saw. He knew where Alfred was, and he bought him. The slaves that he had were capable of building the mansion, but he didn't have a single slave that he considered to be as skillful as Alfred. Alfred couldn't pick up a book, and read it from cover to cover. In fact, he couldn't make out the first word. Yet, he could interpret a blueprint, and turn dreams into reality better than most. Mr. Miller had a clear image of what he had been dreaming of, but he needed Alfred to make it come true.

He had bought Alfred because of his outstanding skills as a builder. Yet, he had defeated his reason for getting him, because he felt like he had to be on the site just to make sure that things were done right. He wanted the finished product to look just like the image that he had in his head.

He had two plantations, a thriving law practice, and he stayed bogged down in politics. He had been trying to juggle his time around, so that he could stay up to-date on everything. He would stop by the construction site each morning on the way to his office, and he would drop by several times during the day.

Alfred could have given Mr. Miller just what he had been wanting; he just needed to leave him alone so that he could do it. If it had been necessary for him to be there to supervise construction, he would have had to take down the shingle at his law office and resign his seat in the Tennessee Legislature. It was plain and simple, he didn't have the time.

Realizing how particular Mr. Miller had been, construction would sometimes slow down, or even stop until they could consult with the boss man—that's what some called him. As the construction project continued, eventually it had reached the point where no one sat around and waited on him to stop by so that he could clarify things. They didn't need him around so that he could tell them how to do this or that, or what the next step was.

Within the work crew, but unbeknownst to Mr. Miller, Alfred had already become the decision maker. The only thing that Mr. Miller had to do was to make sure that they had the necessary building materials, stay out of their way, and then move in when they told him that the job had been completed. Even Elizabeth knew that supervising the construction of a big fancy house was not a job for him. Her opinion had been that with a little help, he could have built a nice little tree house out back for the kids, or maybe a lean-to for whatever purpose, but a stately mansion was out of his reach.

When the building had started taking shape, the townspeople could see that it would be impressive. He had attained prominence in law, and in the political arena. Aside from that, he had become a successful landowner and planter, and he had found a position among society's elite. When finished, he would have a house on the same scale. He had once said to Elizabeth that it might be a little grandiose, but what the heck. Elizabeth didn't know the meaning of grandiose, but to her, it had to be something that was highfaluting.

Elizabeth and Sophia could watch from the window or the front porch, and see passersby traveling up and down the street. Peering from the window, Elizabeth had spotted a man headed into town driving a team of horses. He looked familiar, but she couldn't be certain about who he was. Later that day when she saw him again, she had figured it out, it was Alfred.

Elizabeth remembered Alfred from back when they belonged to the Taylor family, but she hadn't seen him in a long time. In fact, she had thought that he was gone forever—gone from her life anyway. Looking at him from the window, she remembered how he used to make eyes at her, and she never had objected to his advances.

Several days had passed, and Elizabeth saw Alfred again as he was headed into town with the team of horses. Mr. Miller was not at home. Elizabeth had gone out onto the porch, and boldly shouted his name. When she waved at him, Alfred knew who it was, and he pulled back on the reins. Elizabeth was glad that she had her eyes on him again, but not more so than Alfred.

Alfred had been one of Mr. Miller's slaves for several months. Shortly after getting there, he had found out that Elizabeth was his housekeeper—he just hadn't seen her. Through the years, Alfred had always hoped for a chance to see her again, but like Elizabeth, he had never really expected to. The route via Mr. Miller's house had not always been the most direct route to Alfred's destination, but it had become the preferred route.

When they were together on the Taylor plantation, neither of them had ever expected that their relationship, if it had ever been a relationship, to be anything more than what it had always been. As long as they had known each other, their moments together had been limited to nothing more than a few subtle flirtatious gestures sparsely scattered here and there. However, they were in love with each other, and they had been for a long time, but they had never said it.

Elizabeth had always worked in the master's house, and she had never had much contact with Alfred. He had always worked outside. Consequently, they rarely had the chance to see each other, but as time passed, things had changed. The balance had been tilted a bit in their favor when Mr. Miller decided that he needed Alfred's carpentry skills to build his mansion. Though the odds were against them, Elizabeth and Alfred had hoped that building the mansion might give them the chance to bridge the gap that had kept them apart.

While the new house was under construction, there had been occasions when Mr. Miller would have Alfred come to the house that he lived in to do minor repairs— he had to keep it looking nice so that he could sell it. None of it had ever been the kind of work that required much time, but still, those had become the times when Elizabeth and Alfred could talk. Due to the circum- stances, their encounters had usually been limited to idle chit chat. However, there had been a few times when Mr. Miller wasn't around, or when Sophia wasn't look- ing, that Alfred could hold her in his arms, if only for a moment.

Sophia and Elizabeth had been thrilled as much as Mr. Miller about the idea of moving into a beautiful new home. Of course, their interest in the place would be nothing more than the usual day to day activities associ- ated with housekeeping. Still, they liked the idea of living in a mansion. Since things had been the way they were for so long, they didn't even consider that their presence would be due only to the accepted political and social standards of time and place—they would be there to do the cooking and cleaning, because they were his slaves.

After a while, Elizabeth's feelings for Alfred had become more obvious. While working around the house, hardly a teamster could go past that she wouldn't check out to see if it was him. Still, she had managed to pretty much keep her feelings to herself. Try as she did, some had seen the glimmer in her eye whenever he was around. She didn't want Sophia to see her acting like a teenager in love, but Sophia had already figured it out.

Meanwhile, Mr. Miller had kept himself busy trying to supervise things at the construction site as much as possible. Elizabeth had said that he must really think that he knows how to build a house. However, when she said something like that, Sophia would remind her that he had worked his way through law school while working as a carpenter. Elizabeth had always felt like the reason for him becoming a lawyer had been because he wasn't good enough to earn a living as a carpenter. She had seen his handy work around the house, and she wondered why he hadn't let someone else do it so that it would look decent.

Alfred had known from the beginning that Mr. Miller didn't trust them to the point that he could leave them alone to do the job. Every slave that he had working at the site knew that he was just in the way whenever he stopped by. Still, he was there, walking around, and looking at things as if he knew exactly what he was doing.

Considering how particular Mr. Miller had been about the quality of work, he had always been pleased with what had been done while he was away. After a while, he realized that supervising the construction, and taking care of his other business interests had gotten to be more than he could handle. Therefore, he decided that he had to leave it up to Alfred. He didn't tell Alfred that he was in charge. However, it had become evident from the fact that he didn't spend so much time at the site anymore.

Sometimes, Mr. Miller would be gone out of town for the entire week, but whenever he returned, he could see that construction had progressed according to his plan. Every piece of timber and every red clay brick had always been placed exactly where it should be. He wanted the mansion built to his specifications, and to his satisfaction—he was getting exactly what he had wanted.

Mr. Miller had purchased him based on his reputation as a builder, but Alfred had turned out to be even more impressive than he ever expected. All during construction, Alfred would talk to him about his construction plans, and throughout the construction process, the building plans had been continuously modified. Most of the modifications had been based on input from Alfred, because what Mr. Miller had drawn up wouldn't work.

Flaws in Mr. Miller's plan had mostly been structural in nature. Alfred and the work crew could make the necessary modifications without changing the look that Mr. Miller had in mind. The general appearance of the new mansion in town had been Mr. Miller's idea, but it was Alfred and his work crew that had fashioned the beautiful mansion located on Main Street.

Sophia had gotten a shovel, and she had dug up the rose bush that Mr. Miller had given her to plant in memory of her friend, Amanda. She had placed it on the porch, and as soon as Mr. Miller saw it, he knew exactly what it meant. She had dug it up so that it could be transplanted at their new place of residence—it had been for her best friend, and she was taking it with her.

Only a few of Austin Miller's friends knew that he and Mary Jane McNeal had been planning their marriage. Mary Jane had been married once before to the late Albert McNeal. They had two children together, a six year old boy named for his father, and a four year old girl named Mary. Mr. Miller would have probably been satisfied with his old place of residence, but Mary Jane had been the main reason for the elaborate new home that he had built—only a mansion would satisfy her life style.

Mary Jane had been accustomed to the finer things that money could buy, and Mr. Miller wanted her to keep the silver spoon that she had. When the time came to carry her across the threshold, he wanted it to be at the door of their new mansion. It had taken more than a year to complete. After the last brick had been laid, and the last piece of trim had been put in place, it was nothing less than what he had wanted.

Mary Jane had been eying the new place all while it was under construction. Mr. Miller had taken her there from time to time so that she could see what would soon be hers. On the day that they were married, he took her in his arms, and carried her across the threshold just as he had planned. When her feet had been planted on the hardwood floor, he introduced her to their house servants. They had been strangers, and it was time for them to make that first impression.

First, Mr. Miller introduced his wife to Elizabeth, and all went well. Mrs. Miller had always preferred to distance herself from the lower class—she had put slaves at the top of that list—but with some imagination she managed what could be interpreted as a smile. Next, he introduced Sophia, and when he did, it became apparent to the bystanders, Mr. Miller and Elizabeth, that a go-between would have to be around until they could become better acquainted.

Sophia was only sixteen years old, but age didn't matter. She and Mrs. Miller had been standing there looking at each other. Mrs. Miller didn't say anything, but she had surveyed Sophia from top to bottom. Mrs. Miller had an attitude, and so did Sophia. She looked at Mrs. Miller with the same arrogance, and disapproval that Mrs. Miller had for her.

Mr. Miller and Elizabeth had both noticed the stare down. However, they were strangers. They were sure that they just needed some time to get used to each other, and then things would be just fine—there was nothing to be concerned about.

With the mansion completed, Mr. Miller's had one last contribution. His well-conceived idea seemed trite at the time, but it would be most appropriate, and long lived. It was a small tree seedling that he had brought home during one of his many trips to Mississippi. He and Mrs. Miller had selected the perfect spot in the front yard, and they watched as Alfred planted the seedling. It had not been by chance that the small seedling was a magnolia, because he had long since decided that he would christen the new mansion as Magnolia Manor.

The grounds around the mansion had to be landscaped and maintained. That had become Alfred's job. Being the yard boy would put him closer to Elizabeth, and that was exactly what the two of them had been wanting—little by little, the parts to their puzzle kept falling into place.

Alfred and Elizabeth felt like the odds of bridging the gap that had kept them separated continued to get better and better. After a while, the increased frequency of being near each other had made them want to be together even more. Alfred had mustered up the courage to ask Elizabeth if she would marry him. It didn't take long for her to say yes, but as soon as she had said it, they both knew that as slaves, marriage would be rather farfetched. However, they conceded that there had been a few steps that favored them. Yet, they were inching forward so slow that it was hard to tell that they were moving.

Alfred and Elizabeth considered themselves engaged, but they didn't tell anyone. Rarely did they talk about it amongst themselves, because they couldn't be sure that it would ever take place anyway. Still, they loved their verbal commitment to each other, and it would be something to dream about. Just the promise of marriage had made life more exciting, and it had made them feel like they belonged together.

When no one was around, which was seldom, they would hold each other close and daydream. Yet, with their arms around each other, they were still far from where they wanted to be. They had always been kept separated by that slaveholding state law that prohibited slaves from being legally married—they wanted to do more than jump the broom.

If they had been allowed to just jump the broom, it wouldn't have changed anything. Elizabeth was a house servant, and she was in the big house every hour of every day. Marriage would not have changed her work schedule. She would not have gone home to be with her husband at the end of the day, and he certainly was not going to move into Magnolia Manor. Elizabeth granted that she had said yes to Alfred's proposal, but in a way they were still in the same place that they had always been, and nothing had really changed—in a way, it had been more like make believe, a game that children would play.

Mr. Miller's routine stayed about the same after moving into Magnolia Manor. He was out of bed early each morning, he always had at least two cups of coffee, and occasionally, he ate breakfast—a little anyway. He never ate much, just enough to make Elizabeth feel like it had been worth her time to cook.

The biggest change had been for Elizabeth and Sophia. They had always taken care of things around the house, and they had always done it pretty much in the way that they saw fit. In addition, they had always done things on their own schedule. After their marriage, Mrs. Miller had become the one in charge of the house, and she insisted on having everything done just one way, and that was her way.

Caroline and Emily hadn't visited Sophia since they had moved into Magnolia Manor. Sophia had gone out to meet them when she saw them coming down the street, because she was sure that they were coming to see her. They had stopped at the bottom of the steps to talk. Eventually, Magnolia Manor had become their topic of conversation.

Caroline and Emily had seen the construction progress from grading of the site, all the way to completion. Since it had been completed, they were curious to know what it looked like on the inside. They were still standing near the steps when Mr. Miller walked out onto the porch. Hearing enough of their conversation to figure out that they had been talking about his new home, he invited them inside. He had asked Sophia if she would like to show them around.

Mr. Miller knew that the main reason why Caroline and Emily had come over was to see Sophia. He realized that they would probably like to walk through and have a look at the house, but they didn't really care if they saw it or not. As they were about to start the tour, they met Mrs. Miller near the entryway.

Caroline and Emily had been acquainted with Mrs. Miller even before she had married Mr. Miller. They didn't know her personally, but she was someone that they recognized whenever their paths had crossed. They did know her well enough to know that she had a personality that was very different from that of her husband. Their knowledge of Mrs. Miller's character had been the reason why they hadn't stopped by sooner to visit Sophia—they didn't want to be around her.

Standing in the entryway to the mansion, Mr. Miller introduced Caroline and Emily to his wife. When he had finished with the introductions, he told Mrs. Miller that Sophia was about to show them around the house. Mrs. Miller said that she would do that, and then she told Sophia to get a rag and start dusting the furniture. Sophia looked at Mr. Miller as if she had been expecting him to say or do something, but he didn't. Mrs. Miller had gone inside, taking Caroline and Emily with her.

Reluctantly, Caroline and Emily followed Mrs. Miller. When Mr. Miller had asked Sophia to show them around, he was just doing what he had always done, allowing them to visit with Sophia. He knew exactly why Caroline and Emily had come over, and it was not to see the mansion. The tour would just be something to do while they were together, and its' only purpose had been an excuse to be there.

Reluctantly, Sophia walked away, but before she did, she had another look at Mr. Miller. He understood clearly that her eyes and her expressions had been telling him that he should have done something. Although she had wanted him to do something, or more than likely, she had expected him to do something, he didn't know what it was that he could have done. In the short time that he had been married, it had become clear to him that his wife had no use for Sophia, and Sophia felt the same about her.

The problem that Mr. Miller had was one that he had let develop, and it had been a long time in the making. When he bought Elizabeth and Sophia from Mrs. Taylor, Sophia was just a little tot, but she had become a teenager. Sophia's lifestyle up to that point had been more like that of Amanda, Caroline and Emily rather than like that of a slave. As a result, she had pretty much lived a life of leisure, and she had always done pretty much as she pleased. That being the case, the thing that had pleased her most was been being with her friends. Mr. Miller had always known that, and he had never seen anything wrong with it—he simply let it be.

Although Mr. Miller owned Elizabeth and Sophia, it had usually been Elizabeth that told Sophia what to do. She had always been a slave, but the reins on her had always been slack, and Mrs. Miller, she never had any. Therefore, trying to keep them in check had gotten to be a handful. Mr. Miller had been caught in the middle, and he didn't know how to work his way out. On one side, Sophia had been expecting him to intervene on her behalf, and on the other, Mrs. Miller had been wondering how long it would be before he put that slave in her place.

Mrs. Miller had her own caste system, and she hung with the upper crust—the well to-do—and the likes of Sophia were at the tail end. Through the years, Sophia had learned to read and write just from being in the company of Amanda, Caroline and Emily. Her vocabulary and vocal expressions reflected the influence of those whom she had grown up around.

Mr. Miller had not been blinded by the fact that the atypical lifestyle that he had endorsed was the reason why Sophia was what she was. Furthermore, he didn't care, and it had always been fine with him. However, that which had been fine with him had never been fine with Mrs. Miller—therein was the problem at Magnolia Manor.

Through the years, Mr. Miller had become fond of Sophia and her mother. Therefore, he didn't want to suddenly become rude or insensitive, because of something that he had allowed to develop. At the same time, he wanted an agreeable relationship between them and Mrs. Miller. Most importantly, he didn't want to, nor could he allow the situation to alienate himself from his wife. Clearly, there was a huge divide between Mr. Miller's wants and reality. To cap it all off, he had no idea about how to go about resolving the issue, or even how to tone things down. He had decided that maybe things would eventually calm down, and mellow out with time.

Mrs. Miller took advantage of every opportunity to show off Magnolia Manor. Slowly, and therefore taking far more time than necessary, she had dragged Caroline and Emily through the mansion. She showed them every nook and cranny, both upstairs and downstairs. When she had finished, they stood on the front porch, and talked for a few minutes, and then they said goodbye. They had come over to visit with Sophia, but Mrs. Miller had tossed a monkey wrench into their plan. Instead, they had gotten the grand tour of Magnolia Manor, and their much too thorough tour guide had bored them to death.

Mr. and Mrs. Miller stood on the porch and watched, as their visitors walked away. While standing there, he had the opportunity to explain, and clarify a few things for the next time that they stopped by. He had told Mrs. Miller that Caroline and Emily had only come over to visit Sophia, and that they hadn't really been interested in seeing the mansion. Mrs. Miller said that they had most certainly come over to see the mansion, she was sure, because before she walked up, she said that Sophia was about to take them on a tour.

He agreed with her, but he explained further that the tour would just be something to do while they walked around and talked. After he had said that, she made it clear that she would not have a slave showing anybody around her house, especially Sophia. She said that they had her for housekeeping, and they didn't really need her for that—they could go ahead and get rid of her.

While they were on the subject, Mrs. Miller emphasized that white girls should not be visiting a slave anyway. When she asked Mr. Miller why he had allowed such a thing to happen, he had to think about it, because he had never given it any thought. Before he could come up with an appropriate response, she had gone back inside. She had slammed the door behind her like she was trying to take it off the hinges.

Mrs. Miller didn't see anything wrong with the way that she had handled things. Overriding Mr. Miller's offer that Sophia show Caroline and Emily around had been the right thing to do as far as she had been concerned. Contrary to what anyone else might think, she didn't feel that she had been rude to Sophia; if Sophia felt like she had been rude to her, then so be it. In her mind, she had simply exercised her authority as lady of the house. She not only felt that her intervention had been acceptable, she felt like it was exactly what should have been done—she was through with it.

Mr. Miller didn't like the idea of his wife insisting on taking Caroline and Emily on a tour of the mansion, but he had handled the situation in the way that was right for him. However, what happened was exactly what he had been hoping to avoid. It had become obvious to him that such run-ins would be hard to control. He had been left alone on the porch to think about things. When nothing came to mind, he decided that he would think about it later.

Even with the belief that slaves were an inferior class of people, Mrs. Miller always insisted that slaves be treated with kindness—a philosophy that twists the brain when thinking about it. Her definition of kindness was one that she had forged. Although being kind to a person that's kept as a slave seems utterly impossible, perhaps a hint of humanity was better than none at all. Still, it was a thing of the mind, but like dust in the wind, there to drift aimlessly and then settle with no real consequences—just an empty idea to help justify the permitted wrongs of legal injustice.

Whenever they were around each other, Mr. Miller would have thoughts about the two hot heads in the house, but he had decided to place it on the back burner. He had taken the wait and see attitude more than a few times, because it was the easiest thing to do. He knew that he couldn't just walk up to his wife, and tell her to back away from Sophia. Mrs. Miller had told him that he was guilty of letting Sophia be whatever it was that she had become.

The way he saw it, what Sophia had become was an intelligent teenager that had grown up mostly in a white society rather than in the cotton fields. He had never had a problem with her, and he couldn't understand why his wife had such a problem—the beds had always been made, and there was no dust on anything—she should have been satisfied.

Had he wanted to, he could have taken control of the situation right from the start. He had two options, either of which would have ridded the problem, and calmed the storm. He could have simply told Sophia to get in her place and stay there, or he could have put her on the block and auctioned her off to the highest bidder. The second option would have satisfied Mrs. Miller completely, but he didn't care for either.

Elizabeth was well aware of what had been going on between them, yet she hadn't said anything to Sophia. She didn't expect Mr. Miller to do any more than what he had already done, which was nothing. Elizabeth had always known what Sophia was like, and she had been getting to know Mrs. Miller. She had come to the conclusion that if things continued the way that they had been, Sophia with her nonchalant and sometimes fiery attitude, would eventually clash head on with Mrs. Miller. They could clash hard enough so that fixing things could have grave consequences for both her and Sophia.

When Sophia had first become a teenager, Elizabeth found it necessary to remind her that she was a slave, and that she should conduct herself as a slave. After Elizabeth had reminded her, she apologized when Sophia said that she always remembered, and that she didn't have to be reminded. Still, Elizabeth truly believed that sometimes Sophia either forgot, or for whatever reason, she had never been mindful of the fact that she was owned by Austin Miller—she was his property. She had always been like that, but it had never bothered him—he just let Sophia be Sophia.

Elizabeth hadn't known Mrs. Miller very long. However, she had known her long enough to know that she was more satisfied working for Mr. Miller before Mrs. Miller had arrived on the scene. When he was single, he very seldom told her or Sophia what to do. If he wanted something, they knew him well enough to sometimes have it there in front of him before he had to ask. Realizing that Mrs. Miller was more of a slave driver than Mr. Miller, Elizabeth had already made the necessary adjustments to satisfy her expectations. She had expected that Sophia would do the same.

Sophia was still angry, because she had been denied the opportunity to visit with Caroline and Emily. Elizabeth didn't have to look at her to see that she was fuming, because Sophia had already told her so. Since Caroline and Emily had always come over to Mr. Miller's house to see her, she couldn't understand why things had changed.

Eventually, Elizabeth got around to telling Sophia that she wouldn't be seeing much of Caroline and Emily since Mrs. Miller had moved in. When she told her, Elizabeth couldn't believe that Sophia was shocked by what she had said. Sophia had the expectation that

Caroline and Emily could come over to visit her whenever they wanted to, whether Mrs. Miller liked it or not.

Elizabeth had recognized the fact that Mrs. Miller was not going to allow Caroline and Emily to come to her house, and socialize with Sophia. Aside from that, the rule had always been that slaves don't receive visitors anyway—not at the big house. Mr. Miller had never cared, and he still didn't, but it wouldn't happen with Mrs. Miller standing watch. Sophia had been friends with Caroline and Emily for a long time, and neither she, nor they had ever guessed that it would end because someone disapproved. It was something that they had never even thought about.

Elizabeth questioned who had to be the worst, the person that owned slaves, or the one telling her daughter that she should be a good slave. Still, she had to make Sophia understand, because Mrs. Miller could be very persuasive. It had not been inconceivable that with the right leverage, she might be able to convince her husband to exercise one of his options and take control. That option being to put Sophia on the auction block and get rid of her. It was a frightful thought for Elizabeth, because she had seen it, and it was horrible. It would be more horrible if she had to watch her daughter being sold—she would rather die first.

Sophia was still just as angry as when Elizabeth had first started talking to her. Elizabeth realized that she may have been a little harsh, but she didn't have much concern for how Sophia might feel. Foremost in her mind was to get her daughter's feet on the ground, and in case she had missed it, introduce her to the real world.

Sophia had gotten a little too mouthy with Elizabeth when she had been told that she could get herself into a lot of trouble. Sophia said that if she did get in trouble, she had never heard of a house servant being flogged over it. That was the wrong attitude to have, and as soon as she had made the statement, Elizabeth's temperature started to rise. Elizabeth conceded that she may have been right about not being flogged, because when it was over, Mrs. Miller would still have to look at her. Putting her on the auction block would have been more in line with what Mrs. Miller wanted, and Elizabeth told her so.

Elizabeth had been a product of slavery for so long that she knew the system, and she knew it well. In addition, she knew what to do, and when to do it. On the other hand, Sophia had always seemed to be just the opposite, even though she was just as much a slave as Elizabeth. Elizabeth had tried to keep her away from Mrs. Miller as much as possible, but she soon learned that the house wasn't big enough for that.

While Elizabeth had been lecturing her, Sophia's attitude had been indifferent. It was like the words had flown right past her ears, but later on Elizabeth felt like they may have started to sink in. Sophia had never thought about it, and since she hadn't, her assumption had always been that the relationship shared by her, Caroline and Emily would never change. They were the only friends that she had, and the supposition that it might be over had been very depressing.

Later, Elizabeth realized that she had been unsettled as much as Sophia by the things that she had said. She didn't know if she had made things better or worse. She did know that what she had said to Sophia regarding Mrs. Miller was true. She hoped that she had been wrong about Sophia's relationship with Caroline and Emily. However, she believed that to be true as well.

The chores had been done, and Elizabeth and Sophia had gone to their room. The time had been too short for them to forget about the heated exchange of words that they had earlier. Although they still remembered, they didn't talk about it anymore.

Mr. Miller had been busy in his study while Mrs. Miller walked through the house. She had been bouncing ideas back and forth in her mind regarding new furniture, and artwork for the mansion. Her goal was to get rid of almost everything that they had in the mansion, and replace it with the best that she could find—she didn't care where she had to get it from.

While creating a mental image of her refurbishing plans, Mrs. Miller had walked past Elizabeth's room, and she heard Sophia's voice. To her, the inflections didn't sound like that of a person engaged in conversation. Without knocking, she opened the door, and looked inside. She saw Elizabeth sitting in her rocking chair, while Sophia sat on the side of the bed reading the Bible to her. She didn't say a word to Elizabeth or Sophia. Instead, she quickly left the room.

Mrs. Miller had found her husband, and she told him that she had just caught Sophia reading the Bible to Elizabeth. He leaned back in his chair, and explained that it was nothing to get excited about. He said that she had been doing that for years, because Elizabeth couldn't read. She asked him if he would explain what he had just said. He said that there wasn't anything to explain other than Sophia read to Elizabeth, because Elizabeth didn't know how to read. Sophia and Elizabeth could hear them. Mrs. Miller had raised her voice, when she said that Elizabeth isn't supposed to know how to read, and neither is Sophia.

Since she had been so surprised about Sophia knowing how to read, Mr. Miller decided that he should bring his wife up to-date. He explained that Sophia had learned to read and write years ago from playing with Amanda, Caroline and Emily. He told her about how they used to sit out back, and pretend that they were at school. One would act as the teacher, and the others would be the students. He concluded by letting her know that Sophia had a box of books stashed somewhere in the mansion that Amanda, Caroline and Emily had given to her.

Mrs. Miller was flabbergasted when she found out that her husband had allowed a slave to learn how to read and write. She wanted to know what he intended to do about it. When she had asked him, he said that there's nothing that he could do about it, because she had already learned how. He told her that when he finished with his newspapers, he had always passed them along to her, simply because she enjoyed reading them.

He suddenly remembered an article that Sophia had read in the newspaper a few years ago, one that was funny, but one that he had missed. He wanted to tell his wife about it. As soon as he had started telling her about the article, he started laughing. He had not gotten far into the story when she had thrown her hands in the air, and walked away.

Mrs. Miller had made a few steps down the hallway, but then she stopped, and walked back to his study. Mr. Miller was still sitting at his desk, and he was looking at her standing in the doorway. He was waiting for her to speak, because he had assumed that she had come back to say something, but she didn't. With a firm grip, she took hold of the door, and slammed it shut. Talking to herself, she said that she was going back to do something that she could understand. That made the second time that she had slammed the door on him—Sophia had been counting.

Sophia had closed the door to their room. She had been watching and listening to the goings on from Mr. Miller's study. He was as far from resolving the issue between his wife and Sophia as ever. He hadn't done anything, because it was something that he didn't want to be bothered with. He had pretty much come to the conclusion that it was nothing more than bickering, and ill feelings. As long as things didn't get any worse, he could live with it if they could.

Albert and Mary, Mrs. Miller's two children from her first marriage, were the only people in Magnolia Manor without a wish list—they hadn't started thinking about Christmas, because it was too far away. Mrs. Miller had wished that she could somehow get rid of that ever-present unwanted nuisance in her house. If only she could wave bye-bye to Sophia, things would be just the way she had hoped they would be. Mrs. Miller knew that her husband had been blocking the door for Sophia. Anybody else would have shoved her out a long time ago. She had already talked to him about getting rid of her, but he had told her that he wouldn't separate Sophia from Elizabeth.

Sophia's wish had been simple, at least to her. She just wanted things to be the way that they used to be. Had it been left up to her, after Mr. Miller had carried Mrs. Miller across the threshold, she would have then had him turn around and carry her back out onto the porch, and toss her over the side.

Sophia, Amanda, Caroline and Emily had always been able to sway Mr. Miller when need be. They had been very successful at getting him to lean in their direction whenever they thought that Elizabeth might stand in their way. They couldn't finagle anymore since Mrs. Miller had moved in. Sophia was sure that Caroline and Emily had pretty much taken Magnolia Manor off their list of places to visit. If they had, then it had to be because of Mrs. Miller.

Mr. Miller simply wondered why his wife had been making such a big to-do over nothing. He had been around Sophia almost her entire life, and he had always found her to be interesting. He could never tell what she might be thinking, and she had never talked to him very much, but they never had any problems.

He and Sophia had similar wishes—he wished that things could be like they had once been. He loved his wife, but he also loved the peaceful household that he once had. Things were far from being to the point where he and Mrs. Miller had any thoughts about splitting up— they had just gotten married. Still, he liked it when the only fussing around the house had been when Elizabeth got on him about not eating breakfast, or when she got on Sophia for lagging with her chores.

While Mrs. Miller and Sophia had a self-centered attitude, and a personal vendetta to go along with it, Elizabeth had an unselfish wish. She only wanted Sophia and Mrs. Miller to stop doing what they had been do-ing, and bury the hatchet. Elizabeth's fear had been that Sophia would do something that might give Mrs. Miller the upper hand that she needed to coax her husband into selling her. She didn't know what Sophia would have to do to make Mr. Miller go that far, but it was something that she had to think about. In a way, Elizabeth's wish had been like Mr. Miller's wish. She just wanted Sophia and Mrs. Miller to stop—they wouldn't have to shake hands, she just wished that they would stop.

Four

When Mr. and Mrs. Miller moved into their new mansion, they used the old furniture from his old house, and Mrs. Miller had some as well. As the months passed, the old furniture slowly disappeared, and it had been replaced by the new. The interior décor had been coordinated by Mrs. Miller. Since she was in charge, and since nobody had said no, she exercised her responsibility with artistic flair, and elegance of style that were as good as any.

Mrs. Miller had crates of furniture, rugs and artwork arriving from everywhere. Mr. Miller worked in his office during the day, and Mrs. Miller had him, Elizabeth and Sophia all sliding furniture around at night. She thoughtfully considered the perfect placement of each piece. When they slid it to where she wanted it, she would change her mind, and have them slide it again.

Eventually, shuffling and sliding things around in search of that perfect spot had become such a burden for Mr. Miller that he passed the job along to Alfred.

Whenever Mrs. Miller needed help, she would send for him. It was a process that continued for a long time. Mr. Miller was glad that he had delegated Alfred to help with the furniture, because he doubted if he could hold out with his wife cracking the whip the way she had been.

When everything had been finished, Magnolia Manor was beautiful, stately constructed and well appointed. To cap it all off, Alfred had the grounds around the mansion perfectly landscaped with perennials and annuals that offered year-round splendor. Mr. Miller's dream had given birth to the mansion, and at last, it was real and complete. The Millers had been thoroughly satisfied with their family seat on the edge of town, but for those that had tendered the sweat from their labors, there reward had been simply, another job well done.

Mr. Miller had always seemed to be more involved in things than most people ... law, politics and whatever else he could wiggle into. He had two plantations. Even though he had overseers to manage the plantations, he still made frequent trips to both places just to make sure that things were right.

He had been reelected to the State Legislature, and he had always been serious minded when it came to the affairs of state. He was usually well composed, maintaining the qualities of a gentleman, and embracing the dignities expected from a man of his stature. Yet, he was not reluctant to push those qualities aside, especially in defense of his own integrity, his allegiance to duty, or protecting what was his.

Several years before he had married, Mr. Miller had been involved in a brawl, and of all places, in Nashville during a meeting of the Tennessee Legislature. He had the floor, and while speaking, he had been critical of some members of the assembly saying that they had been wasting the time of the House of Representatives. While he still had the floor, a member of the legislature had made a couple of clever remarks that Mr. Miller had considered to be offensive.

Regarding the remarks as insults to comments that he had made, Mr. Miller started walking over to where the House member had been seated. As he got closer, it had become obvious that Mr. Miller had no intentions of walking over to talk. Consequently, the other House member had grabbed a chair to use in his defense. Before he could raise the chair, Mr. Miller had jumped on top of him, and both ended up literally on the floor at the State House.

After they had knocked each other around for a while, they were separated by their colleagues. When things had settled down, the other House member tried to offer an apology. He explained that his comments had been taken out of context, and in no way had they been intended as insults. Mr. Miller had no interest in listening to his apology, because he had turned his back and walked away before he could finish explaining.

Mr. Miller didn't tell anyone at home that he had been involved in a fight. Although it had been some time back, while browsing through one of his dated newspapers, Sophia had seen an article that described the incident. She had asked him if he really had been in a fight. He willingly confirmed that he had been, and then said that he should have slapped his face, given him his choice of weapons, and told him to meet him out back.

Elizabeth understood Mrs. Miller's husband better than she did. She knew that he had never been quick to back away from a challenge. What others had shunned, he willingly courted. Whenever Mrs. Miller would tell him that he had too many irons in the fire, Elizabeth knew that it would be just a matter of time before he would start heating another. He had always been comfortable when bogged down in debates over legislation in Nashville.

Whenever house members needed to be swayed, he could get it done. In the business arena, and even around his adopted home town, he had been regarded as being stern and assertive, but erroneously unsociable. Others saw him that way, but his step children didn't. To Albert and Mary, he was kind and gentle, and they could sway their step-father as well as he could sway sentiments at the State House. To them, he was daddy.

Sophia loved Mrs. Miller's children, and she spent more time with them than anyone, including Mr. or Mrs. Miller. Albert and Mary were young, and therefore impressionable. After a while, they had come to view Sophia more as a family member, and in spite of Mrs. Miller's teachings, less as a slave or a nanny. Their view of Sophia had gone against Mrs. Miller's philosophy. Yet, she had found it impossible to manage her children's feelings toward Sophia, because they were always with her.

Taking care of the kids had been exactly what Mrs. Miller expected of Sophia. However, she didn't want her children getting confused when it came to Sophia's position around the house, or when it came to their affections for her. She had been and always would be less than their equal, and she wanted her children to get the facts fixed in their minds.

Mrs. Miller wanted her children to be cognizant of the fact that Sophia was a slave and nothing more. If they cared for her, let it be no more than a fondness. Albert and Mary's concepts of society's social strata had been undeveloped, and therefore, they couldn't, or they didn't interpret things in the same way that their mother did.

Mr. or Mrs. Miller would usually let Albert and Mary know when it was time for bed, but it was Sophia and Elizabeth that had always helped them prepare for bed. Once they had been tucked in, Mrs. Miller would stop by their room and kiss them goodnight. However, her goodnight kisses had always been tendered after Elizabeth and Sophia had planted theirs.

Sometimes guests at the mansion had made the wrong assumption regarding Sophia. Some had thought that she might be Mr. Miller's daughter by another woman, and some had taken her to be a relative from Mrs. Miller's side of the family. Such blunders did more than just ruffle Mrs. Miller's feathers; they made her down right angry. Mr. Miller had learned that part of his wife's hostile attitude toward Sophia had been due to the fact that she looked too much like a white girl. He knew that she had a problem with it, because she had told him so— more than a few times.

Mrs. Miller had blamed her husband for Sophia's bold attitude, because she felt like he had been too lenient with her. If she had had her way, she wouldn't have put her in the cotton fields in order to get her out of the house. Instead, she would have stuck a cheap price on her—still being willing to negotiate—and sold her as is. That way, she would have gotten her out of the house and out of her life.

The Sabbath day being the Lord's Day, everybody went to church, including Elizabeth and Sophia. Sophia looked forward to going, because it gave her the chance to see Caroline and Emily. Sometimes, circumstances might allow them to talk a little, but usually they didn't. Still, they could say hello to each other without saying a word. Sophia wouldn't dare put Caroline and Emily on the spot, nor would they create an unpleasant situation for her by being overly friendly in public. There were too many other people around that had the same attitude as Mrs. Miller.

Although they were careful not to be overly friendly in public, they had their way of communicating, even at church. They would write notes, usually while at home, and they delivered them while at church. They simply folded the handwritten note, placed it in the palm of their hand, and passed it off as they walked past each other. Magnolia Manor had become pretty much inaccessible to Caroline and Emily, because they knew that Mrs. Miller didn't want them coming over to visit Sophia. Since they had stopped going there, their almost weekly exchange of handwritten messages kept them informed.

Although it was Sunday, Elizabeth and Sophia didn't go to church. They had stayed at home to prepare dinner for the guests that would arrive during the afternoon. It was one of the not so rare get-togethers that Mrs. Miller loved to host. She had planned the menu, and Elizabeth and Sophia had the task of making sure that everything would be ready when their guests arrived. Mrs. Miller had told Elizabeth to set the table with some of her finest imported chinaware, because she wanted it to be very special. Her guests included some of the town's most elite, and her goal had been simply to impress.

When the Millers had returned from church, Mrs. Miller quickly made her way to the dining room to do an inspection. She found everything to be exactly the way that it should be. The only thing that she had to do was to wait for the arrival of her guests. She had arranged for Albert and Mary to spend the afternoon with their friends down the street.

By early afternoon, the guests had arrived. The women sat in the parlor, and the men had gathered on the porch to talk and sip brandy. Mrs. Miller had excused herself so that she could talk to Elizabeth and Sophia. Finding that everything was ready, Mrs. Miller returned to the parlor, and told the ladies that they could proceed to the dining room. As the ladies were leaving the parlor, she went to the porch, and invited the gentlemen inside.

When everyone had entered the dining room, Mrs. Miller took charge of the seating arrangement. She loved what she was doing, and she knew how to do it. Everything was going just the way that she had planned. She waited until everyone had been seated, and then she found her place at the table. On the table next to her, she had placed the small bell that she would use to summon her servants.

After being seated, the men continued with their conversation while still sipping brandy. The women had been busy flattering Mrs. Miller. They had been showering her with compliments regarding her beautiful mansion, and its magnificent accessories. While her guests talked, she mostly listened, because they had been saying just what she wanted to hear. After all, that had been her reason for having them over. After a while, Mrs. Miller summoned Elizabeth to let her know that her guests were ready to be served. Elizabeth politely acknowledged her command, and the process began.

Stylishly, Elizabeth and Sophia placed the main course on the table as if it was a five star restaurant. Elizabeth noticed that Sophia had gotten the attention of some of the guests—although it was a guess, she believed that she knew why—but they had kept their curiosity hidden from Mrs. Miller. They dared not say anything that might offend their host, and most certainly not their hostess.

When it was time to serve dessert, Elizabeth had placed the appropriate pieces of chinaware onto a tray, and she had asked Sophia to take it to the dining room. Mr. Miller had excused himself from the table to fetch a bottle of wine, one that he wanted to serve with dessert. He had gotten the bottle of wine, and he was on his way back to the dining room. When he entered the hallway, he had made a few steps, and then he met Sophia. Elizabeth had been following closely behind. Sophia saw Mr. Miller walking toward her, and she looked up at him, but only for a moment. When she did, the tray that she had been carrying tilted, and all of the chinaware ended up on the floor.

Mrs. Miller heard the noise, and without a word to her guests, she had quickly gotten up from the table, and stepped into the hallway. She was furious when she saw Sophia standing in front of her holding the empty silver tray. On the floor lay her beautiful chinaware, all of it in bits and pieces.

Mrs. Miller had walked up to Sophia, and she stood very close to her, like in her face. When she spoke, she told her to look at what she had done. Mr. Miller had been standing there watching. He decided that if Sophia had ever needed to be rescued, then was the time; he had to jump in and get her. He told Mrs. Miller that it had all been his fault. He said that he had been reading the label on the bottle of wine when he accidentally walked into her, and thereby causing the accident.

Mrs. Miller stared at her husband with an expression that said, "I don't believe you." Yet, she didn't question his account of what had taken place, because she had no way of knowing for sure. To calm her down and take her attention away from Sophia, Mr. Miller said that they would just have to order another set.

Elizabeth had been standing in the background, quietly and bewildered. She didn't see everything that had happened, but she had seen enough to know that it didn't happen the way that Mr. Miller had explained it to Mrs. Miller. Dropping the chinaware had been an accident, but it was Sophia's fault—no one had bumped into her.

Finally, and after Mrs. Miller had exhausted all of the expletives that she could utter without completely losing her dignity, she returned to the dining room and her guests. She had left Mr. Miller, Sophia and Elizabeth standing in the hallway. They had looked at each other, but they didn't say anything. Then, with a nod of his head, somewhat like St. Nick in Moore's Christmas classic—he didn't go up the chimney—Mr. Miller bypassed Elizabeth and Sophia, and again joined his guests in the dining room.

When he had returned with the bottle of wine, his already tipsy friends teased him about being in hot water for being so clumsy. Their antics had been ignored by Mrs. Miller. She had never thought it to be amusing, she was angry, and she was still pretty sure that it had been Sophia's fault—her husband had been covering for her.

After dinner, the ladies and their husbands found themselves back in the same separate places that they had been in before dinner. Again, Mrs. Miller had started talking about how unreliable Sophia was, and how she didn't care for her personality. Elizabeth and Sophia could hear her talking, because she didn't try to hide what she had to say. Her guests mostly listened, but they quickly agreed with her whenever they felt like it was time to do so. After a while, she had finished with her assessment of Sophia, and she had asked her guests to excuse her manners. She tried to erase the last hour or so from her memory, and move on to something that they could all talk about.

Elizabeth and Sophia had been busy with the usual after dinner cleanup. The men had one or two more after dinner drinks, some had already had one or two too many, and then they left. Elizabeth and Sophia were glad that they had gone. They had to go everywhere that they had been, so that they could pick up what they had left behind—everything from empty glasses to spent cigars.

FIVE

The slaves had their own church, and it was located within walking distance of Magnolia Manor. It had gotten to be well into the afternoon, but they were still there and going at it. When the chores had been done, Elizabeth had to speak with Mr. and Mrs. Miller. They had been sitting on the porch. First, she apologized for the broken chinaware. Mr. Miller said that an apology wasn't necessary since it had all been his fault. Mrs. Miller looked at him, but nonetheless, she still had her doubts. Since she didn't know for sure, she had decided to forget about it, and do like he had suggested, order another set.

The chinaware ending up on the floor had not been that much of a concern to Elizabeth. She had brought it up to help pave the way for what was to follow—it was her way of buttering up Mrs. Miller, letting her think that she had connected with her. Elizabeth wanted to get permission for her and Sophia to attend church with the slaves. Just when she had started to ask for permission, Mr. Miller excused himself, and he had gone back inside. Then, only Mrs. Miller and Elizabeth were left on the porch. Since Elizabeth had already started with her question, she had to continue. When she had finished, Mrs. Miller responded to her question by asking a question. She wanted to know why they were interested in going to church with the slaves.

Elizabeth had gotten herself caught in the very position that she had already considered, and she had already made plans to avoid such a snag. After all of her planning, she had gotten stuck between the proverbial rock and a hard place. Since she had thought about it ahead of time, she had planned accordingly—it just didn't go the way that she had it set up.

Like Sophia, she too had learned that if they wanted something, it was better to ask Mr. Miller, and if they had to ask Mrs. Miller, make sure that Mr. Miller was there to listen. When Elizabeth had first gone out onto the porch, she saw that Mr. and Mrs. Miller were there together—right where she had wanted them. However, just as she had started to ask her question, Mr. Miller missed it, because he had to go inside.

Mrs. Miller could have simply said yes or no to the question, and that would have ended it. Elizabeth had the notion that she was probably leaning more toward saying no—to her, it seemed like she was. Yet, Mrs. Miller didn't seem to want to tell Elizabeth that she couldn't go to church with the slaves, perhaps because it didn't sound right. Elizabeth had been the one with a question to ask, but things had flip-flopped. Mrs. Miller had started asking the questions, and Elizabeth was trying to provide the answers. While Mrs. Miller and Elizabeth had been trying to move around without really stepping on the other's foot, Mr. Miller returned.

Mrs. Miller had been looking at Elizabeth, and both seemed like they might be confused. Consequently, that prompted a question from Mr. Miller. He had asked what was wrong. Mrs. Miller said that the slaves were still having church, and Elizabeth wanted to know if she and Sophia could go down there. He thought that it was a good idea, because they had missed out on going to church with them. What he had said was good enough to get Mrs. Miller to agree.

The church where the slaves had assembled was what they called a bush harbor. Poles had been placed in the ground with a lattice framework across the top. On top of the lattice framework, they placed freshly cut tree branches that protected them from the sun. It was crudely built, but it served the purpose.

Elizabeth would rather have been going to the bush harbor all along. She liked it because it was a place where they could not only worship, but they could also socialize. Earlier, Mrs. Miller had told Elizabeth and Sophia to stay at home, and prepare for the dinner party. As soon as Mrs. Miller had said it, that's when Elizabeth started thinking that the dinner party just might get her and Sophia a pass to the bush harbor. Since she and Sophia had skipped the regular church, she felt like the Millers would be more than likely to say yes, and she had it figured right.

Most of the people that Sophia knew were people that she had gotten acquainted with at Mr. Miller's house. Alfred was the only black person that she knew other than Elizabeth. Therefore, Sophia wanted to go to the bush harbor just to see some other faces.

Foremost on Elizabeth's mind had been the hope that she would be able to see Alfred. Although the hope of seeing him had been her foremost reason, she still hadn't placed Alfred above the Almighty, she wouldn't dare. She kept Him on the main line—Alfred had been placed on a side track. She definitely had no intentions of letting Sophia be privy to her personal life, especially when it came to Alfred. Therefore, Elizabeth let Sophia think that they would be going to the bush harbor for religious reasons only. Any other reason for going was none of Sophia's business.

Elizabeth and Sophia had been dressed in their finest for Mrs. Miller's dinner party, and they saw no need to change into anything else. The gentle grade sloping toward the bush harbor favored a rapid pace, and they used the advantage. Although she had never been to a bush harbor before, Sophia had already decided that it just might be the place for her. If she found someone to talk to, a boy perhaps, then she could do so—maybe.

The congregation had been singing, but at the same time they had been watching the two people, seemingly strangers that were headed in their direction. When they had gotten close enough, some amongst the flock had recognized them. Realizing that it was Elizabeth and her daughter, the spirit under the bush harbor had suddenly been elevated to a level higher than the preacher had ever taken them.

Elizabeth and Sophia had found a place amongst the crowd, and they had started singing along. Sophia had been familiar with the songs that they sung when they went to church with the Millers, but she was not familiar with the songs at the bush harbor. Still, she hummed along, and did the best that she could. At the same time, she had been curious, and she had been looking around at all of the black people that she had never seen before.

She didn't know anybody, but she thought that it was great.

After a while, the singing had gotten louder, and like never before their voices blended and rang out under the bush harbor like a broadcast from Heaven. Mr. and Mrs. Miller could hear them clearly, as they sat on the porch back at the mansion, transfixed by a harmonious rhythm that was rare in their church. They had heard them sing before, but on that day, the sound was sweeter.

Service had ended, at least that session had. The congregation hung around, and everybody had started talking. That in itself was good enough reason for them to love being where they were. Sunday was the catalyst of life that charged their will to even want to make it from one day to the next. They didn't have much else to look forward to that might boost their spirits. Sundays had always been welcomed, because it was alright to sit down without the fear of being punished.

The bush harbor congregation was a mixture of slaves from the nearby area. Elizabeth knew some of them, but most of them, she had never met. She did have a few relatives there—cousins that had made the trek with her and Sophia from North Carolina.

She had been walking around talking and getting acquainted, but her eyes had been scanning the crowd looking for Alfred. She knew that he had to be around somewhere. Nevertheless, she didn't want to make things appear too obvious by asking of his whereabouts, because she didn't want to have anybody thinking the wrong thing—more than likely, their thoughts would have hit the nail right on the head. Before Elizabeth and Sophia arrived, Alfred had gone to the spring down the way to fetch some drinking water.

Elizabeth and Alfred could see each other whenever he was at the mansion taking care of the grounds, but that was about it. Seldom did they have the chance to talk. Usually they just watched each other as they went about their work. They both knew what the consequences might be if the lady of the house found them doing anything that might resemble socializing. If they had been caught up in a moment of intimacy, Mrs. Miller might have had Alfred flogged, and then relegated to being a common field hand, and Elizabeth ... it would be hard to say.

When Alfred returned with the water, he couldn't be sure, but he thought that he had seen Elizabeth standing amongst the crowd over at the other side. After he had gotten a better look, he was sure that it was her—she had showed up unexpectedly. Unassumingly, and with no apologies, he pushed and shoved his way through the crowd to get to her. When he approached from the rear and said hello, she had been surprised, because she didn't know that he was there.

Alfred took Elizabeth by the hand, and timidly kissed her on the lips. No sooner than their lips had touched, Elizabeth started looking around, hoping that Sophia hadn't seen anything. They wanted to be alone, so they had walked off to the side, and sat down next to each other on one of the makeshift benches. At last, and for the first time in a long time they were both contented just sitting there together, and away from the eyes of Magnolia Manor.

Sophia didn't see Alfred kiss Elizabeth, in fact, she hadn't even been thinking about them. She had her own agenda. People were moving around like ants, and Sophia was right where she wanted to be, smack dab in the middle. The people that she saw were complete strangers to her, but she didn't care. Never in her life had she experienced the feeling that she then had, and never before had she felt so free. It was like she had spent a lifetime locked in a room, and then someone opened the door. She had fallen in love with where she was.

Sophia was a teenager, but she had never had a boyfriend, and she didn't know what it might feel like to be in love. She realized that the bush harbor might be the one place that could give her that much need social boost that had been missing from her life. She remembered to be polite when strangers walked up to her to talk, but quickly, she had learned to carry on a conversation while still searching the hoard of people. Her eyes had been scanning the crowd, and she had noticed the boys looking at her, but that was all that they had done. Her intuition had suggested that they probably wanted to talk, but they were just too shy.

While she walked around, Sophia had been making a conscious effort not to wander too closely to Elizabeth and Alfred. She didn't want to see them, and she didn't want them to see her. She had been stopped several times, mostly by older people that knew who she was only because they had known Elizabeth. Her eyes kept scanning the crowd to see who was there. However, she wanted to do more than just see who was there. She had been hoping to see someone who could become that special someone in her life. Eventually, one particular boy had gotten her attention. He had been standing off to the side by himself, and Sophia could tell that he had been watching her.

Alfred had Elizabeth occupied, and she had been giving him her attention, but not all of it. She had been trying to keep an eye on Sophia. It wasn't that she didn't trust her daughter, she just felt like she needed to keep an eye on her—mothers are like that. Elizabeth knew that she had placed Sophia in an environment that was new to her, and therefore, she felt like she probably had to be a little uneasy. Elizabeth didn't know it, but from the time that they arrived, Sophia had been on cloud nine, and lost in the new world that she had found—she felt good.

After some mingling, and a lot of talking, the preacher had made his way to the front of the bush harbor. He had made the call for everyone to be seated. He was ready to deliver his final sermon of the day.

Elizabeth and Alfred remained seated in the same place that they had been after moving off to the side to be alone. Sophia had stayed on the opposite side of the bush harbor—away from them—and she had placed herself there by choice. The fact that Sophia wanted to roam around a little on her own had been alright with Elizabeth. Besides that, she didn't want Sophia around in case Alfred decided that he wanted to hold her hand. However, Sophia didn't have anyone to hold her hand, but she had been working on it.

Sophia looked around for the boy that she had been eying—the one that had been standing off to the side watching her. She searched in the direction where she had last seen him, but he had moved. Her first thought was that she had let him get away. She was surprised when she found him. He had seated himself on the end of a bench just ahead of where she had been standing. She wondered if he had been deliberate in choosing his seat, so that he could be closer to her—she hoped so.

Nonchalantly, she walked up to where he was seated, and politely asked that he move over a bit, so that she could sit down. When he had moved over, Sophia then sat down on the end of the bench next to him. She had her eyes directed toward the preacher, but she couldn't see him. From the corner of her eye, she could only see the boy sitting next to her.

Sophia and the boy sat there together, each of them afraid to say anything, but both wanting to talk to the other. Still, they sat there, and they kept looking straight ahead. Sophia had been hoping that he would say something to her, just anything, she didn't care what. She knew that it might appear too bold if she spoke first, but she did want to talk to him.

After a while, she had come to the conclusion that he was not going to say anything, so she bent over and leaned forward to avoid being seen or overheard. She told him that her name was Sophia, and she asked him what his name was. The boy leaned forward and whispered that his name was Daniel. Then she felt like the door had been opened, and she wanted to walk in, but it was just too soon to make a move like that.

The preacher had started getting into his sermon, and the congregation had been responding with shouts of encouragement and jubilation that could be heard all the way to Magnolia Manor. Yet, the preacher was at the other side of the world as far as Sophia and Daniel had been concerned. Even with all of the noise from the preacher and the congregation, the loudest noise that they could hear had been their heartbeats.

All of the sounds from around them had given Sophia and Daniel the advantage that they needed. It made it possible for them to speak softly without being heard. They had just gotten acquainted, but Sophia's sixth sense had told her that Daniel liked her as much as she liked him.

The preacher had been stirring the congregation for quite some time when Sophia, still leaning forward to conceal her whispers, noticed Daniel's hand resting on the bench near his side. She knew that it was not ladylike, and it was still too soon, but she wanted Daniel to know that she liked him, and time was running out. Time was running out, because it wouldn't be long before things would end, and they would part ways. Not only would they part ways, she wouldn't see him again until next Sunday, if then.

Daniel's hand was still resting on the bench. Being ever so gentle, with much reluctance, scared to death, and making it seem like she was unaware, Sophia had placed her hand on top of Daniel's hand. When she did, they both kept looking straight ahead, and they never flinched. She wondered what he might be thinking.

Sophia placing her hand on top of Daniel's had been an innocent gesture, but maybe a rush act, she thought. Yet, for the very first time, both had experienced a feeling of passion that neither had ever known. With her hand resting on his, Sophia could feel that Daniel was nervous, and she wondered if he could feel the same tingle from her hand. Staring at the preacher, but still not seeing him, she wondered if Daniel might think that she had been too forward. Even so, she hadn't planned on backing away, not unless Daniel had asked her to.

Sitting there next to him, Sophia's intentions were all pure, but it was the very first time that she had ever been that close to a boy, and she felt good. It wasn't long before her thoughts about whether or not she had been too forward had gone away. Then, clutching each other's hand, she hoped that no one would hear what they were feeling for each other.

Things were winding down under the bush harbor, and Sophia and Daniel were still holding hands. They didn't let go, not even when everyone had stood. They were sure that no one paid any attention to them since it had been so crowded. When the preacher had dismissed the congregation, Sophia told Daniel that she would see him the next time, but she didn't know for sure when that might be. Daniel had told her that he came to the bush harbor every Sunday. She had taken that to mean yes, he wanted to see her again.

Sophia and Daniel had been trying to get in a few last words before leaving. At the same time, Sophia had been scanning the crowd to try and locate Elizabeth. When she spotted her, she and Alfred hadn't moved; they were still at the other side of the bush harbor. Elizabeth hadn't seemed to be in a rush to leave, and neither had Sophia. Therefore, she and Daniel kept on talking. They couldn't hold hands anymore, because people had started moving around, and they couldn't hide.

Sophia had been attending church on Sunday with Elizabeth longer than she could remember. Never before had she been to a church where the entire congregation was nothing but black people. She loved it, and she wanted to do it again. She was sure that Elizabeth had enjoyed the day the same as she had.

In order to keep on seeing Daniel, she would have to talk Elizabeth into making the bush harbor their church of choice every Sunday. To make sure that Elizabeth would opt for the bush harbor, Sophia had decided that she had to wait for that perfect moment when her mom would be in the right mood.

Daniel had said goodbye to Sophia, and he had walked away, because Elizabeth and Alfred had started walking in their direction. Daniel had mixed himself in with the crowd, and Sophia had started talking with some of the girls. She had decided that what she was then doing would appear innocent enough. She didn't want to have to explain Daniel to Elizabeth. With Alfred still at her side, Elizabeth had said that it was time for her and Sophia to leave.

They had no reason to hurry as they made their way to Magnolia Manor. Sophia was in a good mood, and she was sure that Elizabeth had to be also. They had been walking along quietly, and then Elizabeth started talking. She had asked Sophia if Daniel seemed to be a decent young man. After Elizabeth had asked the question, Sophia didn't say anything for a few seconds, because she had been startled. She realized that somehow, Elizabeth had found out that she had been sitting next to Daniel. Not only that, she also knew his name.

Sophia felt like she and Daniel had been so careful not to be noticed. However, she had to remain calm, so that she wouldn't appear guilty of any wrong doings. When she had gotten her thoughts together, Sophia said that Daniel seemed to be a very nice boy, and that she had talked to him a little. Sophia thought that Elizabeth would be upset with her, but she didn't seem to be. After all, Sophia was sixteen years old, and Elizabeth felt like it had probably been alright, especially with all of the adults around—they couldn't do much in church, even at a bush harbor.

Elizabeth had told Sophia that Daniel was not one of Mr. Miller's slaves, and that he attended church every Sunday at the bush harbor. She said that she had met his parents, and that they seemed to be nice people—the surprises kept on coming. Elizabeth had told her that two of the girls that she had been talking to were Daniel's sisters.

Daniel hadn't said anything at all to Sophia about his parents, or his sisters being at the bush harbor. Sophia didn't know where Elizabeth had gotten her information from, but she had decided not to ask. Regardless of where she had gotten it from, she had it right. She couldn't believe that Elizabeth knew more about Daniel than she did, and she was the one that had been talking to him. Then she wondered if any of Daniel's other relatives might have been sitting near them while they were whispering and ignoring the preacher.

Elizabeth then told Sophia that it wasn't right for her and Daniel to be sitting in the back of the church talking, and she told her that she should learn to keep her hands to herself. Sophia had been completely shocked. She couldn't say anything in her own defense, because everything that Elizabeth had said was true.

Sophia thought about how she and Daniel had been so careful to keep things hidden. Then she felt like they may as well have been standing up front with the preacher for everyone to see, because it seemed like they had anyway. Most of all, she wondered how Elizabeth knew that they had been holding hands.

Since Elizabeth had all of the information, and since all of it had been correct, Sophia concluded that someone sitting near her and Daniel had to have told her, but someone seeing them holding hands remained a mystery—they had been sitting down with their hands at their sides. Regardless of how Elizabeth had found out, Sophia had to let it be, because she didn't want to ask any questions, and she wanted Elizabeth to hurry up and finish.

Sophia didn't tell Elizabeth that she wouldn't whisper or hold hands with Daniel anymore, because she didn't want to lie to her mother. However, she did vow to herself that she would have to be more careful the next time. Everything that Elizabeth had thrown at her was true. The best thing that she could do was to listen and be quiet. After Elizabeth had said what she had to say, she was through with it.

Earlier, Sophia had thoughts of how she would ask Elizabeth about attending the bush harbor every Sunday just so that she could see Daniel. Suddenly things had changed. Then she had to wonder if she had done enough to make her first trip be her last. She hoped not, because it had been the single most breathtaking day of her life—she had been close to a boy for the first time, and it felt good.

When Elizabeth and Sophia arrived at the mansion, Mr. and Mrs. Miller had been sitting on the porch watching Albert and Mary play in the backyard. Mainly to get away from Elizabeth, Sophia had gone over and started talking to the kids. Mrs. Miller wanted to know what they thought of the bush harbor, hoping that their thoughts would all be negative. Elizabeth told her that it had all been worth the trip, and she thanked them for letting her and Sophia go. Even so, in sort of an apologetic way, Mrs. Miller told Elizabeth that she and Sophia wouldn't have to go to that place often. It would only be when there's a conflict that prevented them from attending the church in town.

Elizabeth had asked if there was anything that she needed to do in the mansion. Mrs. Miller said if anything needed to be done, it could wait until tomorrow. Elizabeth then excused herself, and she had gone to her room. It seemed to her that Mrs. Miller had forgotten about the incident that had happened earlier during the day—the broken chinaware. After a while, Elizabeth had sat down in her rocking chair where it was quiet, and she stared outside from the window. She was alone, but she felt good thinking about the afternoon that she had spent with Alfred.

Sophia was still in the yard, sitting on the bench with the kids. It had gotten late in the day when Mary asked Sophia if she would read a story to them from one of the storybooks. Sophia asked Mrs. Miller if it would be alright if she got a book from the shelf. When Mrs. Miller said yes, Sophia and the kids went inside to get one. Albert and Mary tagged along just to make sure that she got the right one.

When they had made their way back to the porch, Mr. Miller asked to see which storybook they had chosen, and Sophia showed it to him. He didn't really care about which book they had, he was just doing something to show the kids that he was interested. Cordially, and like a father, Mr. Miller told them that the book that they had chosen was a good one. Albert and Mary followed Sophia down the steps, and they had gone back to the bench. The three of them sat down next to each other with Sophia in the middle. They had thumbed through the book, and found one of their favorite stories.

Meanwhile, Mr. and Mrs. Miller hadn't moved, they were still sitting on the porch. Mrs. Miller had started talking about the fact that she just couldn't understand how Sophia had ever learned how to read and write. She looked at Mr. Miller, and told him that he should have never allowed it to happen. Again, Mr. Miller had to explain how it had come about—she had learned social etiquette and how to read and ... from Amanda, Caroline and Emily.

He couldn't understand why she kept on asking him how it had come about. He had explained it to her lots of times, but it never made any difference. Although he had explained how she learned, Mrs. Miller didn't care about the how part; her only point was that it should have never been allowed to happen—slaves weren't supposed to know how to read and write.

Mrs. Miller said that a slave didn't need to know anything about social etiquette. She insisted that it just didn't seem right for slaves to be doing that sort of thing, looking and acting like white people, as she had put it. Furthermore, she said that if Amanda, Caroline, Emily and Sophia hadn't been allowed to spend so much time together, they wouldn't have grown up acting like they were sisters. She couldn't imagine a white family that would let their daughter get that close to a slave. Saying that some people just don't know how to raise children, and probably shouldn't have them in the first place got Mr. Miller's attention, but not enough for him to say anything.

Sophia had been reading to Albert and Mary, but she could hear Mr. and Mrs. Miller talking. She never looked up when she overheard Mrs. Miller say that it was embarrassing when people come to the mansion and mistake Sophia as being a relative of theirs. It was so humiliating, she had thought.

Mr. Miller had seen guests at the mansion mistakenly assume that Sophia was a relative of his—he had told her so—but he had never let it drive him up the wall when they did. He had told Mrs. Miller that the best thing to do when something like that happened would be to let it go in one ear and out the other. She said that she couldn't inside. It had started to rain, and in just a few minutes, it had become a torrential downpour.

Frightened by the bellowing wind sweeping through the trees, and around the mansion, they had all hunkered down in the hallway. Mr. Miller had his arms around Mrs. Miller and Albert. Elizabeth, Sophia and Mary were hugging each other, and hoping that it wouldn't be the last time. Since back when she was a little girl, Sophia had always been very frightened by stormy weather. Elizabeth had a bigger task trying to keep her calm than she had with Mary.

After a while, it had quieted down outside, but they kept sitting on the floor looking at each other. Finally, Mr. Miller said that it must be over. He had stood up, and he had taken Mrs. Miller by the hand to help her up. Then he helped Elizabeth. Sophia was still crouched on the floor, as frightened as ever with Mary standing next to her. Mr. Miller had taken her by the hand, and he told her that it was over. Still, she didn't make much of an effort to stand, so he literally pulled her to her feet. They all looked at each other for a moment, and then walked out onto the front porch.

They looked around, and surveyed the damage that had been done. It had all happened so quickly, trees had been downed, houses damaged, and debris had been strewn everywhere. Soon, it seemed like the Heavens had apologized. The clouds had parted, and made way for blue skies and sunshine. A few shaken souls, and a scarred landscape were the remnants of the storm, and that had been enough.

A few days of vacation with his wife hadn't changed things around town for Mr. Miller. Whenever they had let it go in one ear and out the other. Although it had happened once or twice, she said Heaven forbid that anyone else should ever think that she was a relative of hers. He said that he hadn't noticed anything like that. She told him that the only reason why he hadn't noticed anything was because he didn't pay enough attention to what goes on around the house.

Sophia had finished reading to Albert and Mary, and she had taken the book back inside. She was ready to go to her room, but like Elizabeth, first she asked Mrs. Miller if there was anything that she needed her to do. Mrs. Miller responded very bluntly. She told her that she didn't need her for anything. Mr. Miller looked at Sophia, and then at Mrs. Miller, but neither of them had looked at him—they just looked at each other.

Mrs. Miller had gotten up from her seat and gone inside, leaving Sophia standing on the porch with Mr. Miller. Just for a few seconds, Sophia didn't move. She let her eyes follow Mrs. Miller until she had gotten completely out of sight. When she could no longer see her, she looked at Mr. Miller. Still, she hadn't said anything; she just looked at him; and then she went to her room.

Sophia understood Mrs. Miller's remark about not needing her for anything, and she knew that she had said exactly what she meant. Still, Sophia didn't care, because she didn't need her for anything either.

The evening had been quiet. Elizabeth was still sitting in her rocker, and thinking about what a wonderful time she had had at the bush harbor. Sophia could tell that she loved having the chance to get away from Magnolia Manor for a while.

Sophia could sense that Elizabeth had been in a good mood, probably thinking about Alfred, she considered.

She knew how much her mom cared for him; Elizabeth just didn't know that she had been aware. Since Elizabeth seemed to be in a good mood, Sophia decided that it might be the right time to talk about going to the bush harbor every Sunday.

Sophia had considered the fact that Elizabeth might still be thinking about how she and Daniel had been carrying-on. Yet, she was in a good mood. Therefore, she had decided to cross her fingers, hope that Elizabeth would say yes, and know that the answer could very well be no.

After Sophia had asked the question, Elizabeth didn't say anything. Instead, she just sat there with Sophia waiting for her to reply. Since she hadn't replied, Sophia thought that she might be getting her thoughts together, so that she could get on her again about Daniel, but she didn't.

When Elizabeth spoke, she said that she did like listening to the preacher, and the beautiful singing. She told Sophia that she had always been more accustomed to the way slaves practiced religion than she had been to the customs of white people. Elizabeth had given Sophia a long line of well thought out reasons for attending the bush harbor, none of which included Alfred. Still, she seemed to be a little undecided to Sophia—she hadn't said yes or no.

Sophia realized that Elizabeth may have been absolutely right about her reasons for being interested in the bush harbor. Although she hadn't mentioned his name, she knew that Elizabeth would love to spend a few hours at the bush harbor on Sundays with Alfred. Sophia had been cognizant of the fact that Elizabeth had done an excellent job of explaining her reasons. Yet, she didn't really care about Elizabeth's reasons for going, so long as she went.

After all of her talk, Elizabeth still hadn't said yes or no to the question. Sophia wanted the answer to be yes, and she felt like Elizabeth might need a little push to help make up her mind. She knew that Elizabeth was very religious, and since she was, maybe she had inadvertently failed to consider the social rewards of going to the bush harbor. Therefore, she told Elizabeth that going to the bush harbor would give her more time to be with Alfred.

Sophia's suggestion about spending more time with Alfred had gotten Elizabeth all stirred up. She had just finished explaining that her reasons for considering the bush harbor had been for religious reasons only. If she wanted to see Alfred, she said that she could just look out the window, and see him working in the yard. Her only interest in going to the bush harbor had been so that she could worship in the way that she had always been used to doing. She then ended the conversation by asking Sophia what was it that had made her think that she wanted to see Alfred on Sunday anyway.

Sophia could tell that her mom had gotten more than just a little edgy in defending herself, and she knew that things would probably go a lot smoother if she just forgot about it for a while. She didn't want to twist Elizabeth's arm to the point that the bush harbor would become off limits. She wanted to see more of Daniel, but she had decided to talk about it later—she needed to give her mom a chance to settle down. Elizabeth's reason for wanting to go to the bush harbor had been no different from Sophia's reason. She wanted to see more of Alfred, but that was her business, and she didn't need any help from Sophia.

Sophia had made Elizabeth upset, but she stayed in the room with her. She found one of Mr. Miller's newspapers to read while she lay sprawled across the bed. After a while, Elizabeth had cooled off, and they had gotten back on friendlier terms. Elizabeth said that she would speak to Mr. and Mrs. Miller to see if going to the bush harbor would be alright with them.

That was the response that Sophia had been waiting for, but for a while she thought that she might have ruined things by being too pushy. Elizabeth said that if Mr. and Mrs. Miller did let them go, it would only be during fair weather. She had been to many such gatherings, and she knew that in foul weather, you may as well be standing outside in it. The bush harbor protected them from the hot sun, but from nothing else.

Elizabeth told her about the people that she had met earlier at the bush harbor. A few of them were relatives, and some of them were friends that she had known for a while. She promised Sophia that she would introduce them to her the next time, provided that there would be a next time—going to the bush harbor every Sunday hinged on what Mr. and Mrs. Miller might say.

If the Millers decided to let them go to the bush harbor each Sunday, Sophia felt like she definitely needed to know the people. She had to know exactly who the person was that she might be next to. It would be a precautionary measure. She didn't want the wrong eyes seeing her doing anything with Daniel, because the dust hadn't really settled from the first time.

Sophia had asked Elizabeth why they hadn't been going to the bush harbor all along rather than going to church with the Millers. Elizabeth didn't have a good answer. She simply said that she didn't know why, but she guessed that since it had started out that way, they just kept on doing the same thing.

Sophia had gone back to reading the newspaper. Once in a while, she would read something, and then tell Elizabeth about it. Bedtime had crept upon them before they realized it, probably because they had been thinking and talking about the good time that they had had that day.

Mr. Miller was up early the next morning. With a cup of coffee in one hand, he had been rambling through his study looking for only he knew what. When walking past the dining room, he would stop just long enough to stand over his plate, and eat a bite or two. While he nibbled, Elizabeth fussed at him about not sitting down, and eating a proper breakfast. He didn't pay much attention to her about fussing at him regarding his eating habits, because he had gotten used to it. She fussed at him every morning about the same thing, and she had been doing it for a long time. After he had finished his coffee, and found whatever it was that he had been looking for, he headed to his law office.

In town, he had noticed a group of people standing around on the streets talking. When he had made it to where they were, he found himself engaged in conversation regarding the current political issue, the legality of slavery. For several years, the issue had been on the mind of every slave-owner in the country. Some that didn't have a single slave wanted to keep things the way that they had always been, if for no other reason, simply because they felt like black people just ought to be slaves.

Although slavery had been a big concern, the issue was tied in with states rights versus federal rights. Some states wanted to have the right to decide for themselves whether or not they were willing to accept certain federal laws. However, the federal government wanted all states to be bound by the same federal laws. Should there be a federal law declaring slavery to be illegal, it would apply to both North and South—the entire country.

Since Mr. Miller was a member of the State Legislature, if he was there, then he was usually in on the conversation, not because he wanted to be, but because they dragged him in. Being a member of the legislature had him on the inside, and he had the answers, at least his constituents expected him to have them.

Mrs. Miller had asked Mr. Miller if he thought that slavery was legal. He told her that whether or not it was legal depended pretty much on where you lived and on how you interpreted the Constitution. Most people living in the South, including slave owners and many non-slave owners, believed it to be legal, while most Northerners believed it to be illegal. He said that both sides had been reading the same document, and each side had their own interpretation. They had taken it to mean what they wanted it to mean.

The slave holding states promoted the idea that the right to have slaves was protected by the Constitution, and they wanted Congress to recognize that right. If Congress did not, then their recourse would be to secede from the Union. Mr. Miller had made it clear—to his satisfaction anyway—that the country would forever be better as a Union of States than it would be if they were to separate. He had made it clear to himself, but it was not himself that had placed him in a seat at the State House.

West Tennessee had more slaves than any other region of the State. That had been because West Tennessee had the most fertile soils, and therefore, was most suited for growing cotton. Cotton had been the crop of choice, because it had been the most profitable.

Anyone that had slaves was a supporter of slavery, and they wanted to maintain that right. However, that was the question. "Did anyone have the right to own slaves?" That was the question that they couldn't agree on, or more than likely, the question that they had been unwilling to agree on.

Austin Miller owned many slaves in both Tennessee and Mississippi, and slave labor had made him a wealthy man. Yet, he had openly opposed any concepts promoting the idea that the slave holding states be willing to dissolve all ties with the Union for whatever reason. He had been cognizant of the fact that such a move would be nothing short of treason.

Mr. Miller's popularity had gone downhill with his constituents, because he had been on the wrong side of the fence. As a result, business at his law office had declined, but he could live with that. He had other interests that he could focus on.

Elizabeth and Sophia had overheard Mr. and Mrs. Miller discussing politics, and the issue of slavery a lot. They usually pretended not to be interested, or they acted as if they had not been paying attention. However, they did pay attention, and when they were alone, they had their own discussions regarding what they had heard. Even though they had their discussions, they knew that what they thought didn't make any difference, because nobody cared about what slaves thought anyway.

Sophia had asked Elizabeth if she thought that it was right for people to have slaves. Elizabeth told her that she should know better than to ask a silly question like that. She said that people are supposed to be free, so that they can do whatever they like as long as they do the right thing. Thinking about all of the slaves in the country, Sophia didn't know how they would be able to make it if they were all set free, and suddenly had to eke out a living for themselves

Elizabeth had already thought about the snags and glitches that would stare them in the face had someone opened the door and said go, you're on your own. She knew that the white people still wouldn't want to get in the fields, and do what had to be done. Farming could still be a job for black people. She had seen many slaves that were skilled professionals—Alfred for one. If they had been paid for their work, they could have earned a decent living. Then she asked Sophia if she thought that Mrs. Miller would do the cooking and cleaning if she didn't have slaves to do it for her.

Sophia had let their conversation take her imagination to some place far away. She looked out the window with a sweeping stare—she had been daydreaming. She said that if she could be free, she would get on a train, and ride off to see the world. Elizabeth told her that the only world that she was going to see would be the one that she had been looking at from the window.

After a while, Elizabeth had to end the conversation, because as she put it, Sophia had been asking too many crazy questions, and they had work to do. Elizabeth wanted Sophia to stop talking to her about slavery, because it had always been something that she had never cared to talk about—it was too depressing.

It had been a constant bother to Elizabeth when she thought about her own relatives, scattered all over the South and working in somebody's cotton fields. She supposed that there had to be some who at one time or another had felt the strikes of someone's lash across their naked back. She had even heard stories of parents that had been forced to hold their own child while they were being flogged by someone that didn't care.

Mr. Miller had left his office a little earlier than usual, because he had gotten fed up with things in town. He and Mrs. Miller sat on the porch. He talked about how difficult the day had been, because he couldn't get anything done with all of the interruptions. People had been in and out of his office all day questioning him about why he had opted not to jump on the band wagon. Mrs. Miller didn't say much, she just listened to him so that he could get rid of his frustrations.

After a while, Mr. Miller had walked over and peered around the corner of the house to see the evening sunset. It seemed like it had become a ritual with him. If it was striking, he didn't want to miss it, and if it was, he would watch until it ended. More often than not, the beautiful sky would remind him of the day when Amanda's father had come over bearing news of his daughter's death. To him, it was strange that such a beautiful scene on the horizon—the sun announcing the end of another beautiful day—could sometimes be so depressing. It had been a dreadful flashback, one of which he wanted no reminders, but it had become one that he couldn't forget. He had supposed that it would be stuck in the crevices of his mind forever.

The light of day had almost gone, but enough remained for Sophia to fulfill Albert and Mary's request. Like Mr. Miller, they too had a daily ritual—reading from the storybook. Mrs. Miller could hear her, and as usual, it just didn't set well with her, a slave reading a storybook to white kids. She said that they should be reading to her.

Furthermore, she just couldn't understand why the kids always wanted Sophia to read to them rather than asking her.

Elizabeth had gone out onto the porch to talk to Mr. and Mrs. Miller. She didn't beat around the bush. She had a question to ask, and she had thrown it on the table—can she and Sophia go to the bush harbor every Sunday? If Elizabeth had known that Mrs. Miller had already been frustrated over the fact that Sophia had been reading a book, she would have definitely waited until another time—catch her when she was in a better mood.

Mr. Miller had responded to her question, and she was glad that it had been him rather than Mrs. Miller. He said that he didn't realize that she cared that much for going to the bush harbor. Elizabeth told him that it had been a long time since she had been to a bush harbor, and that she did like it. Mrs. Miller just couldn't understand why anybody would prefer going to a place like that rather than to a real church.

Elizabeth had said that she and Sophia had relatives that went to the bush harbor, and that she liked seeing them again. It was important to her to let Sophia have the chance to know who she was kin to—even if most of them were distant cousins. Elizabeth knew that it couldn't be wrong—but more than likely, it had been unintentional—when she let her words be a little more assertive than ever before. She said that people need to know people other than those that they are stuck in the house with, and Sophia only knew three, Caroline, Emily and Alfred.

Neither Mr. Miller nor Mrs. Miller could disagree, and they didn't argue the point. Yet, Mrs. Miller did remind her of how uncomfortable the bush harbor could be sometimes. Elizabeth agreed, but she said that on days like that, they would go with them to the church in town. Mr. Miller had said that he didn't mind. Maybe she didn't care, or maybe she had been unable to come up with anything that might be a reasonable objection. Therefore, Mrs. Miller said that it would be fine with her.

Elizabeth had held back on the facial expressions that wanted to take over—expressions like those that a child might have on Christmas morning. She didn't want the Millers to even wonder if there might have been some other reason for the sudden interest in the bush harbor—Alfred for example. Her opinion was that they didn't need to know any more than what she had told them.

Elizabeth had walked away, and was out of sight, but she could still hear Mr. and Mrs. Miller talking. She had heard him say that it's probably a good thing to let them go to the bush harbor on Sundays. If for no other reason, he said that it's probably a big relief for them to just get away from the mansion, and away from them for a few hours every once in a while.

As soon as Mr. Miller had said that it's probably a relief for them to get away for a while, Mrs. Miller wanted to know what he meant by such a statement as that. He said that he didn't mean anything other than they just needed to get away from them, so that they could be with their own people now and then like everybody else. Mrs. Miller granted that he had probably been right. After that, they sat quietly, and watched the daylight fade away.

The day had ended. Albert and Mary had been tucked in, and Elizabeth and Sophia had gone to their room. Elizabeth told Sophia that she had gotten permission for them to go to the bush harbor on Sundays. Upon seeing how happy Sophia had been after she had told her,

Elizabeth knew that it couldn't be because they had permission to practice religion at their own church—Sophia believed in God, but Elizabeth knew that she couldn't be that holy. She didn't care so much about Sophia having a boyfriend, or sitting near him on Sunday. On the other hand, she did want her to remember that the bush harbor was their church, and not Sodom or Gomorrah.

Elizabeth didn't let on, but she had been just as happy as Sophia, and for the same reason that Sophia had mentioned to her earlier—a chance to be with Alfred. She wanted to see him, and she wanted to see him somewhere other than at Magnolia Manor. Like always, she didn't want Sophia to be privy to her feelings or her desires, especially when it came to Alfred. Elizabeth loved spending time with him at the bush harbor, but she didn't feel like she had to explain it to anybody.

SIX

It had become obvious to Mrs. Miller and to Elizabeth that political issues had been weighing heavily on Mr. Miller's mind. Yet, he never had much to say regarding the subject when he was at home.

Mrs. Miller had suggested that they take a trip—go someplace where they could relax, and forget about things for a while. Her idea appealed to him. He had asked her if she would like to visit the plantation in Mississippi, and they could spend a little time in Memphis since it would be on their route.

Mrs. Miller had never visited the plantation in Mississippi, and she had no desire to do so then. When she had said take a trip, the plantation was not what she had in mind. To her, all plantations were alike, big fields of cotton filled with the sight of slaves. She had seen it, and she didn't feel like it would be worth a trip all the way to Mississippi to see it again. On the other hand, she had never been to the city of Memphis, but the idea of going there, and doing some shopping had its' appeal.

Therefore, she agreed to the dreary trip to the plantation in Mississippi just to appease her husband. She had decided that she could tolerate a day or two at that place if that's what it would take to get her to Memphis.

Some time in Memphis would be just what she needed, a chance to see what the city was like, and do some shopping. Mr. Miller had suggested that they go to the plantation first, and then stop in Memphis on their way back. He knew that shopping meant handling lots of packages, and by doing it on the way back, he wouldn't have to handle them as much.

When Mrs. Miller told Elizabeth and Sophia about their trip plans, Elizabeth asked if they had planned on taking Albert and Mary with them. The answer to that question was absolutely not. She said that they would have been as pestilent as politics. Mr. Miller told Elizabeth that his wife had suggested the trip so that he could get away, and relax for a few days. Since coming up with the idea, it seemed to him that the reason for the trip had shifted from him to her.

They had decided to let Alfred take them to the train station in Grand Junction with the carriage. From there, they could board that westbound train for Memphis, and then cruise down the Mississippi to the landing at Austin.

For the trip to Grand Junction, Elizabeth had packed a basket with far more food than they really needed, so that they wouldn't have to stop. Everybody knew that it was virtually impossible to find a decent place to eat when traveling—pulling in at some off the road eatery would more than likely be some rough-and-ready slipshod operation, and a bad experience to say the least. If the food wasn't bad, you might have to eat with bad company, and sometimes you might have the misfortune of having to do both.

The road to Grand Junction had been rather rough, but they took it slow to avoid being bounced around too much. Besides, the train didn't leave until the next morning, and they had no reason to hurry. After Alfred had dropped them off at the hotel, he headed home. Mr. Miller had told him when to pick them up on their return trip.

Mrs. Miller didn't care much for the hotel that they had, and they hadn't chosen the wrong one—it was the only one in town. Mr. Miller had promised that he would make it up to her in Memphis. His promise had given her enough staying power to tolerate one night in Grand Junction.

The train ride to Memphis didn't take long, it wasn't dusty, and they enjoyed the view. They did have to listen to the constant click clack of that little spot where the rail is tangent to the wheel. Still, it had been far more comfortable than Alfred's carriage ride.

Mr. Miller had sent a telegram before leaving home to make sure that someone from the plantation would meet them at the landing in Austin. He had made the trip many times, and that had always been his way of doing it. From the landing at Austin to the plantation would be about a thirty minute ride.

While waiting for the steamboat in Memphis, Mr. Miller sat down and he had started reading a newspaper. Mrs. Miller had not been quite as calm as he. She had been feeling anxious as she looked around at the place that she had never seen before.

After a while, they heard the horn of the south bound steamer approaching the landing. It was a little ahead of schedule, and it had been a welcoming call for Mrs. Miller. She had gotten bored with hanging around, and waiting. She wanted to go somewhere, even if it had to be the plantation in Mississippi.

The day had been beautiful, just right for traveling on the river. All of the passengers had gotten aboard, and started mingling around on deck. It wasn't long before the giant steamer, laden with manufactured goods from the industrial North, had started meandering its' way down the Mississippi. Soon after departure, it seemed like everyone on-board had found the clique that was right for them, and they stayed in their circle all the way to Austin.

The landing at Austin would be the first stop. The steamboat ride downriver had seemed too short for Mrs. Miller, because she had placed herself in the company of some of society's elite, and that had always been the perfect spot for her. It was the one place where she was most at ease. In addition, she had enjoyed the slow, smooth ride on the steamer, the scenery along the river had been beautiful, and there had been no dust in her face—only a gentle breeze that she had found most comforting.

Mr. Miller was always paying attention to things, even when it seemed as though he wasn't. He had noticed that when the boat pulled in at the landing, first time acquaintances tendered heartfelt farewells—at least they had gone through the motions—and then they parted ways. He knew that the verbal expressions and the physical gestures that come with saying goodbye had sometimes been exaggerated. He had said to Mrs. Miller that if it is pretentious, you do it anyway, because it's the right thing to do.

Isaac, one of the slaves from the plantation in Mississippi, had been sent to the landing to meet them. It had always been Isaac that picked him up at the landing. If it had been anyone else, he would have thought that something was wrong. Mr. Miller recognized him, and he had walked over to where he had been waiting. Mrs. Miller had been standing at his side, but she looked past Isaac as if he didn't exist. Although, she had looked past him, it had not been a predetermined cold shoulder, she just didn't see him.

Mrs. Miller had been looking much further than Isaac, and she had been wondering what on earth could possibly be out there in that God forsaken place. She could see for miles, but the only thing that she could see was flat fields of farmland. She questioned who would even want to live in such a place. Mr. Miller had noticed her scanning the landscape. He had told her that he could hear what she was thinking. When she didn't say anything, he took her by the arm, and said that it's really a nice place.

They were standing in the town of Austin, Mississippi. The town had been named Austin, because Austin Miller had donated the land for the purpose of building a town to serve as the county seat of Tunica County, Mississippi. Mrs. Miller was not surprised that he had a town named for him, because she had been told about it many times, she just hadn't seen it before. Although she had known about the town, after she had given it the once over, she could see that it just wasn't quite what she had expected.

She never did let him be aware of her assessment of his namesake. She didn't say anything about it, at least not to him. After all, it had been a trip that she had suggested to simply get away from home, and relax for a while. It had been his idea to drag her to Austin, Mississippi, and she had decided to just make the best of things. Yet, she kept thinking about where he had taken her. Her thought was that she had been dropped off in the middle of nowhere, and was about to get a lesson on how to survive.

Where she was standing was nowhere close to what she had in mind when she had said take a trip. Yet, she settled back and decided that she could tolerate the place for a while. After all, it would only be for a couple of nights, and then she would be headed back to civilization. Still, she had found it hard not to think about where she was.

Isaac had placed their belongings on the buggy, and Mr. and Mrs. Miller had climbed up to their seat. Once they were on the road, Isaac kept the pace slow, so that he wouldn't stir up the dust and have it settle on his passengers. The ride to the plantation house had been a short one, less than two miles.

Isaac had stopped the buggy near the house—just at the edge of the yard. Mr. Miller had stepped down, and he had reached for his wife's hand, but she hadn't moved. She was still sitting, and staring around at the vast countryside. When she did notice him, she gave him her hand, so that he could help her to the ground.

The plantation house was nothing like Magnolia Manor, and she had never expected it to be. It was good enough to serve as a home away from home, but it was not a place where Mrs. Miller wanted to be stuck forever. It had been occupied only when Mr. Miller was there, otherwise, it remained empty. Inside, it had been adequately furnished she supposed, but rather common. She concluded that her husband had to be the person that coordinated everything, because it looked like something that only he would do.

Jenny, a middle-aged slave woman on the plantation was his part-time housekeeper, and she had been
anxiously awaiting their arrival. Mrs. Miller was still
awed by the vast flatlands that surrounded her, and all
the while she had been pretty much alone except for
her thoughts. Jenny had welcomed them to their second
home as if the place belonged to her. She had told them to
come in and make themselves comfortable.

After supper, Mr. and Mrs. Miller had gone outside
to sit on the front porch. While they were talking, the
overseer of the plantation walked up. Mr. Miller spoke
to him, and then he introduced him to Mrs. Miller since
they had never met. She had thought him to be somewhat of a grubby looking fellow, but respectable enough.
Therefore, she supposed that he couldn't be all bad. He
and Mr. Miller had talked briefly, and then he left.

It had been a long day, first the train ride from Grand
Junction to Memphis, the steamboat trip down the
Mississippi, and then the horse and buggy from the boat
landing. It was earlier than usual, but shortly after eat-
ing supper, the Millers had decided to get ready for bed.
Their belongings had been placed in their room, and
Jenny had unpacked their luggage. Everything had been
properly placed when they walked into the bedroom.
The covers on the bed had been turned back, and Jenny
had placed a single red rose on each pillow.

Jenny stayed in the main house with the Millers
while they were there. Her room was located toward the
back. Mrs. Miller had been impressed at how thorough
she had been with her duties as housekeeper, and the red
rose ... it was obvious that Jenny had been someone else's
housekeeper prior to Austin Miller, because such was
not his style.

The next morning, Mr. Miller was up and about at first light. Jenny sensed that he would be, and when he walked into the kitchen it was just like at home—his cup of coffee was waiting. Jenny could read him almost as well as Elizabeth, because she had been his part-time housekeeper for a long time.

Mrs. Miller always slept late, but since they had gone to bed so early, the smell of Jenny's coffee had roused her attention, but it didn't wake her up. Going to bed early had to have been the reason why she had gotten up so early. The same coffee aroma spread through Magnolia Manor every morning, she just wouldn't let it get her out of bed. A few minutes sooner, and she would have seen something that would have been a rare sighting for her, the sun just on the horizon.

While she was getting dressed, Jenny entered her bedroom, and placed a cup of coffee on the stand near her bed. Mrs. Miller thanked her, and said that she would be dressed shortly for breakfast. When she had gone to the dining room, Mr. Miller was already there waiting for her. Granted, it was very early for her, but she was feeling good. She had complimented Jenny for being so thoughtful, and she especially liked the red rose that had been placed on each pillow.

After breakfast, Mr. Miller said that he would be outside for a while. He had made plans to ride around with his overseer to have a look at things. He loved his Mississippi plantation, located on some of the most fertile soils in the country, and therefore, making it just right for farming.

They rode around for hours, he and the overseer. When they returned, it had gotten well into the afternoon. The overseer had offered to take care of the horse and buggy, but Mr. Miller said that he was going to take Mrs. Miller for a ride later, and show her around the place.

When she had first suggested that they take a trip, going to Mississippi was his idea. Mrs. Miller had been watching him, and she didn't know if she had ever seen him be so into something as he had been with their Mississippi plantation. Before they had left home, she had thought about talking him into going someplace else, but she was glad that she had given in, and let him drag her to the one place that he apparently loved most.

Although she lacked the emotions that he had for that part of the country, she was happy that it pleased him. However, she still preferred being at Magnolia Manor rather than one and a half miles from Austin, Mississippi. Yet, for her husband's sake, she realized that it was a good place to have, because it seemed to be the only place where he could truly be contented.

Mrs. Miller realized that there was nothing wrong with the plantation other than it was just in the wrong part of the world for her. The area was sparsely populated, she didn't know if there were any neighbors or not— she hadn't seen any—and the nearest town was the one named for her husband. She could be satisfied with just a quick look at it, and she didn't feel that she needed to see it very often. Yet, she had decided that she had to give him her attention whenever he talked about it, because he was in love with it.

After Mr. Miller had said that he was going to take her for a ride in the buggy, she didn't hesitate. He helped her up to her seat, and off they went. He had been taken away by the bountiful crops growing on the beautiful flatlands, and she could tell that he had been.

After riding around for about an hour or so, he drove the horse and buggy up a winding road to the top of one of the tallest hills on the place—there weren't many, it was rather flat. They had stepped down from the buggy. He had told her that it was his favorite spot on the plantation, because he could stand there and see so much. She looked around and wondered what it was that he could see so much of, but she had chosen to stand there and look at it with him.

Then he told her to look as far as she could see, and then turn around in a complete circle, and continue looking. She did as he had asked, and then she wanted to know why. He told her that she had looked as far as she could see in all directions, and everything that she had seen was theirs. Still, she hadn't seen it all, because her eyes couldn't see that far. Then, Mrs. Miller had been impressed by their Mississippi plantation.

The place was huge. Yet, she maintained her first perception, it was not Magnolia Manor, but she was glad that they had it. The place that had failed to impress her when she had first seen it would secure their financial status and social standing all the way to the end. She said that those flatlands located in that out of the way place had taken on a different look—she could see the dollar signs.

Mrs. Miller talked all the way back to the plantation house, and Mr. Miller felt good. He could then see her in the way that he had always wanted her to be, full of life and fun to be near. When they had returned to the plantation house, Isaac took charge of the horse and buggy. Mrs. Miller even had a few nice words for him—she was better than he had first thought—although it was the first time that she had said anything to him since arriving.

Again, Mr. and Mrs. Miller sat on the front porch, and that time for the first time, they looked at the beautiful flatlands together. It was the same flatlands that she had seen earlier, the same place that had her stuck out in the middle of nowhere, but the view had changed along with her opinion.

Jenny had asked if she could get them something to drink, but Mrs. Miller didn't say anything. Her mind had been bogged down in the fertile fields of Tunica County. Mr. Miller suggested a cool drink of water. Jenny fulfilled his request, but she had done it with a tall glass of iced tea which surprised Mrs. Miller. Jenny told Mrs. Miller that the overseer had sent Isaac into town to get a large block of ice just for her. Jenny had also given her a fan, so that she could make the warm temperature a little more tolerable.

Mrs. Miller had been unusually polite with her housekeeper. She thanked Jenny, and told her that she and the overseer had been so thoughtful. Mr. Miller had wished that he could keep her forever just the way that she was then.

Whatever it was that had been favoring them in Mississippi, he would love to put in a bottle and take it home to be uncapped in Magnolia Manor. However, in his mind, he was always cognizant of the overly aggressive attitudes that existed back at home between his wife and Sophia. They didn't care for each other. Furthermore, he had come to the conclusion that they would probably be like that forever.

After they had eaten, they sat on the porch and talked until the sun had disappeared. Jenny had brought out a glass of ice containing a double shot of bourbon for Mr. Miller. He didn't have to ask for it, because she knew how much and when. He always kept several bottles of something around the house just in case he needed it, or just in case he wanted it. Jenny had asked Mrs. Miller if she could get anything for her. She had never really cared for alcoholic beverages, but on that day, she let abstinence fly with the wind. She had told Jenny that she would have a glass of sherry with ice.

Mr. Miller had made the short walk over to the overseer's house. He had some last minute details that he needed to talk about. He had been gone for about an hour. When he returned, Mrs. Miller had gone inside. Correctly, he had assumed that she would be in their bedroom.

As soon as he had entered the house, he could hear Mrs. Miller and Jenny laughing and talking as they packed the luggage. Listening to them made him think again about things back at home. Once more, he thought about the beautiful sunsets, and his oftentimes accompanying thoughts of depression. In a small way, he had likened it to his wife's attitude in Mississippi and what it would no doubt be when they returned home. If only she could stay the way that she had been in Mississippi, then every day at home—blue skies or gray—would be like a beautiful sunset.

They had to be at the landing in Austin the next morning, so they didn't stay up late. Mrs. Miller wanted to be fresh when she arrived in Memphis, and Mr. Miller had to be rested so that he could keep up with her. She wanted to shop around during the afternoon, because they would be on that train to Grand Junction the next morning.

They had slept well during the night, no doubt aided by the two shots of sherry that Mrs. Miller had, and Mr.

Miller's two strong shots of bourbon. When they got up the next morning, Jenny had breakfast ready for them. They both had sat down at the table together—two mornings in a row. That was unusual, because more often than not, their schedules didn't match. Mr. Miller was up at dawn, and therefore, didn't miss many sunrises. On the other hand, Mrs. Miller would skip breakfast if it meant getting out of bed early. She had granted that they're beautiful, and that she loved to see them, but she would much rather sleep than to see the morning sunlight sparkle on the horizon.

After breakfast, Mr. Miller walked out onto the front porch, and he saw Isaac waiting with the horse and buggy. He walked out, and struck up a conversation with him. Soon, Jenny had come out, and she told Isaac that he could start putting the luggage onto the buggy.

The overseer had come over just to see them off. He and Mr. Miller had been talking when Mrs. Miller interrupted them. She thanked the overseer for his kind gestures to help insure their comfort—maybe thinking about what Mr. Miller had said a couple of days earlier, "It's just the right thing to do."

The Millers had said goodbye, and they had climbed aboard for the ride to Austin. Mrs. Miller turned around to give the house one last look, and again, she waved goodbye to Jenny. She said that if they had her back at Magnolia Manor, they wouldn't need Sophia in the house.

After she had made the statement, Mr. Miller had no comments. If he had said anything that sounded like he was defending Sophia, she would fly off the handle like the blade of an ax. She had given him two of their best days together, but it was obvious that the source would soon run dry. That unseen aura that had been with them in Mississippi, whatever it was that he wanted to put in a bottle and take home, would be left in Mississippi.

There were other people waiting at the landing in Austin to board the steamboat, several of whom Mr. Miller had shaken hands with, because he knew them. When the steamboat arrived, Mr. Miller said goodbye to Isaac and so did Mrs. Miller.

When the cargo and passengers were all on board, the giant steamer got back on the Mississippi, and made its way upriver toward Memphis. Before rounding the bend, Mrs. Miller looked back at the town of Austin, but not to get a permanent image fixed in her mind so that she could remember. She looked at it and wondered what kind of people could be satisfied with living in a place like that— she was sure, it just wouldn't work for her.

On the way to Memphis, they had put together a simple two-part plan for the afternoon, check in at the hotel, and then go shopping. Upon arriving in Memphis, Mr. Miller hired a carriage and driver. He had agreed to provide transportation for them as long as they needed him.

Patiently, the driver waited while they checked in at the hotel, one that Mr. Miller had been familiar with, and one that met Mrs. Miller's approval. When she had first seen the hotel, she said that no one had to tell her that she was in Memphis, and not in Grand Junction— she was referring to the substandard accommodations that she had to tolerate a few days earlier when Alfred had dropped them off. Then she remembered that her husband had promised her an upgrade for their stay in Memphis—he had kept his word.

Mr. and Mrs. Miller had been shown to their room, and when they entered, both were pleased with the scenic overview that was afforded from the window. Since

Mr. Miller had been a frequent guest, the hotel manager had made sure that he had one of their finest rooms. Mrs. Miller stood at the window—eying the city of Memphis. She loved it, and she had already dreamed about all of the possibilities for the afternoon.

Mr. Miller had suggested that they freshen up and get downstairs, because their driver had been waiting. Quickly, Mrs. Miller agreed, and after a few minutes in front of the mirror, they had left their room. They had told the driver of their interests, and he knew where to take them.

Mr. Miller had planned on just accompanying Mrs. Miller, but while she had been shopping around, he had found something that he wanted. A black suit had gotten his attention. When he had made up his mind to get it, Mrs. Miller felt good, simply because he was doing some shopping for himself. Then, she didn't feel like it would be such a one sided affair with him just following her around.

When the shopping spree had ended, they returned to their hotel, and had their purchases taken to their room. Mr. Miller could see that they had about three times as many bags as when they left home. He never asked their chauffeur about his fee for chauffeuring them around all afternoon; instead, he just gave him some money. Mrs. Miller didn't know how much he had given him, and she never asked, but she could tell from the expression on his face that he had been well paid.

Mrs. Miller loved expensive things, and she had no financial barriers. While shopping, whenever she found something that she liked, she got it without even looking at the price tag—she might put it back on the shelf for being too cheap, but not because it was too pricy. She and her husband were among society's upper crust, but unlike her husband, she had no reservations when it came to flaunting where they stood on the ladder.

Mr. Miller had been stretched out on the bed, somewhat tired, and not saying much. He just looked at her. She was happy, and that had made him happy. Beautiful reflections from her had been shining in his eyes all day. Yet, deep down, or maybe not so deep down, he knew that he had to make the most of being with the person whom he had enjoyed so much—the good feelings, and the upbeat attitude would soon fade away for sure.

Toward nightfall, they had walked down the street to one of the city's finer restaurants. Since it was early evening, and only a few patrons were present, the Millers were showered with attention. Still, it had been no more than Mrs. Miller expected. It had been a day that she would remember, and one that she could talk about for a long time. It would stand out because of the high end experiences that she had had—a lifestyle that had been more to her liking than what could be offered back at home—excluding the plantation in Mississippi.

After dinner, they walked arm and arm back to the hotel, and sat in the well-furnished lobby engaging each other in small talk. After a while, Mr. Miller entertained himself in the same manner as when at home, reading the newspaper. Mrs. Miller's attention had been drawn to the beautiful artwork, and lavish décor, as she strolled around the lobby.

Later during the evening, Mrs. Miller met another woman that had been doing the same as she, admiring the hotel's beautiful works of art. After getting acquainted, the other woman pointed out her husband to Mrs. Miller. She identified him as being the man standing over there, surrounded by a bunch of whisky drinking, cigar smoking gentlemen, discussing politics.

Still reading the newspaper, Mr. Miller had also become aware of the whisky drinking, cigar smokers, but he never looked around. He kept his head buried in the newspaper, holding it so close to his face that anyone seeing him would think that he had lost his eyeglasses—he didn't want to be recognized. He had no desire to be in on whatever they had been talking about. He had been engaged all day, and he had no desire to be further occupied. After all, his reason for being away from home was so that he could forget about the political issues that had been racking his brain.

After a while, Mr. Miller decided that they should escape to their room before they got dragged into something of which that they had no interest. He had gotten up from his seat, and walked over to where Mrs. Miller had been. She introduced him to the lady that she had been talking to. After a few cordial words, they said goodnight. Mr. Miller then walked over to the hotel clerk, and asked him to send a bottle of wine to their room.

Shortly after getting to their room, their bottle of wine arrived. While teasing their taste buds with a glass of French import, they listened to the clock mark time, and they watched the lights glimmer along the streets of Memphis. Mrs. Miller admitted to her husband that at first, she didn't care for his idea of visiting their Mississippi plantation. However, after seeing it, she had changed her mind. She loved having the place, and she realized that it had to be among the best. Still, she didn't want him to ever suggest that they move to Austin, Mississippi.

After having breakfast the next morning, they headed to the train station. They had been sitting around the station waiting. The approaching train was not in sight, but they had heard the whistle blow. Everyone had stood and started moving about as it got closer. Some had gone outside so that they could get a better look as the massive engine huffed and puffed its' way to the station. When it came in and slowed down to a stop, it belched out a cloud of black smoke, and then released a surge of steam that was a little unnerving for those standing too close. Many would be passengers had stayed inside the station to avoid the sooty ash that had been discharged with the smoke, and then drifted down from above.

No sooner than the train had stopped, people began stepping off while others began loading and unloading cargo. Everything was moving fast, because the engineer wanted to stay on time. It was to his satisfaction when he found himself ahead of schedule, but a mark against him when he was running late.

When given the signal, the engineer engaged the throttle, and pulled away from the station. At first, the forward motion had seemed to be like that of an old man on a walking cane, as it struggled to make its way along the tracks. Within a few minutes, it had gotten up to speed, and had started beating out that familiar click clack rhythm of metal on metal. The slow start had become like an effortless motion as the roaring steam engine sped along the seemingly, never ending rails. Every now and then, the engineer sounded the whistle to clear the tracks ahead, and sometimes he let it squall just to satisfy his ego.

Trains had made traveling a lot easier, and a lot more comfortable. Still, Mrs. Miller had her own thoughts regarding the so called modern era of transportation. She had been annoyed by the constant noise of the engine, and she didn't like the sound of metal on metal while rolling down the tracks. She said that it was enough to drive a person crazy. Mr. Miller had noticed that it didn't seem to bother her quite so much until they were headed home. The trip had been uneventful, except for Mrs. Miller's occasional expressions of dissatisfaction about this and that. She had complained about the noise, but the train was by far her favorite mode of travel. Letting her head rest on her husband's shoulder, she had decided that she would just sit there, and be happy about being where she was ... just make the best of it. Mr. Miller had tried to pacify her by saying that it wouldn't be long before they would be in Grand Junction.

His comment didn't make things any better. For her, a quick trip to Grand Junction only meant that she would be climbing onto that carriage with Alfred sooner. Then, she would give up the noisy train for a long dusty ride all the way home. She had supposed that Alfred knew the location of every bump in the road, because he didn't miss many. When they arrived in Grand Junction, Alfred was there and waiting at the station. He secured their luggage and all of Mrs. Miller's purchases safely on the carriage. Mrs. Miller had been rushing him so that she could get away from the sooty ash falling from the sky after it had been discharged with the black smoke.

Alfred had kept the team moving at a lively pace in order to shorten the travel time, knowing all the time that it would be rougher, and that it would stir up more dust. Yet, since no one had said anything, he kept it moving. Like Mr. Miller, he also knew that Mrs. Miller wanted to end the carriage ride as soon as possible. Therefore, no one said slow down, and they just sat there so that it would hurry up and end.

They had decided not to stop anywhere to eat along the way. They would much rather wait, and eat whatever Elizabeth had waiting for them at home. Mrs. Miller had been bounced around a bit more than she cared for, but she didn't complain. She had made up her mind to make the sacrifice, and tolerate the lack of comfort for a quicker trip.

Comfort had always been at the top of her list, and it had been like that for her entire life. That being the case, what really had been a rather quick, and not so bad trip for Mr. Miller and Alfred, seemed like a journey across Hell for her. She had just never gotten used to that sort of thing.

The long dusty ride was about to end. Mrs. Miller could see the town in front of her, and she would be eying Magnolia Manor as soon as Alfred made that left turn ahead. After he had pulled in at the mansion, Alfred stopped the carriage at the end of the walkway. He held the team, and kept his position while Mr. and Mrs. Miller stepped down.

After planting themselves on the ground, they both stood there for a while and squirmed around a bit. They had to get used to being on their feet again. Alfred said that he would be careful taking their belongings inside. He could have just been quiet, because when Mrs. Miller headed toward the mansion, she stopped and turned around to tell him to be careful with those bags.

Elizabeth had heard them outside, and she had gone to the door. When she saw Mrs. Miller bent over and lumbering, she went out to meet her, and she had taken her by the arm. Slowly, they walked toward the mansion.

Elizabeth told Mrs. Miller that she must be completely tuckered out from having to make that ole long rough carriage ride. Mrs. Miller said that train rides were not a lot better.

Elizabeth's caring attitude had been just what Mrs. Miller needed, and it was just the way that she loved being treated. Leaning against Elizabeth, she was undoubtedly tired. At the same time, theatrics had to have been part of her presentation, simply because they had always been—it was just her style. Still, she felt good, because she was back at home, and as soon as she could get rid of some of the dust and rest for a while, she could reclaim the roost.

Sophia had been out back with Albert and Mary. When they heard voices out front, the kids ran ahead of Sophia, stopping first at Mrs. Miller, and then moving on to Mr. Miller. Sophia had stepped aside to let Elizabeth and Mrs. Miller pass. She said hello to Mrs. Miller, but she didn't say anything back, she kept on walking with Elizabeth holding on to her arm, and Sophia kept walking toward the carriage.

Mr. Miller and Alfred had placed all of the luggage and packages on the ground near the carriage. Mr. Miller was tired, but he had picked up a piece of luggage and carried it in with him, leaving the remainder for Alfred. Sophia had a bag in each hand. Alfred told her that he could take care of them, but she held on to them anyway.

It was almost mealtime, but Mr. and Mrs. Miller wanted to freshen up a bit first. That gave Elizabeth time to put a few finishing touches on some things in the kitchen. When Mr. and Mrs. Miller did sit down at the table, Mrs. Miller told Elizabeth that she was about to starve. She said that she had eaten breakfast in Memphis, and she ate nothing but dust all the way from Grand Junction.

Mrs. Miller's comments had made Elizabeth side with her. Elizabeth looked at Mr. Miller, and she asked him why he didn't see fit to stop long enough so that she could eat something, and stretch her legs; it had been much too far for her to ride in that ole dusty carriage without stopping. Mrs. Miller was glad that Elizabeth had said something on her behalf, but she had never really expected to stop at some squalid eatery along the roadside.

Elizabeth had been fussing at Mr. Miller, and she kept standing there waiting to hear what he had to say, but he didn't say anything. Elizabeth looked at him and said that you men are all alike. Then she threw her hands up, and walked away.

After dinner Mr. and Mrs. Miller sat out back. They purposely avoided sitting out front, because they didn't want any passersby to see them, and pull in for a visit. They didn't want to chit chat with anyone; instead, they just wanted to be left alone. Albert and Mary had been their biggest nuisance—question after question about the trip.

After a while, Elizabeth told Sophia to take the kids and do something with them so that Mr. and Mrs. Miller could relax. They had both heard Elizabeth's request to Sophia, and apparently they approved—neither of them objected to Sophia getting them off the porch.

Elizabeth finished cleaning up in the kitchen, and then she walked out onto the porch. She told Mr. and Mrs. Miller that she was preparing a warm bath for each of them, and it would be ready in a few minutes. Mrs. Miller said that a warm bath was exactly what she needed. Mrs. Miller had decided to leave their luggage and the purchases that she had made in Memphis right where they were—they would put them away the next day.

Sophia and the kids had been out in the yard. It had gotten close to sundown, and it was time for her to read them a story. There was still enough daylight for them to sit on the bench in the yard, and see well enough. From the porch, Mr. and Mrs. Miller could hear Sophia reading, and they both sat there listening just like the kids.

Elizabeth had noticed them. She felt like they had gotten into the story just as much as Albert and Mary, listening and eagerly waiting to find out how it ends. After a while, Mrs. Miller's attitude had changed. She told Mr. Miller to listen to her out there reading a book just like white people. She had said that the worst part about it was that she was reading to her children. Mr. Miller had already laid back and propped his feet up. Mrs. Miller had said, "Listen to her out there reading ...." He did just like she had asked—he kept on listening to her read. He had shushed her, because he really did want to hear how the story ended.

Later, Elizabeth walked to the door, and told them that their bath tubs were filled with warm water and waiting. They both got up at the same time as if trying to get ahead of the other. When Mr. and Mrs. Miller had finished with their bath, Elizabeth and Sophia threw Albert and Mary in the tubs with the same water, so that they could get rid of some grit and grime before getting into bed. It was still rather early, but Mr. and Mrs. Miller had gone to bed. Albert and Mary lounged around with Sophia for a while.

Quietly, Elizabeth took a walk through the house to make sure that everything was alright. Later, she and

Sophia had tucked Albert and Mary in, and they had gone to their room. Since it wasn't late, they sat around just to while away the time.

Elizabeth had gotten her sewing kit down, and started stitching on a blanket that she had been making. She had asked Sophia if she would take her Bible down from the shelf and read to her. Sophia asked her if there was anything in particular that she wanted her to read. Elizabeth said that it didn't matter, and that she could just find something that she liked and read it to her.

Sophia's reading took her to the verse where David slayed the giant, Goliath. She had stopped reading so that she could ask Elizabeth if she thought that it was really possible for a small person like David to slay a giant. Elizabeth had never questioned what was written in the Bible. She said that it just goes to show what you can do when you have God on your side. Sophia still had her doubts. She said that she just couldn't see how a person like David could slay a giant.

Elizabeth had stopped sewing. She looked at Sophia, and told her that she should stop questioning the Bible. She said if the Bible says that he did it, he did it, and that was good enough for her. Sophia read for a while longer, and then she placed the Bible back on the shelf. Elizabeth was glad that she had put it away. She felt like Sophia reading the Bible, and then doubting what she had read didn't make it worthwhile.

Sophia had told Elizabeth that she was looking forward to going to the bush harbor on Sunday. Elizabeth reminded her that she should go there with something on her mind other than Daniel. Sophia said that they didn't do anything other than sit there and hold hands. Elizabeth told her that holding hands was more than she ought to be doing in church—although she held onto Alfred's hand every Sunday.

Sophia had granted that she was probably right, and therefore, she had chosen not to argue the point. Yet, Sundays at the bush harbor were the only times that she could be with Daniel. If she couldn't sit near him then and hold his hand, she never would. They couldn't take the horse and buggy, and go on a Sunday picnic.

Still trying to get Elizabeth off of her back, Sophia added that she always paid attention to the preacher. None of what Sophia had said could make Elizabeth bend in her way of thinking. Sensing that she had probably pressed on a nerve, and one that might cause Elizabeth to let her know that she was still the boss, Sophia decided that she should probably change the subject. It was conceivable that Elizabeth might have had her sitting on the other side of the bush harbor between her and Alfred on Sunday.

Sophia had asked how it came about that black people had to be slaves. Elizabeth said that she really didn't know how it had come to be. Yet, she said that some people are greedy, and they want things. Sometimes they want more than they need, and they don't care who they hurt so long as they get what they want. Elizabeth had grown tired of Sophia's questions, she told her to put her night clothes on and go to bed.

The next morning, Mr. Miller had gotten up early; and while getting dressed, he walked around humming a tune. When he sat down at the table, Elizabeth felt good, because he had decided to sit down and eat rather than nibble.

He had asked Elizabeth if she and Sophia were still stuck on the bush harbor. When Elizabeth said that they were, Mr. Miller said that's good. He reminded her that whenever the weather got too uncomfortable, they could go to church in town with him and Mrs. Miller. He and Elizabeth kept on talking all while he was eating breakfast. Sophia had been helping Albert get ready for school. Mrs. Miller and Mary, they were still asleep.

Albert had walked in, and sat down at the table across from Mr. Miller. Shortly afterwards, Mr. Miller had finished, and he had gotten up and gone to his office. Sophia made Albert rush through breakfast so that he wouldn't be late for school. With Mr. Miller and Albert out of their way, Elizabeth and Sophia began their daily routine, being careful not to disturb Mrs. Miller.

Sophia and Elizabeth had almost finished cleaning up in the kitchen when Mrs. Miller walked in. She had said good morning to Elizabeth, but as usual, she kind of ignored Sophia. Mrs. Miller sat at the table, but she only wanted a cup of Elizabeth's coffee. Realizing that Mrs. Miller would much rather be around Elizabeth than around her, Sophia walked away to start cleaning and straightening up the bedrooms.

Elizabeth had asked Mrs. Miller how she enjoyed the trip. She said that she couldn't imagine how large the plantation was in Mississippi, but that it was stuck out there in the middle of nowhere. She knew that her husband loved it, and she supposed that nothing else mattered. She said that the best part of the trip had been their layover in Memphis.

Mrs. Miller had finished her coffee, and then she told Elizabeth that she could use some help unpacking the luggage. Mrs. Miller showed her the things that she had purchased while in Memphis.

Elizabeth had picked up one of the dresses, and she held it up against Mrs. Miller so that she might picture herself in it—it was a good thing to do to help stay on the good side. Mrs. Miller had been looking in the mirror, and admiring the view just as Sophia had walked past the door. She stopped and went back to have a second look. Always aware of the fact that Mrs. Miller had never cared much for her, Sophia walked into the room, and told Mrs. Miller how beautiful the dress was. Sophia had said the right thing, and Mrs. Miller thanked her for noticing. She may have spoken the words without thinking ... saying thank you to Sophia.

Mrs. Miller had spent a lot of money shopping, but she had it to spend. She knew that when the next occasion presented itself, all eyes would be on her from the moment that she entered the room. She had told Elizabeth that if someone didn't throw a big bash so that she could wear one of her new outfits, she would have to throw one herself.

Elizabeth had been curious about riding on the steamboat. Mrs. Miller said that the steamboat had been the best part of traveling. It had been so smooth that she could hardly tell that they were moving. Elizabeth said that she wouldn't want to ride on a steamboat, because it might sink. Mrs. Miller said that they were pretty safe. Elizabeth still wouldn't change her opinion. She said that she didn't know how to swim, and she would never get on a boat.

Mrs. Miller asked Elizabeth if she knew that her husband had a town named for him in Mississippi. Elizabeth said that she did know, and she even remembered when he had to make a trip there for a dedication ceremony in his honor. Mrs. Miller supposed that it was an honor to have a town named for him, but she said that she was glad that they didn't see fit to add her name on it with his.

SEVEN

T he sky had been beautiful all morning, but toward noon, dark clouds had started to move in. No one had paid much attention, other than thinking that they were going to get that long awaited for rain that would end the dry spell. By mid-afternoon, the skies had become threatening, and the wind had started to blow. Occasional flashes of lightning followed by claps of thunder could be heard off in the distance.

From his office in town, Mr. Miller had been watching the storm build, and he decided that he would lock up and go home. After he had left his office, he stopped by the school to get Albert. When he and Albert arrived at the mansion, Mrs. Miller, Elizabeth, Sophia and Mary were all standing on the porch, watching and wondering what the weather might do.

The sky kept on getting darker, and the sounds of thunder and flashes of lightening increased as the storm got closer and closer. Mr. Miller had told everyone to go

the chance, people still cornered him. They wanted his frame of mind to be like theirs.

Those that were in favor of states rights had started talking more about secession, and they wanted Mr. Miller to start talking the talk with them. Since he had chosen not to, they felt like he had turned his back on them, and therefore, was a traitor to the South. He had questioned whether or not they knew that secession would make them a traitor to their country, and along with it might come severe consequences.

Mr. Miller went about his business, and after a while, most of the cutting remarks regarding his political stance had seemed to lessen. Still, there were some that had been too blinded by their unwillingness to see things any way other than their way. At the end of a long and busy day in his office, he had started home. He was accompanied by a friend that lived just down the street past his house. He felt good as they walked together, because neither of them found it necessary to talk about anything that involved politics.

Even though Sophia's friends, Caroline and Emily lived within walking distance, they didn't talk to Sophia nearly as much as they used to, but it had not been by choice. Caroline and Emily both knew that Mrs. Miller didn't want them in Magnolia Manor visiting Sophia. In fact, they hadn't been on the Miller's property since the time when Mrs. Miller took them on that tour of the mansion. There had been occasions when they would see each other from a distance, but rarely did they have the chance to talk.

Whenever they did talk, it was only for a few minutes, and that was usually when they were passing by, and happened to see Sophia in the yard with the kids.

They could talk a little, but while doing so, they had to keep one eye out for Mrs. Miller. She wouldn't have said anything to Caroline or Emily if she had caught them, but for sure she would have gotten on Sophia.

Sometimes Sophia would talk to Elizabeth about Caroline and Emily. She would tell her about how much she missed having them come over to visit. Elizabeth knew that she couldn't help but miss them, because they used to be together almost every day. Yet, she had explained to Sophia that it would be like that sooner or later. Sophia had come to know that, but she still missed them, and she wished that things could be the way that they had once been. Yet, she had come to the conclusion that her mother was probably right. Things would never again be the way that they used to be.

Sophia still had the letter that Amanda had written to her, the one that she had been afraid to read. For whatever reason, she had decided that the time had come. She had been in the room with Elizabeth, and she had gotten up quietly. She took the small box down from the shelf in the closet, and found the letter in amongst some of her other things. She had sat down and started opening it. When Elizabeth realized that she was opening the letter from Amanda, she sat and watched.

Sophia read the letter. When she had finished reading it, she read it again, and then, again. When she didn't say anything, Elizabeth asked if that was the letter from Amanda, knowing all the time that it had to be. Sophia told her that it was. Then, Elizabeth didn't know if she should ask what it said, or whether she should wait and see if Sophia wanted to tell her.

Finally, Sophia told Elizabeth that Amanda had written something for her. She wanted Elizabeth to know that she had been thinking about her a lot, and that she never did thank her for all of the times that she had taken care of them when they were kids playing in Mr. Miller's yard. In the letter, Amanda had asked Sophia to tell Elizabeth that she loved her, and when she comes home, she would stop by and give her a big hug. Sophia didn't tell Elizabeth anything else that Amanda had written. Whatever it was, she had decided to keep it to herself.

Elizabeth didn't say anything for a while, so Sophia asked her if anything was wrong. Elizabeth said that she had just been thinking about Amanda's words in the letter. She told Sophia that she could understand why they had been best friends.

Sophia and Elizabeth had attended church at the bush harbor all summer, and well into the fall. In fact, they both had become more interested in the bush harbor than ever before. There had been more than just the bush harbor that pulled on them like a magnet. It was Alfred that had been attracting Elizabeth and Daniel had been pulling on Sophia.

Alfred and Elizabeth always sat in the same spot as if it had been reserved for them—their seat at the far side had always been available. Most of the time they would hold hands while listening to the preacher. Whenever they did, Elizabeth had to have been reminded of the times when she had hounded Sophia about holding hands with Daniel.

Sophia and Daniel always sat at the opposite side and as far away from Elizabeth and Alfred as possible. Undoubtedly, Elizabeth had to have known why, but it had gotten to the point where it seemed to be alright with her. Not only did Sophia and Daniel sit at the opposite side, they also sat near the back—the very back if possible—and they were there on purpose.

Sophia had learned who was who, and therefore, where to sit. She didn't want to be near anyone that was kin to her or Daniel, and she didn't want to sit near anyone that was a close friend to Elizabeth. It was a preconceived strategy to reduce the likely hood of some blabbermouth feeling the need to keep Elizabeth updated on what she might be doing.

No one talked about the affair between Elizabeth and Alfred, but Mr. Miller knew about it anyway. He could tell just from the way they acted whenever they were around each other. Although he knew, he had chosen to keep it to himself. He didn't even talk about it with Mrs. Miller, and if she knew, she never talked about it either.

Sometimes Austin Miller did things that seemed to go against the grain. Elizabeth had at one time wondered about him, what was it that made him the way that he was, but she had quit thinking about it—he had been like that ever since she had known him. He was aware of the unwritten policy that slaves were not allowed to learn how to read and write, or to take part in any aspect of formal education. Never in his life had he seen another slave owner that would let white girls into their home so that they could fraternize with a slave girl. It was absolutely unheard of, but he did it.

Sophia had lived her entire life in an environment that allowed her to ignore the double standard of rules and customs of the day, infractions in a society that had usually resulted in severe punishment. Austin Miller had always let Sophia be Sophia. He did it with the attitude that what's mine is mine, and I'll manage it as I see fit. Mrs. Miller had always criticized him for not putting his foot down and being more stern with Sophia, but no one else would dare.

Mrs. Miller was the only person that would question how he handled anything that he considered his. When he had to, he could handle her questions as well.

Of course, there had always been Elizabeth. She didn't mind giving him a piece of her mind. She had been taking care of things around the house for him so long that maybe she felt like she had earned the right to be heard. In return, maybe he felt like he owed her, at least, the obligation to listen. Then, there were times when he would pretend to be listening, and at other times he just completely ignored whatever had been said.

Whatever the case, with consideration to time and to circumstances, Mr. Miller and Elizabeth had maintained a good relationship. She couldn't read him like a book, because she couldn't read, but she could almost always tell what he was thinking. Without a doubt, she had gotten to know him better than anyone else.

Sunday morning had been rather cool. Mr. Miller had asked Elizabeth and Sophia if they wanted to go to church in town so that they would be more comfortable. Elizabeth said that she had been outside, and she didn't think that it was all that bad. She would just put on something a bit heavier to be on the safe side.

Mr. Miller had it right, it would have been a lot more comfortable at the church in town than sitting under a bush harbor, but Elizabeth and Sophia were not ready to call it quits, not yet. If they felt a chill in the air, Elizabeth could sit a little closer to Alfred, and Sophia could slide over closer to Daniel. That would be enough to make them comfortable. If they had any goose bumps, it wouldn't be because of the chill in the air, it would be due to the stirred up emotions of sitting near the one that they loved.

Sophia and Elizabeth had gotten Albert and Mary dressed for church. When the kids had been taken care of, Elizabeth checked to see if the Millers needed them to do anything else before they headed off to the bush harbor. The Miller's didn't need anything, and they were about to leave themselves.

Before leaving, Mrs. Miller had told Elizabeth how beautiful the dress was that she had on. Sophia had been standing next to Elizabeth with a look that most girls dreamed of having. Nevertheless, Mrs. Miller had chosen to ignore her. As soon as Mrs. Miller had complimented Elizabeth on her appearance, Sophia had anticipated that there would be no words to flatter her. She had consciously turned, and walked away a couple of seconds before Mrs. Miller had finished talking. Mrs. Miller had noticed what she thought might be a brazen move by Sophia, but she couldn't be sure. Therefore, she let it be.

Although she wasn't sure, Mrs. Miller had been correct when she considered that Sophia's body language might be interpreted as a sign of contempt. When it came to Mrs. Miller, Sophia had pushed respect and disrespect so close together that it had gotten difficult to tell where one stopped, and the other started. She had become very skillful at walking the narrow line that separated the two. As a result, it was almost impossible for Mrs. Miller to translate the true intent of her actions. Therefore, she had often times been left wondering, and not knowing.

Elizabeth had noticed Sophia's behavior in front of Mrs. Miller, and she had also noticed Mrs. Miller's reaction. When the Millers had left the mansion, Elizabeth and Sophia headed off to the bush harbor. On the way, Elizabeth mentioned to Sophia that what she had done in front of Mrs. Miller was not polite. Sophia had pretended that she didn't know what Elizabeth was talking about, but she knew exactly, and what she had done had been deliberate.

As they approached the bush harbor, some of their kin had walked out to meet them, but Alfred and Daniel stayed off to the side and watched—they would have their chances later. Alfred never had been one to be too obvious with displaying his feelings for Elizabeth, and she didn't want him to, yet it was no secret. Daniel ... he was just shy, but he was also leery of Elizabeth. He had always been unsure as to what her thoughts might be about him spending so much time with her daughter every Sunday. Whenever he saw Elizabeth moving toward him, he would shift and move in another direction. If standing near Sophia, he would step back if he saw Elizabeth looking at them.

Whenever Elizabeth and Sophia arrived at the bush harbor, they usually received the same welcome. They all acted like it was the first time in a long time, when it had only been seven days ago. Elizabeth would talk with everyone that was around her, but all the while she would be making her way through the crowd like a politician stumping for votes—slowly making her way to Alfred. She didn't have to try and locate him amongst the crowd, because he would always be in the same place—standing at the far side.

Elizabeth had walked up to Alfred, and he smiled at her without speaking. Holding her hands, he then leaned forward, and kissed her lips—a bold move for him, one that had completely surprised Elizabeth. With very little effort, she had made it seem as if she had been trying to push him away. The pretense had been to maintain her ladylike conduct, and she didn't want Sophia to see her kissing him. If Sophia had happened to see her, she would have at least been able to say that she had tried to push him away.

Everybody that had seen Alfred kiss Elizabeth applauded, including the preacher. Sophia had heard the commotion, and she had looked around to see what was going on, but she was none the wiser. She had missed it all.

Sophia had been standing at the other side of the bush harbor with Daniel. They wondered why everybody had applauded, but not enough to think about it for more than a few seconds. After a while, the preacher had asked everybody to have a seat so that they could get started.

Elizabeth and Alfred sat in their usual place, but when Sophia and Daniel walked up, the only place left to sit was at the very back. Yet, that had been by design. The empty seats were always at the back. To get one, just wait and be the last to sit down. They were right where they wanted to be, and if anyone asked why they were sitting in the back, namely Elizabeth, they could easily explain why—all of the other seats had been taken.

The preacher had started getting into his message— Heaven's Gates will be opened only for the pure at heart. Although Sophia and Daniel had chosen to sit at the back, they knew that they should have been listening to the preacher, but they couldn't. Instead, most of their time had been spent sitting there whispering to each other with Daniel holding her hand like always.

Sophia and Elizabeth had been going to the bush harbor all summer, and they had continued well into the fall.

Since the weather had started to turn, it had become obvious that they would soon have to start going back to church with Mr. and Mrs. Miller. Sophia knew that, and so did Daniel, because they had been talking about it before the preacher told everybody to be seated.

Sophia and Daniel were both teenagers, and they were in love. Yet, neither had ever told the other. It had remained an unspoken agreement between them—consummated by sitting near each other and holding hands.

Sophia knew that Daniel was shy, but she was as well when it came to courtship. No one had ever talked to Daniel about girls, and Elizabeth had said very little to Sophia about boys. Therefore, they didn't know for sure if they had been doing things the right way, but they had been figuring it out as they went along—playing it by ear and hoping that they were on the right track. Sophia had heard Elizabeth say that love is something that you don't rush into. Neither Sophia nor Daniel had the feeling that they had been rushing things, but Sophia knew that they had probably been moving a little too fast for Elizabeth.

Sophia and Daniel had spent a lot of Sundays holding hands at the bush harbor. Realizing that their Sundays together were winding down, Sophia had the urge to clearly express her feelings to him. Still holding hands, she had leaned forward, and in a barely audible whisper, she told Daniel that she loved him. Daniel had already been gripping her hand, but when she told him that she loved him, he gripped it tighter, so tight that it hurt, but she didn't want him to let go.

Daniel had never said the words before, and since he had been so shy, they were hard for him to say then, but like Sophia, he wanted her to know. He whispered back, and told her that he loved her too. Then, they both sat there, unaware of everything except for the constant echo of their just spoken words of affection.

On the way back to the mansion, Elizabeth and Sophia both felt like they had become a little lighter on their feet—lifted by love—they had experienced something that had them feeling good. While the preacher was delivering his message, Elizabeth had turned around several times to check on Sophia. Each time that she did, she could see that she and Daniel had their eyes focused toward the front. Elizabeth had no doubts ... although they had been sitting at the very back, they had been listening to the preacher.

As they walked together, Elizabeth recalled that little talk that she had had with Sophia about paying attention in church. Back when she had spoken to her about it, she didn't think that Sophia had paid any attention. To herself, she reckoned that something had happened, because it seemed obvious that her words had finally sunk in. She was sure that the preacher's sermon had moved Sophia, and that her daughter's soul had been filled with the Holy Spirit. If she had only known the truth, that her daughter and Daniel had been ....

Mr. and Mrs. Miller had returned home from church, and it was time for Elizabeth and Sophia to start cooking. However, Mrs. Miller told Elizabeth that she and Mr. Miller had been invited to dine with some of their friends; they were going to leave Albert and Mary at home. It would be a while before it was time to go, so Mr. and Mrs. Miller just lounged around the house.

It was still a little cold, but Sophia had taken Albert and Mary outside to let them play in the backyard—she knew that they wouldn't be out there very long. She could still hear Daniel's words. It was the first time that a boy had said I love you to her, and she wanted to remember the words forever.

Elizabeth had put her apron on, and started taking care of the chores. Mrs. Miller had been back and forth in the mansion, and she had seen Elizabeth sitting on the side of the bed. She stopped and asked her if something was wrong, but Elizabeth said that it was nothing. However, Mrs. Miller insisted on knowing.

Elizabeth said that she had been wondering what might become of Sophia after she was gone; she would never know what it feels like to have a husband, and raise children of her own. Elizabeth didn't see Sophia's life as being any different from what hers had been. She would probably be someone's housekeeper, and never be able to marry, or more than likely, never be allowed to marry.

Mrs. Miller had never considered that a slave would express such personal thoughts to their owner. However, Elizabeth never had any intentions of letting Mrs. Miller in on her personal thoughts in the first place. It was Mrs. Miller that had insisted on Elizabeth explaining why she had been so down and out.

Mrs. Miller had sat down on the bed next to Elizabeth. She understood exactly what Elizabeth had said, and she probably knew that it was all true. Still, she didn't know what to say. Elizabeth had expressed concern about what might happen to Sophia after she was gone. Mrs. Miller didn't really care about what might happen to Sophia, but that's what had Elizabeth feeling depressed.

Mr. Miller had seen Mrs. Miller sitting on the bed with Elizabeth. He stopped in the doorway to ask what was wrong. Mrs. Miller said that it was just women talking, and that they could take care of it. He had taken that to mean that he should leave them alone.

The truth was that they couldn't take care of it, because Mrs. Miller didn't even know how to respond to what Elizabeth had said. They kept sitting there, and Elizabeth had done most of the talking. Mrs. Miller had been listening, but she couldn't say anything that would help Elizabeth.

Mrs. Miller and Elizabeth were still sitting on the side of the bed with Elizabeth still doing most of the talking. Mr. Miller had walked to the door again. That time, however, he had stopped to say that it was time for them to go. Mrs. Miller was glad that it had gotten to be time for them to go, because Elizabeth had her in a position that had her feeling a little uncomfortable. She was uncomfortable, because she knew exactly who had been responsible for Elizabeth's feelings regarding Sophia— she and her husband.

When the Millers had left, Elizabeth continued with her chores, but she still had a lot on her mind. The only thing that she knew to do was to pray, and ask God if he would see to it that everything worked out alright. When she had finished cleaning the house, she decided to go ahead and prepare something to eat for Sophia and the kids.

When they had finished eating, Albert asked Sophia if she would go back outside with them, so that they could play a little longer—Sophia thought that they had gotten cold enough when they were outside the first time. She didn't want to go outside again, but she did. Elizabeth told her to go ahead, because she didn't want to be bothered. She just needed to be alone for a while.

Having finished with the chores, Elizabeth went to her room and sat in her rocker. From time to time, she could see Sophia and the kids outside, but she didn't pay much attention to them. To help relax her mind, and maybe think about something else, she reached for the quilt that she had been working on, and she got her sewing kit down from the shelf in the closet. Once in a while when it got noisy outside, she would look to see what was going on, but other than that, she stayed in her rocker. She had let her mind go back to the time earlier in the day when she had been with Alfred.

When the Millers returned home from their dinner engagement, the kids were in the room with Elizabeth and Sophia. Elizabeth was still sitting in her rocker and working on her quilt, and Sophia was sitting on the side of the bed reading a book. Mrs. Miller strolled through the mansion until she had found them. The door to the room had been left open. Mrs. Miller looked in just to say that they had returned. She stayed for a few seconds just to stare at Sophia and the kids sitting on the bed.

Albert and Mary were sitting right next to Sophia—like kids sit near their mother. Elizabeth had noticed Mrs. Miller looking at them. Albert and Mary were focused on the story that Sophia had been reading, and they never noticed Mrs. Miller. The only sound in the room was that of Sophia reading to the kids. When she had seen enough, Mrs. Miller walked away, but clearly, she had been agitated.

Mrs. Miller had met Mr. Miller in the hallway, and she had bumped into him. She had seen him before she had gotten to him, but she walked into him anyway. He knew then that she was upset. She said that she just couldn't understand why Albert and Mary were so in love with Sophia; every time you see them, they're right under her. Mr. Miller said that they probably liked her, because she had spent so much time with them. Mrs. Miller said that she's in the room with them right now reading to them like she's a school teacher.

Like Mrs. Miller, he knew that Sophia had always read to the kids. He was glad that she did, otherwise, it would have been something that they would have had to do. He had suggested that she relax, and not let things like that bother her. He told her that Albert had always been a good student, and it was mostly due to Sophia spending so much time helping him. Again, Mrs. Miller reiterated that she just didn't like the idea of a slave teaching her children; she hoped that Albert didn't tell anyone at school that his mother's slave helped him with his homework. Then she wondered why things had to always be so different at their house.

Mr. Miller had asked her to have a seat. He had gone to get a cup of hot tea to help her relax. When he returned with the cup of tea, Mrs. Miller took it from his hands. Then she said that if their servants were any good, one of them would have seen to it that she had a cup of tea. When she had asked him to guess where they were, he said that he didn't know. She said that they're in their room, relaxing as if they were guests in the house. She then wondered if they even had any servants, and she was sure that they didn't have any slaves—at least not in the mansion. Mr. Miller didn't say anything. He had already sat down beside her, and picked up his newspaper.

Further into the fall, Elizabeth and Sophia had kept on going to the bush harbor. They both could feel that it was all about to end, because it had already gotten too cold to be sitting outside. Yet, they had bundled up for the trip anyway, realizing that it would probably be the last time until the following spring.

On their way, Elizabeth told Sophia that it would probably be the last trip. She didn't mention Daniel's name, but she knew that Sophia would get the hint, and let Daniel know that he probably wouldn't be seeing her again until the weather warmed up again. Elizabeth would be able to see Alfred from time to time during the winter, because one of his jobs was to maintain a stockpile of wood at the mansion. Still, she would miss the closeness that they had become accustomed to when they were together at the bush harbor.

Again, Sophia and Daniel sat on the last seat at the very back. It seemed as if that spot had become theirs, and many had figured out why. Sophia had already told him that she probably wouldn't see him again until the weather turned back warm. He had already heard others talking about it being time to shut things down for the winter.

Like always, when the preacher started, they held each other's hand and whispered. They sat very close to each other, partly to keep warm, but mainly to create a memory that would last until next spring. The preacher had really gotten the crowd stirred up—maybe trying to give his flock enough food for thought to last them through the winter. Sophia knew that it was not the place, but she had made up her mind, and she did it anyway. She leaned over toward Daniel, and kissed him on the lips. It had been a very brief one, but when they looked at each other, it was followed by one that was more passionate—far more passionate. Then she wished that they had tasted each other's lips much sooner.

Kissing Daniel at the bush harbor had been a gutsy move by Sophia, one that she had come to believe that Daniel wouldn't make. Even though it was just a simple kiss, Sophia felt like it had been so improper, because they were at church. Yet, she had spent the Sundays of summer sitting next to him and holding his hand. He was the first boy that she had ever loved. He was the one that could give her the first kiss of her life, and she didn't want the chance to pass her by.

Elizabeth had told Sophia time and time again that the church was no place for stuff like that. When she kissed Daniel, she remembered her mother's words. However, she had decided that maybe she would be forgiven if indeed it is wrong to let someone know that you love them—even at church.

When service had ended, everyone stood around heavily wrapped to shirk the cold, but still shivering because they were. Yet, it was comfortable enough to not rush away. After a while, the preacher had announced that it was the last time under the bush harbor until next spring. The announcement had been followed by sighs of regret, but that was the way that it had to be, and no one had been surprised.

Everybody had stayed around longer than usual. Alfred and Elizabeth were off to the side talking about whatever. The two young lovers were in their space away from any would be eavesdroppers. To them, next spring seemed like a thousand miles away, and filled with an equal number of sleepless nights—lying awake in bed, and dreaming of each other.

Alfred and Elizabeth were still talking, but while they talked, Elizabeth had been watching Sophia and Daniel. Alfred had told her not to worry, and that Daniel was a good boy. Elizabeth knew that she had always been very protective of her daughter, maybe too protective. She had already decided that Sophia could have a boyfriend, and that it was time for her to stop bird-dogging her so much. Still, she found it hard to just turn loose. Sophia was all that she had, and she had not been overjoyed by the thought of having to share her with someone else—not even with Daniel.

The Miller's had already returned from church when Elizabeth and Sophia made it back from the bush harbor. Mr. Miller had asked if they stayed comfortable enough. Elizabeth told him that she had almost frozen. She put the word in that they would be going to church with them until next spring.

He and Elizabeth both knew that it had gotten too cold for them to go to the bush harbor even before they had left the mansion. Yet, he didn't try to talk her out of going, because he knew that she wanted to see Alfred. She just didn't know that he was aware.

Sophia had looked outside, and she saw Caroline and Emily walking down the street near the mansion. She sneaked outside, and walked over near the street so that they could talk. Sophia had told them that Mrs. Miller was in the house so that they wouldn't stay too long. If Mrs. Miller had seen them outside talking, she would have been just as angry as if they had been sitting in her parlor. She was dead set against them visiting, and passing themselves off as being friends with Sophia.

Sophia had to tell them that she had kissed Daniel only about an hour ago. When she did, Caroline and Emily acted as if they had forgotten where they were. Sophia had to remind them to be quiet. When they had quieted down, and even though Caroline and Emily had no idea as to who Daniel was, they still wanted Sophia to describe him. They were so free minded with each other that Sophia even described her innermost feelings that she had when she kissed him.

Emily had asked Sophia where she and Daniel were when they kissed. When Sophia told them, they couldn't believe that she had kissed him at church with so many people around. Sophia admitted that she was scared, but she said that she had to do it.

Caroline had told Sophia that she was getting married on Christmas Eve. Sophia had thought that the groom might be one of the boys that they used to talk about when they were younger. When Caroline told her his name, Sophia realized that she had never heard of him.

Caroline had told Sophia that it would be good if she could attend the wedding. When she did, they didn't say anything. The three of them stood together, and then they put their arms around each other. They knew that a thought such as that had never been worth anything, and there was no need to talk about it. Still, they wanted Sophia to know that if the decision had been theirs, she would be there at the altar with them, simply because they were friends.

Elizabeth had looked outside from the window, and she saw Sophia, Caroline and Emily locked together—hugging each other. Elizabeth kept watching. She knew that Mrs. Miller would be furious if she had seen them, but soon they had left.

Sophia had gone back inside. Elizabeth told her that she had seen her talking to Caroline and Emily. She scolded Sophia a bit, because she didn't want her to do something that might make Mrs. Miller angry.

When Elizabeth had finished, Sophia told her that Caroline was getting married. Elizabeth listened, because she knew how Sophia felt about Caroline and Emily. Hearing about the wedding roused Elizabeth's attention. She had known Caroline since she was a little girl, but she had become a young woman, and ready for marriage. Elizabeth had told Sophia not to mention the wedding to the Millers, because Mrs. Miller would certainly be upset with the idea that her house servants had gotten the news before she did.

Sophia, Caroline and Emily were all about the same age, and Caroline had already planned her wedding. Emily would probably be next, according to Elizabeth's thinking. She had started having the same thoughts that she had when she tried to talk to Mrs. Miller about Sophia. However, she had come to realize that she couldn't do anything to change things, and if she didn't let it go, she would either lose her mind or go plumb crazy.

Sophia's future had always been the single most depressing thought that Elizabeth had to deal with. She had heard talk about freeing the slaves, but she had heard it for so long that she didn't pay attention to it anymore. To cap things off, Elizabeth knew that Sophia had always had an attitude. It was an attitude that wouldn't be tolerated anywhere other than at Magnolia Manor. Had Mr. Miller's point of view been the same as that of his wife, Elizabeth reasoned that Sophia would have been long gone.

EIGHT

The cold dreary days of winter seemed like they would never go away. Yet, they still had more days of winter left in front of them than what they had put behind. Elizabeth and Sophia had been going to church every Sunday with the Millers, but it was so different from being at the bush harbor.

Their shabbily built sanctuary was indeed a sore eye on the landscape, and they knew that it was. However, it was theirs and it was where they wanted to be. Sundays there had proven to be not only good for the soul, but good for the mind as well. It was a place where for a short while, they could almost forget about chains and shackles, and the indecencies imposed on them by amoral legal sanctions levied by one race of people on another.

Christmas had been slowly creeping closer and closer. Alfred had been wrestling with a tree that was definitely too big. It was one that Mr. Miller had selected, and he had told Alfred to set it up in the mansion. Alfred had gotten stuck in the back door with it, and Mrs.

Miller had been giving him a hard time about scratching the walls and scuffing up the floor. Elizabeth, Sophia and the kids were all standing back watching. He kept yanking on the tree until it had funneled down enough to squeeze through the door.

Mrs. Miller had him to place it in the perfect spot that she had selected in the parlor. The tree was standing tall and stately on the stand that Alfred had made. Mrs. Miller told him to fetch the box of ornaments from storage, and place them near the tree. While he was in the mansion, Alfred stoked the fireplaces.

Sophia and the kids had been decorating the tree when Mr. Miller walked into the parlor. When he selected the tree, he had the thought that it might be too big, but looking at, he concluded that it was just the right size. Mrs. Miller told him that Alfred had almost torn the house down trying to get it through the door. Alfred said that he was going outside to get the other tree.

Mrs. Miller had been surprised by Alfred's comment. No one had said anything to her about having two trees in the mansion, and what for, she wondered. Mr. Miller said that it was his idea. He had decided that it would be nice for Elizabeth and Sophia to have a tree in their room for Christmas. Although she hadn't been told, Mrs. Miller agreed that it was probably a good idea to let them share in the Christmas spirit. After all, it was a religious celebration, and she couldn't stand in the way of that, not even with her house servants.

Alfred had taken the second tree inside—it was much smaller than the one that he had set up in the parlor. He had made a stand for it just like the one that he had made for the monster that Mr. Miller had selected. Elizabeth showed him where to put it—they hadn't seen each other for a while, and they felt good setting up the Christmas tree together. Elizabeth didn't do much other than show him where to place it. It had taken far longer than necessary, because Alfred was in no hurry.

After they had finished decorating the tree in the parlor, Mr. Miller surprised everybody when he walked in with an arm full of gifts that had already been wrapped. Christmas was still several weeks away, but since Mr. Miller had been out shopping, Mrs. Miller realized that she had to get hers done. Sophia and the kids placed the gifts under the tree. When they had finished, they all stood back and admired the beautifully adorned cedar with the beautifully wrapped gifts that had been placed underneath.

Sophia had asked Mrs. Miller if there was anything else that she needed her to do. Since there wasn't, she had started to go to her room. As she was about to leave the parlor, Mrs. Miller told her to take the box and the remaining ornaments. She could use them to decorate their tree. Although there were a lot of ornaments remaining in the box, Sophia was surprised that Mrs. Miller had made the offer. She was so excited that she was picking up the box, and thanking Mrs. Miller all at the same time.

With a smile on her face, and the box in her arms, Sophia rushed to show the beautiful ornaments to Elizabeth. On her way, she had slowed down to examine the contents of the box. When she had made it to the room, she suddenly stopped—the door was almost closed, but not enough to obscure the view. She was stunned, and she didn't know what to do. Sophia was standing there in the doorway with her arms wrapped around the box of ornaments, and just in front of her stood Alfred with his arms wrapped around Elizabeth.

Alfred and Elizabeth looked at Sophia. He still had his arms around her—locked in place it seemed. At that moment, all three of them were just standing there staring at each other—as still as statues. Then, Elizabeth and Alfred backed away. They had been separated by the forceful push that each had given the other. Elizabeth had started fumbling around with the Christmas tree.

Everybody had become speechless and jittery. Alfred couldn't say anything, because of the intimate scene that he had been cast in; Sophia because she had seen everything from her front row seat; and Elizabeth because she had been the leading lady. Finally, Sophia decided that the show had ended, and someone had to let the curtain down. She walked in and showed them what was in the box. She had been so casual with her approach that she made it seem like she hadn't seen a thing.

At that moment, Elizabeth didn't care about what Sophia had in the box, but digging through it and pretending to be interested was all that she knew to do. Alfred had been so embarrassed. He quickly finished with the tree, said goodbye, and left.

Elizabeth kept on digging through the box, and admiring its' contents. She had exaggerated her fascination with the ornaments in order to try and get Sophia's thoughts off of her and Alfred. Sophia had pretty much let it go, and it was Elizabeth that needed to forget about what had happened and think about something else.

It was cold outside, but cozy in their rooms. Sophia had started decorating the tree, and Elizabeth was doing just whatever to try and calm down. She was still fidgety, because her daughter had caught her doing something that she would rather have kept from her.

After Sophia had finished decorating the tree, she and her mom sat and looked at it—it was beautiful. It didn't seem to matter that they didn't have any gifts to place underneath. They adored it for what it was truly meant to be, a religious symbol to represent the birth of Christ.

Mr. and Mrs. Miller had made several shopping trips to town during the week. They had a pile of gifts under the tree in the parlor that would fill a wagon. Elizabeth had been busy baking cakes and pies for the holiday season. The aroma coming from the kitchen had spread throughout the mansion, and it tormented their taste buds. To keep the peace, she had to place one of her pies on the table, so that whomever could satisfy their craving, and thereby, avoid a confrontation in the kitchen.

While Elizabeth was in the kitchen, Albert and Mary asked Sophia if she would read them a story, a Christmas story. Mrs. Miller had told Sophia that she could sit in Mary's room while she entertained the kids. Later, when Mrs. Miller was in the hallway near the bedroom, she could only hear Mary's voice. She stood quietly and listened. When she had peeked into the room, she saw a different seating arrangement. The norm had been Sophia in the middle with Mary and Albert on either side. That time, however, Mary sat in the middle with Sophia and Albert sitting on either side of her.

Sophia and Albert listened as Mary read a story to them—The Night Before Christmas. They still didn't know that Mrs. Miller had been listening. Mr. Miller had noticed his wife quietly standing outside Mary's room, and he had eased up near her. Then they listened together as Mary read from the storybook.

Mr. and Mrs. Miller had gone back to the parlor and sat down. She had asked him if he knew that Mary could read like that and he said no. Mrs. Miller said that since Albert and Mary both had learned to read, they wouldn't need Sophia reading to them anymore. He said that the reason why they both could read was because Sophia had been teaching them. He had stood up to go to his study, but before leaving, he said that the best thing to do would be to just leave them alone, and let them keep on doing what they had been doing.

It was still early, but the short daylight hours of winter had gone, and it was dark outside. Elizabeth and Sophia had just finished with their chores for the evening, and they thought that they were through for the day. When Mrs. Miller noticed that they had finished, she told them to dust all of the furniture and book shelves in Mr. Miller's study. Elizabeth wondered why, because they had already dusted things off in his study. Still, she didn't question Mrs. Miller, and she did as she had been told.

After Elizabeth and Sophia had finished dusting in the study, Mrs. Miller told them that they didn't have to bother about anything else—they could go to their room. Elizabeth wondered why Mrs. Miller had them dusting things off when there was no dust on anything ... none of it made any sense.

As soon as Elizabeth and Sophia had walked into their room, they saw the beautifully wrapped gifts that had been placed under their Christmas tree. Sophia wondered where they had come from, but Elizabeth knew as soon as she had seen them. She told Sophia that Mrs. Miller had kept them busy while Mr. Miller placed the gifts under the tree. They picked up the gifts, and wondered what was inside, but they knew not to open them until Christmas day.

The next morning, Mr. Miller walked in looking for his cup of coffee. When Elizabeth and Sophia thanked him for the gifts, he pretended that he didn't know what they were talking about. Elizabeth told him that they knew that he was the one that had put the gifts under their tree. He said that it may have been Santa Claus. Elizabeth laughed, and told him to sit down so that he could eat breakfast.

He ate a few bites as usual, but he had more than one cup of coffee. After grabbing the satchel from his study, he headed off to town. Elizabeth could tell that he had been in a good mood all morning, because when he left the house, he was singing—it was a Christmas song. When he had closed the door, Elizabeth told Sophia that the only way that he could carry a tune would be in a tote sack. She had heard him sing in church, and she could always pick his voice out from the others. He was always too loud, and way out of tune.

The official announcement of Caroline's wedding had been made. Mrs. Miller had never said anything about it to Sophia, but Mr. Miller had told her. When he did, Sophia acted surprised just like Elizabeth had told her to do. Mr. and Mrs. Miller had been invited to the wedding, and that pleased Mrs. Miller. Caroline's family was amongst the higher-ups around town, and Mrs. Miller would have been very disappointed if their names had not been on the list.

While at church, Mr. and Mrs. Miller congratulated Caroline, and so did Elizabeth and Sophia. Caroline never let on that Sophia and Elizabeth had been among the first to know about her wedding. Before leaving the church, Caroline had secretly passed two letters to Sophia, one from her, and one from Emily—Emily wasn't at church. Sophia had passed two off to Caroline—one being for Emily.

Caroline's mother had asked Mrs. Miller if it would be alright if she could get Elizabeth to make some minor alterations to her daughter's wedding dress. It was no secret that Elizabeth had always been a master with a needle and thread. Without asking Elizabeth, Mrs. Miller assured her that she would be able to accommodate her request. A few days later, Caroline's mother delivered the wedding dress to the mansion.

Mrs. Miller was not at home when Caroline's mother dropped the dress off. She spoke with Elizabeth about what needed to be done. Elizabeth told her that she would have to see the dress on Caroline in order to make sure that she got it just right.

Caroline's mother told Elizabeth that her daughter had been in bed with a terrible cold, and she didn't feel well enough to come over and stand for the measurements. She told Elizabeth that her daughter and Sophia were the same size. Therefore, if she altered the dress based on Sophia's measurements, then it would fit Caroline. Elizabeth agreed and said that she would get started on it right away.

Caroline's mom had left the dress with Elizabeth. Sophia was showing her to the door just as Mrs. Miller returned home. Mrs. Miller invited her into the parlor, and she told Sophia to bring them a cup of tea.

Elizabeth had taken the dress to her room, and she laid it on the bed to have a good look at what needed to be done. She could tell just from looking at it that it was a bit large in the waist, but the alterations would be a snap.

Sophia had gotten a silver tray from the cabinet to serve tea to Mrs. Miller and her guest. Thoughtfully, she had also placed a few cookies on the tray, some that Elizabeth had baked.

In the parlor, Sophia had placed the tray on the small table in front of them. Mrs. Miller listened as Caroline's mom talked with Sophia. Sophia knew that Mrs. Miller would rather that she had placed the tray on the table and walked away. Yet, she couldn't because it was Caroline's mom that had initiated their brief conversation.

Caroline's mom liked Sophia, but she had never been around her much. Most of what she knew was what Caroline had told her. She knew that Sophia, Caroline, Emily, and the late Amanda had all grown up together, and that they had spent lots time together at Mr. Miller's house.

Although most of what she knew about Sophia had come from Caroline, she did know that all four of them had always been close friends, and that had always been fine with her. Mrs. Miller sensed that her guest had a fondness for Sophia. To avoid being placed in a predicament where she might have to expend false accolades, she changed the subject so that Sophia could leave.

Elizabeth didn't start work on the dress until the next day. When she told Mrs. Miller what she was going to do, she was reminded to be careful, and not to ruin it. Sophia had put the dress on so that Elizabeth could see exactly what needed to be done. Elizabeth had to tell her to be still and stop moving about. Sophia had been admiring herself in front of the mirror. Elizabeth pulled and tucked to see just what she needed to do. When she had it all figured out, Sophia took the dress off, and Elizabeth had laid it aside. She would wait until the next day to start stitching on it.

Once she had started, Elizabeth worked on the dress off and on—she didn't want to let it interfere with her duties as house servant. After a couple of days of snipping and stitching, she had finished with the alterations. It had gotten dark outside, but still early in the evening. Just to make sure that she had it right, she asked Sophia to put the dress on again, so that she could see how it fit. Sophia was standing in front of the mirror, admiring herself in Caroline's wedding dress. Elizabeth was looking as well. Sophia had said that it was beautiful. Elizabeth had taken a step back with her eyes still fixed on Sophia. She agreed with her daughter, the dress was beautiful. Then she told Sophia that she was more beautiful than anything she had ever seen.

Elizabeth was proud of her work, and she wanted Mrs. Miller to have a look at it. She had told Sophia to stand in the parlor while she went to get her. Mr. and Mrs. Miller had been talking, and they were both in the other parlor—the mansion had two. Elizabeth told her that she had finished with the dress, and they both followed her to the parlor to have a look. When they saw Sophia wearing Caroline's wedding dress, Mrs. Miller was speechless, she just stood there looking at Sophia, and for a few seconds she didn't say a single word.

Mr. Miller had been astonished as much as Mrs. Miller, but for different reasons. With his wife still speechless, Mr. Miller had said something. Elizabeth didn't know if he had said it without thinking, or if he had been flabbergasted, and called it what it was. He had told Sophia that she was as beautiful as any bride that he had ever seen.

Mr. Miller had become accustomed to Sophia's brief responses and quick get-a-ways whenever he tried to talk to her. That time, however, she was completely different. Standing there, she was dashing, poised, and had a faint smile on her face. She thanked him and followed up with a polite curtsey.

In Caroline's wedding dress, Sophia was everything that a well refined southern belle should be—black or white—and she knew it. Mr. Miller had been just like Elizabeth, never before had he seen her so beautiful. For a short while, Elizabeth felt like he may have forgotten about Sophia's rank in life, but on the other hand, maybe he hadn't.

Sophia had always done pretty much as she pleased with little if anything holding her back—that in itself was enough to make her different. Maybe the trace of African heritage in her genetic makeup had been masked to the point that Mr. Miller couldn't see anything other than what she appeared to be. Whatever the reason, he found her fascinating.

Mrs. Miller had been speechless, but not anymore. Had there been a gun in her pocket, she may have used it on her husband. It's doubtful that she would have shot him, but she may have slapped him up side of the head with it, and then pulled the trigger at the same time— when it went bang, he would then think that he had been shot for sure. Anyway, she had chosen to deal with him later. At the moment, she wanted to go right to the core.

First of all, she started with Elizabeth. She had been the one responsible for the mess up in the first place. She was responsible, because she should have never allowed Sophia to wear Caroline's wedding dress. Elizabeth explained that Caroline's mom had said to alter the dress so that it would fit Sophia. If the dress would fit Sophia, it would fit Caroline, because both girls were the same size. Mrs. Miller conceded that she may have said that, but she had never intended for Sophia to put the dress on. She said that the only thing that you had to do was hold the dress up against her to get an idea about what to do, and then do it.

When she had finished with Elizabeth, she started on Sophia. She had told her to get out of that dress, and to get out of it right now. In just a few minutes, Sophia had gone from feeling good about herself to being totally confused. When Mrs. Miller told her to get out of the dress right now, Sophia took it to mean right now—at that very moment. She had started taking the dress off. Mrs. Miller asked her what in the name of hell did she think that she was doing? Sophia said that she was taking the dress off. Mrs. Miller told her to take her damned ass back there somewhere and do it.

Mr. Miller still hadn't left the room. He had been listening to his wife, and even though she was furious, he thought that he could straighten her out—he had never seen her bent so far out of shape.

Very calmly, he said that it seemed like in order to make sure that the dress would fit, someone would have to put it on to see what needed to be done—he had chosen the diplomatic approach. Mrs. Miller told him that he didn't know a damn thing about tailoring. Sophia had already left the parlor, and Elizabeth was on her way out. Subsequently, Mr. Miller had headed for his study, with Mrs. Miller right behind him.

Mrs. Miller was angry—she had gone passed angry—and she had a lot more to say to her husband about Sophia. Mr. Miller had sat down at his desk, hoping that she would soon exhaust herself, but she has not shown any signs of letting up. Again, she rehashed everything that had just happened in the parlor, and he had to listen to it again. After she had said that it was hard sometimes to tell who was in charge of things around here, she got on him.

She had asked him how was it possible that he could stand there and tell Sophia how beautiful she was when she's nothing but a slave. He said that he didn't see anything wrong with complimenting her on her appearance. Mrs. Miller didn't want to talk to him anymore. She had sashayed from his study and found the wedding dress. She placed it on a hanger, and she hung it up to air out any traces of Sophia—hoping that Caroline's mom wouldn't be able to tell that she had it on.

Mrs. Miller was through talking, and she had decided to get ready for bed. First, she had to stop by, and say goodnight to the kids. When she entered Mary's room, she wasn't there. Since she wasn't in her room, she knew that she had to be with Sophia and Elizabeth. When she had opened the door to their room, Mary was sitting on the bed next to Sophia.

Mrs. Miller had walked into the room. No one said anything, but they all looked at her. She looked at Mary, and asked why she wasn't in bed. Mary told her that she had heard her fussing at Sophia and Elizabeth, so she had been trying to make them feel better.

Mrs. Miller had told her to come with her so that she could tuck her in, but Mary didn't move. Instead, she sat there and looked back at Mrs. Miller. Then Mary asked if she could sleep with Sophia. Mrs. Miller had grabbed her by the hand, yanked her off the bed, and was almost dragging her along—moving at a pace that was far too fast for Mary. Curiosity had gotten Sophia up, and she looked down the hallway, hoping that Mrs. Miller wouldn't hurt Mary.

After Mary had left, Sophia started talking about Mrs. Miller, and how she had acted. For a while, Elizabeth let her talk, maybe because she realized that what Sophia had been saying was right. Sophia had said that she acted like they were filthy animals, and she wished that she would go somewhere and just disappear. Elizabeth told her that she shouldn't say things like that, and that she would get over it soon enough. Sophia said that she didn't care if she never got over it. She hated Mrs. Miller just as much as Mrs. Miller hated her; and she didn't see why Mr. Miller had even married her in the first place. Elizabeth told her that she had said enough, and that she didn't want to hear any more about it.

A couple of days later, Caroline's mom had stopped by to see if Elizabeth had finished with the alterations. When she knocked on the door, Mr. Miller let her in. When Mrs. Miller saw her, she walked over and they talked a bit, and then Caroline's mom asked if the dress was ready. Mrs. Miller told her that it was, and then she told Elizabeth to bring it to the parlor. Elizabeth got the dress, took it to the parlor, and held it up for viewing.

Sophia and Mr. Miller had been standing near the entryway to the parlor watching. Caroline's mom admired Elizabeth's skillful work, and then she asked Mrs. Miller if it would be alright if Sophia put the dress on so that she could get a better look at how fits. Then, it got quiet in the parlor.

Mrs. Miller couldn't believe that Caroline's mom would even consider having Sophia put on her daughter's wedding dress—putting it on before her daughter did. To her, it was not just ridiculous, it was stupid. Mrs. Miller still hadn't responded to her request, so Caroline's mom asked again. She reminded Mrs. Miller that if the dress would fit Sophia, then it would fit Caroline, because they were both the same size.

Mrs. Miller knew that Caroline and Sophia were the same size, but she couldn't understand why everybody had missed the point. Mrs. Miller didn't want to clash with her, so she told Elizabeth to help Sophia with the dress. Sophia and Elizabeth had left the parlor while Mr. and Mrs. Miller talked and waited with Caroline's mom. A few minutes later, Sophia stepped into the parlor with Elizabeth trailing behind. Caroline's mom was fascinated. She told Sophia how beautiful she was in her daughter's wedding dress. She then turned to Mrs. Miller, waiting for her to agree.

Mrs. Miller had recognized the look, and finally she had to say yes she's beautiful, but her words had no meaning. Tactfully, Mrs. Miller had directed attention to the beautiful dress, and Elizabeth's stitch work—none of which she really cared about. Yet, she had to avoid dishing out anymore niceties about Sophia. She had already forced one out, but she didn't want to have to do it again.

The showing had ended, and Elizabeth and Sophia had left the parlor. Sophia had taken the dress off, and Elizabeth carefully folded it so that it wouldn't get wrinkled, and then she presented it to Caroline's mom. Before leaving, Caroline's mom asked about the fee for doing the alterations. Mrs. Miller told her that there was no charge.

Elizabeth and Sophia had found something to do just to make it look like they were doing something. They knew that Mrs. Miller had gotten very upset, and the best way to keep her off their back was to be busy. Mr. Miller had walked Caroline's mom to the door. When he returned to his study, Mrs. Miller was sitting at his walnut desk in his high back leather chair. He didn't know why she had chosen to sit there, but he walked in and closed the door.

He looked at her, suspecting that she might want to offer an apology for her earlier behavior. No doubt she had suspected what he had suspected. Maybe she had intended to apologize, and just changed her mind. Still, she hadn't said anything, and neither had he. She had stood up and walked toward the door. He stepped aside to let her pass. She looked at him and kept walking. He knew that she was fiery; she had always been like that.

The following Sunday, they all saw each other again at church. Caroline had gotten rid of that bad cold, and she was there along with Emily. Caroline, Emily and Sophia stood off to the side and talked, no one paid them any attention. Even Elizabeth had found herself tied up in conversation.

The little mix-up from a few days earlier had mostly been forgotten about, or at least, they had pushed it to the side. It had certainly been nothing to dwell on, because it was a common thing around Magnolia Manor. Elizabeth had supposed that it wouldn't be long before they would have something else that would stir up another stink.

It had been a beautiful day, and it felt good to be outside. Church goers stood around and talked a little longer than usual. But eventually, the crowd began to thin out, as people started to go home.

Back at the mansion and toward mid-afternoon, Mr. Miller responded to a knock on the door. When he went to see who it was, he was a bit surprised to see Caroline's mother. He had invited her in, but she said that she only needed a minute. She had two gifts, one for Elizabeth and one for Sophia. She wanted Elizabeth to have something for the alterations that she had made on her daughter's dress. She said that the gift for Sophia was from Caroline and Emily—apparently, Caroline and Emily didn't want to deliver a gift to Sophia, not in person with Mrs. Miller around.

Mr. Miller said that he would see to it that they got the gifts. Just as he was closing the door, Mrs. Miller walked up, and she wanted to know who it was that he had been talking to. He told her, and then he showed her the gifts that Caroline's mom had dropped off. Mrs. Miller wondered why she had gone to the trouble. She took both gifts from Mr. Miller, and said that she would pass them along.

When Mrs. Miller had given the gifts to Elizabeth and Sophia, she was more curious as to what might be inside than they were. She thought that they might open them, so she stood there waiting to see. Instead, Sophia took the gifts, and placed them beneath the Christmas tree. Christmas Eve was cold, the few snowflakes that had been falling had created a splendor outside, and it really felt like Christmas. It would be a perfect day for Caroline's wedding. It was early morning, but Alfred was already outside with a wagon load of firewood. Mr. Miller never had to tell him when to replenish the pile. It was Alfred's job, and he had always made sure that there was more than an adequate supply on hand.

The wood supply had not really gotten low, but making a delivery was an excuse for Alfred to be at the mansion so that he could see Elizabeth on Christmas Eve. Every now and then, Elizabeth and Sophia would peer from the window as he neatly stacked the wood, one log at a time. He had noticed them watching from the window, but he pretended that he hadn't seen them.

Alfred had finished stacking the wood, and then he took some logs inside and stoked the fireplaces. When he had finished downstairs, he did the same upstairs. He had spotted Mr. Miller, and he told him that he had something that he wanted to give to Elizabeth and Sophia for Christmas. He wanted to know if it would be alright if he brought it inside. After Mr. Miller told him that he could, Alfred had to go outside to get it. When he had gone back inside, he didn't see Mr. or Mrs. Miller, so he just headed to Elizabeth's room.

Alfred had knocked on the door. When Elizabeth opened it, he was standing there holding a large something that he had covered with a blanket. When he asked her if he could come in, Elizabeth opened the door wider, so that he could get through with whatever it was that he had in his arms. He had placed the arm full on the floor in the middle of the room. Elizabeth and Sophia stood back looking down at whatever it was that he had under the blanket. Slowly, Alfred removed the blanket, and then he said Merry Christmas.

On the floor in front of them was a beautifully crafted chest that Alfred had made for Elizabeth and Sophia, but mostly for Elizabeth. Again, he said Merry Christmas, and was about to leave when Elizabeth told him to wait for a minute. She had taken a package down from the shelf in the closet, and after giving it to him, she then said Merry Christmas. Like Alfred, Elizabeth couldn't buy a gift, but she had done the same thing that he had done. She had given him a beautiful handmade blanket, one that she had been working on for several months.

Later that day, Alfred drove the buggy to take Mr. and Mrs. Miller to Caroline's wedding. When the wedding ended and they had returned home, both knew that Sophia would want to know how things went. Mrs. Miller wondered why it was any of her business, and didn't feel like they should to tell her anything. Yet, they had both gone to tell her.

After they had walked into their room, the first thing that they noticed was the beautifully crafted chest that had been placed over near the window. Mrs. Miller had asked where it came from, and she could tell that such a beautiful piece would be quite expensive—since Elizabeth and Sophia didn't have any money, she knew that they didn't buy it. Elizabeth told her that Alfred had made it, and that he had given it to her and Sophia as a Christmas gift.

Mrs. Miller hadn't taken her eyes off the chest since entering the room. Still looking at it, she told Elizabeth and Sophia about the wedding, and that everything had gone just as planned. It seemed as though she had forgotten about the incident over Caroline's dress, and her behavior was such that she was kind of nice to be around. Regarding the ruckus that she had created, they all knew that there would never be an apology. Still, Elizabeth felt like the rare, but respectful attitude that she had may have been her attempt to smooth things over—bordering on an apology anyway.

When they were about to leave, the beautiful chest still had Mrs. Miller's attention. She had not been surprised by the fact that Alfred had made it. The only thing that she had to do was to look at Magnolia Manor, and she would see his credentials. Yet, she had no idea that he was so skilled at making furniture.

Whenever Mrs. Miller had something to say she would say it. Sometimes she said it with the boldness of, to hell with tact. She had made the statement that a lot of slave owners would take a fine chest like that, and kept it as their own. Mr. Miller looked at her, probably wishing that she hadn't said it—certainly wondering why she had found it necessary. He had placed his hand on her shoulder, and at the same time he was escorting her from the room. She moved along ahead of him while still eying the beautiful chest, but completely unaware of what he was doing or the reason why.

Sophia told Elizabeth that Mrs. Miller had been trying to be nice. Elizabeth said that Christmas had a way of doing that to people. Sophia didn't care if it was Christmas or a Friday night fish fry. Her attitude was nothing like that of her mother. As far as she was concerned, Mrs. Miller couldn't do enough nice things to offset the wrongs that she had done. She had said that she would never forget, and she didn't want to forget.

Elizabeth had always let her religious faith be her guiding light. Yet, she realized that faith didn't turn wrongs into right, but it did give her the strength to cope. On the other hand, Sophia's attitude seemed to be that she would rather burn in Hell than to rely on Christianity to help her tolerate Mrs. Miller.

It had started getting dark outside when the Millers sat down at the dining room table. The setting was spectacular. Mr. Miller had suggested that maybe they should just sit there and look at it rather than ruin the sight by tearing into it.

The table had been adorned with some of Mrs. Miller's finest china and silverware. Light from the candles danced and created images on the wall that resembled nothing, but yet, they were worth watching. Lined up on the table from one end to the other were Elizabeth's culinary Christmas creations. Stationed in the middle of it all was Mr. Miller's favorite, Elizabeth's baked ham. He wasn't surprised when he saw it, because he had been savoring the aroma all day while it baked in the oven.

They had all pretty much stuffed themselves when Elizabeth placed dessert on the table. She had held it back until the end, because if she had placed it on the table too soon, Albert and Mary would have passed on everything else, and gone right to the sweets. When they had finished eating and had gotten up from the table, Mrs. Miller casually reminded Elizabeth and Sophia to be careful with her chinaware. When she did, Sophia glanced at Elizabeth with a snide look on her face. Elizabeth replied with one of her own. Hers told Sophia to keep a lid on it.

Albert and Mary had gone to bed early, because they had lots of good reasons to wake up early on Christmas morning. However, Mr. and Mrs. Miller had decided to sit up later than usual. It was still snowing outside, and the flames flickering in the fireplace had made it all the more cozy. Mr. Miller found Elizabeth, and he had talked her into helping him make some eggnog. Elizabeth could have done it herself, but he felt like doing something in the kitchen.

When it was time, Mr. Miller spiked it up with a strong shot of bourbon—he didn't measure it, he just held the bottle upside down and let it go chug-a-lug. When Elizabeth told him that he had added enough, he looked at her as if he didn't understand what she had said, and kept on pouring. Elizabeth took the bottle from him, and put it away. When it was ready, Elizabeth poured a cup for him, and one for Mrs. Miller. She left the rest of it on the stove, so that Mr. Miller could have more if he wanted it. With Mr. Miller helping her, they had ended up making far more than was necessary, but they didn't care about that—it was Christmas Eve.

Elizabeth had cleaned things up in the kitchen, and was about to go to her room. Since they had made so much eggnog, she poured a nice cup of it for herself. In her room, she sat near the window, and watched a million snowflakes fall, and then gently come to rest—landing ever so softly as to keep their one of a kind structure. She listened as some collided with the window pane, but not one made a sound. Sophia had flung herself across the bed, and was looking at the gifts under the tree. She wanted to open hers, but she waited so that she and Elizabeth could do it together.

Elizabeth kept watching the snowflakes fall outside, and she kept sipping on the delicious cup of eggnog. She had come to the conclusion that it was certainly one of her better batches—as smooth as it gets—and the far too much bourbon that Mr. Miller added had been suppressed by the nutmeg, the cream, the sugar, and whatever else they had tossed in. It had been a long day, and she had the perfect toddy for bedtime on Christmas Eve.

There was still quite a bit of eggnog remaining in her cup, but she had gotten a bit tipsy, and decided that she should go to bed. Just as she had started to get up, she sat back down. She had changed her mind about going to bed—she would wait a few more minutes. She didn't want to be wasteful by throwing away some of the best eggnog that she had ever made. After she had finished it off, she then called it a day.

The next morning, Elizabeth was up at her usual time, and she got the coffee pot brewing first thing. She knew that Mr. Miller would soon be up and about.

She had noticed the pot that they had used to make the eggnog—it was empty. She had guessed that Mr. Miller had probably downed all that he wanted, and then tossed what had been left.

She had heard the kids making their way to the parlor, anxious to find out what they had for Christmas. Elizabeth watched as they tore away at the wrappings. She had decided that she would wait until Mr. and Mrs. Miller were both out of bed before she made breakfast. She knew that he would be up early, but since it was Christmas morning, she expected that Mrs. Miller would be up early as well. Still, she delayed cooking, because she didn't want to have to serve cold food—there was no reason to eat so early anyway. Since it was Christmas morning, Elizabeth had been excited herself. She had gone back to her room so that she could tear into whatever it was that she had under the tree.

When she walked in, Sophia had already opened all of her gifts. She was sitting on the side of the bed admiring the one that meant the most to her. It was a beautiful friendship ring from Caroline and Emily.

First, Elizabeth opened the gift that she had received from Caroline's mother. Inside the small box that had been hidden with the wrapping paper was a bracelet. Elizabeth was holding the empty box, because as soon as she had opened it, Sophia removed the bracelet. She had been too impatient to wait for Elizabeth to do it.

Sophia was trying to put the bracelet on her own wrist when Elizabeth took it from her, and then placed it on her wrist. Sophia had told Elizabeth that she was going to wear her bracelet the next time they went to the bush harbor; it would go good with her friendship ring. Elizabeth said that she shouldn't count on it.

When all of the gifts had been opened, Elizabeth and Sophia both realized how generous Mr. and Mrs. Miller had been. They each had two new dresses and new shoes. They knew that it had to have been Mrs. Miller that purchased them. After thinking about the gifts, Elizabeth had started having confusing thoughts. She couldn't understand how Mrs. Miller could be so hardhearted sometimes, and at other times, be just the opposite. The two didn't go together, but she was not about to spend a lot of time trying to figure that one out.

Mr. Miller had been in the parlor with Albert and Mary. Elizabeth found him so that she could thank him for the gifts. She had gone to the kitchen to get him a cup of coffee. After filling the cup, she gave it to Sophia so that she could take it to him. Like Elizabeth, she thanked him for the gifts, and then she stood there watching Albert and Mary. For whatever reason, Sophia was not in her usual hurry to walk away.

Like Elizabeth, Mr. Miller thought that his wife would be out of bed since it was Christmas morning. He had gone to the bedroom to wish her a Merry Christmas. When he opened the door, she was still asleep. Quietly, he walked over to the window, and threw open the curtains. He wanted her to be surprised when she saw the beautiful snow covered landscape.

After he had flung open the curtains, the sunlight reflecting off the snow outside shone through the windows so brightly, that Mrs. Miller felt like her bed may as well have been out in the yard. She had told him to close the curtains, but he wanted her to see how beautiful it was outside. Again, she told him to close the curtains, but she had been more persuasive the second time. She told him that she would look at the snow later. It was Christmas morning, and everyone else was up and about, but Mrs. Miller didn't feel good. The eggnog had taken a toll on her.

She could do without alcoholic drinks, but she would have an occasional glass of wine, or perhaps a glass of sherry. Christmas Eve, sitting in the parlor next to her husband and watching the snowflakes fall had created a very romantic atmosphere. The evening had been accentuated by the flames and embers in the fireplace, and the tasty cocktail that may have been a little on the strong side after Mr. Miller had spiked it up. Whether or not it had been due to being spiked up too much, or just having one too many, she had been feeling the after effects. It was the first time in her life, but she was suffering from a hangover.

Mr. Miller had recognized the symptoms, and he closed the curtains so that she could sleep it off. About mid-morning, she had made it to the table. Elizabeth told her that she would have breakfast ready in just a few minutes. She told Elizabeth that she didn't want any breakfast, only a big cup of black coffee. In between sips, she would let her elbows rest on the table, so that her hands could support her aching head.

Elizabeth recognized the fact that she didn't feel good, and when she had put two and two together, she knew exactly why. The person responsible for the empty eggnog container had her head resting on the table right there in front of her. When her cup of coffee had gotten low, Elizabeth filled it again. She then took it to the parlor for her, because she was too unsteady. After she had flopped down on the sofa, she said Merry Christmas, but there was nothing merry about it for her. She was feeling as rough as corn cob. She had sworn that if somehow she would be able to survive, she would never do it again.

After having had several cups of strong black coffee, and then getting two or three hours older, Mrs. Miller had started feeling better. When she finally felt well enough to talk, Elizabeth and Sophia thanked her for the Christmas gifts. Mrs. Miller had noticed the bracelet on Elizabeth's wrist, and she wanted to know where she had gotten it. Elizabeth told her that it was the gift from Caroline's mother. Mrs. Miller took a closer look at it, and said that it was beautiful.

Sophia showed her the ring that Caroline and Emily had given to her, and she liked it as well; she even said that it was beautiful. She still didn't like Sophia any more than she ever had, but at the time she didn't want to put any more stress on her already aching head. Therefore, it was much easier to lower the colors, and declare a temporary truce.

Mr. and Mrs. Miller still hadn't moved from their seat in the parlor. She had started talking, but she had been trying to keep her voice down so that no one would hear. Yet, the hangover had her talking a little louder than she realized. She had told Mr. Miller that the gifts that Caroline's mom had brought over seemed to be too costly for house servants. She had supposed that they were probably the only people in town with slaves that got gifts on Christmas anyway. He just let her talk, probably because he had learned that if she wanted to say it, she would.

Mrs. Miller still hadn't fully recovered from the hangover. She had leaned back and put her feet upon the table near her coffee cup. She said that maybe she had made too big of an issue out of things, and that it really didn't matter anyway. She had decided that she would go back to her bedroom and lie down for a while. When she stood up from the sofa, she said that things were just a little different around their house, and that she may as well get used to it.

NINE

Christmas had come and gone, and the New Year had aged a bit. It had gotten to be springtime, and time to get things back to normal. Albeit, getting things back to normal at Magnolia Manor wouldn't be normal for most other households, it would just be normal at Magnolia Manor. Mr. Miller did feel like the warm weather might give the three women in the mansion a little more space to spread out, and possibly stay away from each other. It seemed to him like his wife and Sophia had been going at it all winter.

They hadn't talked about it much, but Elizabeth and Sophia had been missing those Sundays at the bush harbor. Neither of them had ever felt the need to talk too much about their love life. They had both considered that to be their own private business. Yet, each knew that the other had been having heartaches all winter. Elizabeth had been hoping that their seats would still be reserved; and Sophia, the taste of Daniel's lips on hers had become faint, and she had the need to be reminded of what it was like.

Sophia had been outside with Albert and Mary when she saw Emily walking past the mansion. She walked over near the edge of the yard so that they could talk. She told Emily that she hadn't seen Daniel since they stopped going to the bush harbor last fall. Emily asked her if she had been missing him. Sophia said that she had missed him a lot, and she wondered if he missed her.

While they were talking, Sophia and Emily heard Mrs. Miller say something to Albert and Mary. They didn't know what Mrs. Miller had said, but Emily knew that it was time for her to go. As Emily walked away, Sophia hurried over to where the kids had been playing. When she got to the corner of the house, she slowed down, so that she wouldn't attract attention in case Mrs. Miller saw her. As soon as Sophia walked around the corner of the house, Mrs. Miller did see her. She said to Sophia that she had been wondering where she was. Sophia told her that she had been walking around looking at the flowers.

At the end of the day, Elizabeth and Sophia were in their room. She had never said it before, but Sophia told Elizabeth that she missed Daniel. Elizabeth told her that she would just have to wait until the weather turned warmer, because nobody wanted to be at the bush harbor—it was too cold and damp. Sophia knew that she didn't have any choice other than to wait, but for the first time, she wanted to talk to Elizabeth about her personal feelings. Elizabeth didn't read the message very well, because she had pretty much snubbed what Sophia had said.

Elizabeth's situation had been different from that of Sophia. She had been able to see Alfred off and on all winter, because he was always taking care of odds and ends around the mansion. Therefore, Sophia felt like it was easy for Elizabeth to tell her to be patient, and wait until the weather turned warmer—she hadn't seen Daniel in months.

Sophia had known for a long time that Elizabeth and Alfred were in love with each other, but she knew that Elizabeth didn't like to talk about it. She had tried to talk to her about Daniel. Even though Elizabeth had pretty much turned her away, she supposed that it had more than likely been unintentional. Although she was hesitant, she had decided to try and talk to her again, because it was important to her.

Sophia had told Elizabeth that she loved Daniel, and that she loved him a lot. Elizabeth was surprised that Sophia would tell her that she was in love, but she didn't let on that she had been surprised. She did say that she had suspected as much. Then Sophia was surprised. Elizabeth had seen them sitting together every Sunday at the bush harbor, but Sophia didn't think that she knew anything about how she and Daniel felt about each other. After she had thought about it, she realized that it probably hadn't been too hard to figure out.

Sophia had told Elizabeth that she thought that she had been keeping her feelings about Daniel a secret. Elizabeth told her that mothers had their way of knowing things. She said that a boy and a girl don't sit and hold hands unless they have special feelings for each other.

Sophia had been pretty sure that Elizabeth had known all along that she and Daniel held each other's hand every Sunday. She also suspected that Elizabeth had figured out that they always sat at the back so that they wouldn't be noticed. Elizabeth said that another good sign that you were probably in love was that you were willing to take the risk of kissing Daniel while everybody else was listening to the preacher's sermon.

Sophia asked Elizabeth how she had found out, but Elizabeth wouldn't tell her. She had come close to telling Elizabeth that she was sorry, but she wouldn't. She wouldn't tell her because she knew that saying I'm sorry would be telling her a lie. She knew that it would be a lie, because she had every intention of kissing Daniel the very next time that she saw him. She had been thinking about it too long ... they were going to sit at the back as usual, and wait until the preacher got started.

Sophia had decided that she needed to change the subject, because talking about her love life hadn't gone quite the way that she had intended. In fact, it had sort of backfired on her. She decided to ask Elizabeth about her father. Sophia knew very little about him, because Elizabeth had never told her much. Elizabeth was well aware of the fact that she hadn't said much to Sophia about him, but that had been intentional.

When Sophia was younger and had questions, Elizabeth could say about anything without telling her any more than she wanted her to know. Since she had gotten older, Elizabeth couldn't skirt the issues anymore. The time had come to be honest, and tell her the truth. On top of that, Elizabeth supposed that she had the right to know about her father.

Elizabeth had told her that her father was a white man. Sophia had to have already known that, the only thing that she had to do was look in the mirror. Elizabeth explained that her father was the slave owner that had them when they lived in North Carolina. Sophia was rather naive. She wanted to know if they were in love with each other. Elizabeth told her that there was no love in it, he had raped her.

Sophia didn't say anything for a while. Instead, she sat on the side of the bed staring at Elizabeth, because she had been surprised. When she started to cry, she tried to speak, but her words were sort of scrambled, yet, they were still understandable. She told Elizabeth that she didn't know that it had been like that, and that she was sorry. Elizabeth told her that there was nothing to be sorry about. All while they were talking, Elizabeth had been sitting in her rocking chair, and Sophia had been sitting on the side of the bed.

Elizabeth had put her arms out for Sophia to come to her. She walked over, and sat on the floor in front of her, and then she laid her head on her lap. Elizabeth told Sophia that she was born because someone had raped her. Even though he was dead, Elizabeth said that she still hated him for what he had done to her and to her family. While sitting on the floor near Elizabeth, Sophia found out that both she and Elizabeth had been born, because a slave owner had raped their mother.

Elizabeth had lost track of time, because she didn't know how long she had been talking—although it had been unpleasant for her to talk about, she felt relieved because she had. When she looked down at Sophia, she had fallen asleep with her head still on her mother's lap. She let her stay where she was, as she stroked her hair, and let Sophia's soft breaths soothe her own troubled mind.

While sitting there listening to the quietness, Elizabeth struggled with memories of the past, along with the what ifs and the how tos of tomorrow, knowing all the time that she could do nothing about either. To her, it was a messed up world. While she and Sophia had been getting ready for bed, Elizabeth said that she had often wondered what a place in Heaven might be like when life closes the door for the last time to the evils and wrongdoings of this mean ole world. She said that she wondered because her mind kept telling her that things were supposed to be different, and there had to be a better place somewhere.

It had been a harsh winter, and Elizabeth remembered that first snowfall on Christmas Eve. She had a fleeting memory that made her smile when she thought about Mrs. Miller's ill feelings on Christmas morning after having a little too much eggnog the night before. Since then, life had started anew. The yellow blossoms on the south side of the mansion had been the first hint that springtime and warm weather had arrived. Alfred had already started tending the grounds around the mansion, removing the remnants of last year's finery, and making way for nature's new birth of flora.

Mr. Miller had been in town, but was back at home by noon. After eating lunch, he sat on the front porch reading the newspaper. He had seen Emily walking down the street. Correctly, he had assumed that she would stop at Magnolia Manor. Several weeks prior, Emily's father had told Mr. Miller that he and his family would be moving to Memphis during the spring. Emily's father was an attorney, and he had decided that his law practice might be more lucrative if he relocated to a larger city. As soon as Mr. Miller saw Emily, he realized that he should have told Sophia that they were moving away, but it had slipped his mind.

Emily was well aware that Mrs. Miller wouldn't tolerate Sophia having visitors. Yet, she had made up her mind to stop by anyway. She would ask to speak with

Sophia, and if Mrs. Miller said no, she would leave. She had been talking with Mr. Miller, but as soon as there was an opening in their conversation, she asked if it would be alright if she could speak to Sophia. Realizing that Emily had to be uneasy about being there, he told her that Mrs. Miller had gone shopping, and he invited her inside. Then he went to get Sophia.

Sophia knew that Mrs. Miller had gone to town, but Mr. Miller could tell that both Sophia and Elizabeth were still leery about Emily stopping by to visit Sophia. After assuring them that it would be alright, Sophia followed him to the parlor where Emily had been waiting. Mr. Miller said that he would be on the front porch. They had taken that to mean that he would let them know if he saw Mrs. Miller returning home before Emily left. Mrs. Miller hadn't been gone long, and therefore, Mr. Miller didn't expect her back for quite some time anyway.

Emily told Sophia that she and her family would soon be moving to Memphis. Sophia was surprised, but she and Emily both understood that life had its separations— sadly enough, they had had some of their own. Emily had told her that Caroline was expecting a baby, and that was the good news. They had agreed to stay in touch via the mail, but sensing that they might have been looking at each other for the last time.

They reminisced about things that had happened years ago—way back when it had seemed like growing up would take a lifetime. Then, they wished that they could turn around and go back to the years that they had been so anxious to leave behind. Go back to a time that then seemed to have been far too short, but a time filled with countless hours spent in Mr. Miller's backyard under the big oak tree—the one that they had claimed as theirs. It seemed like those had been their best years together. The four of them had been separated, yet the big oak was still there, but it was no longer theirs—it too had become a memory.

After Emily had gotten up to leave, Sophia walked her to the door. They stood on the porch and hugged each other, and then she put her arms around Mr. Miller. When she had hugged Elizabeth, neither of them had anything to say, but nothing had really been necessary— they had already said it a thousand times.

Emily had made her way down the steps, and then she said that she was not going to look back when she walked away, because if she did she would cry. Elizabeth had looked at Mr. Miller. She could see that he was having regrets. He had turned and walked away, perhaps for the same reason that Emily had chosen not to look back.

Elizabeth had followed him back inside. She said that watching her leave was close kin to being at a funeral. Sophia had stayed on the porch. She thought about them, Amanda, Caroline and Emily, her best friends, all gone away—each taking a part of the other with them.

Later, but before Mrs. Miller had returned, Mr. Miller had to talk to Sophia. He had to tell her that he had forgotten to let her know that Emily would be moving away. Sophia said that it was alright, because it wouldn't have made things any different anyway.

Sophia had gone outside, probably to feel sorry for herself, because to her it seemed like her world—the one that she had shared with her best friends—had become empty. Mr. Miller had told Elizabeth that it seemed like they all should have lived in the same house forever; they had helped raise them, and they were all alike—they didn't know white from black, if they did know, they didn't care, not in their circle.

Elizabeth had a flashback. More times than she could remember, she had heard Mr. Miller say or do things that made it seem like his conscious may have been bothering him. She had often wondered if he might have been troubled by the forced inequalities between white and black people—she didn't know.

She wondered if perhaps sometimes he might have had the thought that he should open the gate, and then tell all of his slaves that they were free to go. If he ever had that thought, then she wondered if he had been influenced—if just to some small degree—by the relationship between Sophia, Amanda, Caroline and Emily. Then, she remembered what Mrs. Miller had always said about things just being different at Magnolia Manor. Elizabeth had started getting the feeling that she was probably right.

Mrs. Miller returned home with the few things that she had purchased in town. Alfred had stopped the buggy out front, and was carrying her packages inside. Mr. Miller had been sitting on the porch. He stood and held the door for her and Alfred. He didn't mention the fact that Emily had stopped by, nor had he intended to—she wouldn't have cared anyway.

Elizabeth and Sophia had been attending church almost every Sunday during the winter with Mr. and Mrs. Miller. However, the weather had turned warm, and the bush harbor would be back in business. Elizabeth had already asked Mr. Miller if it would be alright for her and Sophia to switch over—knowing all the time that it would be. Asking had been nothing more than a formality. When he had mentioned it to Mrs. Miller, she still couldn't understand why they would rather go to something as crude as a bush harbor when they could go to a real church with them.

Mr. Miller knew that Elizabeth went to the bush harbor so that she could be with Alfred. He had always thought that Sophia went, because she was just following her mother. He didn't know that she had found a boyfriend. Still, none of it had ever mattered to him. Unlike Mrs. Miller, he never had attempted to persuade Elizabeth and Sophia to attend their church. If they wanted to go to the bush harbor, or sit on the bank of the river, it would have been alright by him.

Mr. Miller could tell that Sophia had been bothered by the fact that Emily had moved away, and he asked Elizabeth if she had noticed the same thing. Elizabeth agreed, she said that she had talked to her about it, but it hadn't done any good; Sophia had grown up with those girls, and she felt alone. Elizabeth said that things would probably change when they started going back to the bush harbor. She could make new friends. Mr. Miller agreed, but Elizabeth never mentioned Daniel, because that would be telling him more than he needed to know.

Sophia never had much to say to Mr. or Mrs. Miller. She had always done what she was told, she was polite—most of the time—but she had spent very few words on either of them. She had no ill feelings toward Mr. Miller. She just didn't talk to him much—however, she hated his wife.

Mr. Miller had become accustomed to Sophia's personality, and he didn't let it bother him—it was just the way she was. However, Mrs. Miller could have easily done without her. In her mind, Sophia was nothing but a pest. Mrs. Miller had interpreted her behavior as being snide and disrespectful. Her interpretation had been correct, Sophia had no respect for her, and she had a contemptuous attitude to go along with it. Yet, neither could really point a finger at the other, because both were guilty of the same thing. However, Mrs. Miller occupied the high ground, but Sophia didn't care where she stood.

Sunday morning was beautiful. Mr. and Mrs. Miller, and the kids as well, had gotten dressed for church. Elizabeth and Sophia were excited, because it was the first warm Sunday of a brand new season. Soon, Elizabeth would find out if she and Alfred's seats were still available at the bush harbor. Sophia and Daniel, they didn't have a favorite place to sit as long as they were at the back, and hidden from Elizabeth.

Elizabeth and Sophia knew exactly what they would be wearing, because they had been making plans for a long time. They wanted to show off the new outfits that they had gotten for Christmas. Elizabeth had that new bracelet around her wrist—the one that she had gotten from Caroline's mom. Sophia had Amanda's pendant around her neck, and the friendship ring from Caroline and Emily had been placed on her finger.

Elizabeth had the feeling that some would think that they may have been flaunting it a bit, but they had been willing to take their chances. On that day, she was going with the attitude that if you've got it and can't use it, then you may as well not have it.

When they had finished getting dressed, they gave each other the once over, and each had gotten a nod of approval from the other. As they made their way toward the bush harbor, they had more pep in their step than they had had in the past. It was like that because it had been a long time since the last time, and they each had someone special waiting for them at the end of that gentle grade that led to the bush harbor.

A while back, Elizabeth had given Sophia a good chewing out about her carrying on with Daniel while sitting at the back. However, on that day she had decided that she wouldn't remind her of anything, she could sit at the back if she wanted to, and she wouldn't baby sit her. She had chosen not to say anything, because she knew that she had made herself perfectly clear, and therefore, nothing more was necessary.

The boredom of being inside all winter with nothing much to do other than brood about things was about to end. When they arrived, the place looked more like a gathering for a Sunday picnic than it did for Holy reunion—it was a beautiful sight. More than likely, they had all probably been reminded of the preacher's words, "Together at last, one more time and again."

After mingling around for a while just for the sake of keeping up appearances, Elizabeth spotted Alfred. He had been leaning against the support post over near their reserved seats. She had walked over to him, and they held each other's hand. Since everyone had seen them do it before, Alfred smiled at Elizabeth with an attitude that said I don't care. He then held her in his arms, and passionately kissed her with no regards to who might see them, Sophia included. Elizabeth didn't even turn around to see if Sophia had been looking— Alfred had done exactly what she had been wanting him to do.

Sophia had been wandering around in the crowd. She stopped now and then to talk, but still looking for Daniel. When she couldn't find him, she figured that he had just been delayed or something, but she expected that he would show up soon. She had no doubt that he would be there, because he would want to see her just as much as she wanted to see him—she was sure that he would.

Elizabeth had seen her searching, and she had told Alfred that Sophia couldn't seem to find Daniel. As soon as she had spoken the words, she saw the look on Alfred's face. He had asked her to sit down. When she had sat down, he sat down beside her. Then she knew that things weren't right.

Alfred told her that Daniel wouldn't be coming to the bush harbor anymore. Elizabeth had asked him why not. He said that he had just found out, but the man that owned Daniel had sold him some time back during the winter. He had talked to Daniel's parents, but they had no idea as to where their son had been taken. Elizabeth told Alfred about how happy she and Sophia had been when they arrived, but after hearing about Daniel, she felt like somebody had just died.

Elizabeth had stood up, and she could see that Sophia was still walking around searching. She dreaded the task of having to tell her. She had tried to think of a way to do it, a way that would make it easier on Sophia. Then she realized that there was no way of making it easy, and that there was but one way. She knew that she should be the one to tell her, because if it had to come from someone else, they might be too blunt. While she and Alfred were making their way toward Sophia, Elizabeth tried to get the right words together, but her mind seemed to be set on empty.

Elizabeth had pushed her way through the crowd—not giving much consideration as to how she did it, and offering no apologies for stepping on some toes.

When they were standing near each other, Sophia told Elizabeth that Daniel was late, but she expected him to show up soon.

Elizabeth had taken her by the hand, and she was looking at her, but it was hard for her to talk. Sophia had asked what was wrong, but she still couldn't tell her. Finally, Alfred had to do it. He told her that Daniel wouldn't be coming, and he told her why. Sophia had become nervous and confused. Even after listening to Alfred, she kept on looking for Daniel. Finally, Elizabeth told her that he wouldn't be coming—he had been sold.

By then, almost everybody standing around knew what had happened. It was impossible to talk to Sophia, because she wouldn't listen. The preacher had even tried. He told her that God would take care of things and make it alright, but it didn't work. Alfred told Elizabeth that he would help take her back to the mansion. Elizabeth held her hand, and Alfred put his arm around her as they walked along on either side.

They didn't try to talk to her, because there was no use, and she cried all the way. To Elizabeth, it seemed like someone had moved Magnolia Manor to the other side of town, because it was the longest walk of her life—she had to struggle, because that gentle grade had become a mountain. When they arrived, Elizabeth put Sophia in bed, and Alfred suggested that she stay with her while he waited outside.

Although Elizabeth had put Sophia in bed, she knew that she hadn't done anything other than got her off of her feet. She wanted her to sleep for a while, hoping that it might lessen the initial trauma. Elizabeth went to the kitchen, and concocted a potion from the hand-me down recipe that she had learned from her mother—a compilation of medicinal herbs and whatever that would certainly do the trick.

Alfred had been waiting outside. It hadn't really been that long, but to him it seemed like time had stopped. After a while, he looked down the street and saw the Millers on their way back from church. When she had seen Alfred, Mrs. Miller sensed that something might be gone awry, so she had told Albert and Mary to go inside. Alfred explained what had happened.

After Alfred had explained things, Mr. Miller asked how Sophia was doing. Alfred said that she was in pretty bad shape. He told Alfred that he should probably wait around for a while just in case Elizabeth might need him.

Mr. and Mrs. Miller had gone inside, hoping and assuming that Elizabeth and Alfred would be able to take care of things. Besides, it didn't seem to be something that they could help with anyway. Mrs. Miller was sure that Sophia would be just fine in no time. However, Mr. Miller had been more skeptical, but waiting seemed to be the only thing that any of them could do.

Mr. Miller had gone back outside, and was talking to Alfred. He said that Sophia probably had the feeling that things had caved in around her. He had talked about her relationship with Amanda, Caroline and Emily, but Alfred already knew about that. Elizabeth had told him.

Alfred sat on the steps listening to him express his thoughts about different things. While listening to him, Alfred had started having thoughts of his own. He didn't know, but they were the same thoughts that Elizabeth had from time to time. He had seen how some slave owners treated slaves. Consequently, he too had come to the conclusion that if he had to be a slave, he would rather be where he was then than any other place—whether he did or didn't, at least Mr. Miller acted like he cared, and that was more than a slave got from most slave owners.

Elizabeth left Sophia in her bedroom, and she had walked outside. She told Mr. Miller and Alfred that Sophia had fallen asleep. Elizabeth had bumped up the strength of the potion to make sure that Sophia would fall asleep. Since Alfred wasn't needed anymore, he had left. Elizabeth had started telling Mr. Miller about Sophia and Daniel, but he stopped her. He said that Alfred had already told him.

Mrs. Miller had heard Mr. Miller and Elizabeth talking. She walked out to the porch, and started questioning Elizabeth about Daniel. Elizabeth told her that they had gotten acquainted last year at the bush harbor, and that they had started liking each other. Then, Elizabeth apologized for not having dinner ready, and said that she would get right on it. Mrs. Miller told her not to bother with it, and that they could find something to eat without having to cook.

Elizabeth had gone back to be with Sophia. Mrs. Miller had started to go back inside, but she stopped in the doorway. She said that none of it would have happened if they had stayed away from that bush harbor, and went to church with them. Mr. Miller told her that she couldn't blame it on them going to the bush harbor. She said that she could blame it on the bush harbor, because if they hadn't been there, she never would have met that boy in the first place. Mr. Miller said that there's nothing unusual about people liking each other or falling in love, most people do the same thing when they become of age.

Elizabeth could hear them talking, because Mrs. Miller was still standing in the doorway. She said that they had gone to church like they do every Sunday, and then they come home to a big mess, involved in some-body else's love life. She wondered if anybody else had as many problems with slaves as they did, because with theirs, she said that it seemed like something was always going on.

Albert and Mary had heard enough to figure out that something was wrong with Sophia. After Mrs. Miller had gone back outside, and sat down on the porch with her husband, they had gone to find out for themselves. They had eased the door open, and slowly walked in. Elizabeth was sitting in her rocking chair, and they noticed that Sophia had gone to bed. Mary asked Elizabeth what was wrong with Sophia. Elizabeth simply said that she didn't feel good. Mary had asked if she was going to die. Elizabeth told her that it was nothing like that, she just needed some rest.

Elizabeth could see how hard it had been on Sophia, but she felt like she herself had been pushed a few steps closer to her grave. She had decided that she was not about to tell Albert and Mary what the real problem was. She didn't want to be the one telling the kids a horror story about how black people were bought and sold. If they had to know, they could find out from Mrs. Miller. She would be able to explain it to them in such a way that it would sound right.

The brew that Elizabeth had concocted for Sophia did what it was supposed to do. Once she had fallen asleep, she didn't wake up until late in the afternoon. Albert and Mary had returned to check on her. When they walked in, Sophia had been sitting on the side of her bed. She was groggy, had an aching head, and was a long ways from feeling good—the stuff that Elizabeth had given her, wouldn't help her get over Daniel, but it would make her feel so bad that she wouldn't be able to think about anything but herself for a while. She would rather have not had any visitors, but she didn't turn Albert and Mary away. Mary had laid her head on Sophia's lap, and Albert stood next to her.

Elizabeth sat in her rocking chair, and watched Sophia and the kids. She could see the love and admiration that the three of them shared. As she watched, she supposed that the day would come when the social attitudes of their one-sided society would slowly distance them until they be like strangers. Then she remembered having the same thought about the relationship between Sophia, Amanda, Caroline and Emily—she had been wrong about them ... maybe she would be wrong again. Mary had asked Sophia if she would be well enough to read to them tomorrow. Sophia told her that she would be fine tomorrow.

Elizabeth had been thinking about Daniel's family, but she kept her thoughts to herself, because they were not good enough to share. She had been trying to compare the mental anguish that she and Sophia had been going through with how she thought Daniel and his parents might feel. When she did, she realized that the two were not even close. She still had her daughter—hurt as she was—but Daniel had been sold and taken away from his mother and father. She had even put together a mental picture of what it must have been like when Daniel's parents had last seen their son—he was probably walking away and looking back at them, with his hands bound behind his back. Just a probable thought that had made her want to vomit.

Sophia had told Elizabeth that her head was filled with so many things that it seemed heavy. She talked about Amanda, and about Caroline and Emily. She said that when she needed them the most was when they had all gone away. Elizabeth still didn't say anything. She just sat there, and listened to her talk. After a while Sophia laid back down, and again, she had fallen asleep.

Half way out of her mind, Elizabeth had been taking care of Albert and Mary, getting them ready for bed. Mrs. Miller had asked about Sophia. Elizabeth said that she seemed to be doing better. Mrs. Miller said that things like that just take time, and she'll get over it. She had told Elizabeth to go on back and keep an eye on her, and that she would tuck Albert and Mary in bed. Facetiously, Mrs. Miller said that she needed to start doing something for them every now and then anyway, just to remind them that she was their mother.

Before bedtime, Elizabeth decided that another shot of that hand-me-down tonic that she had made would probably be good for Sophia. It might not get rid of her aching heart, but she wouldn't be walking the floor all night keeping her awake. Sophia downed the brew—it wasn't as potent as that first dose that Elizabeth had given her—and then she and Elizabeth sat around and talked for a while. When Sophia could no longer keep her eyes open, she got in bed. Elizabeth didn't see any need to throw away the remaining bit of the potion that Sophia hadn't consumed, so she downed it herself.

The next morning, Mr. Miller was up and about, and he had asked Elizabeth about Sophia. She told him that the potion that she had given her last night had her still sleeping. He knew that Sophia would be in bed for a while, because now and then, he had downed some of that stuff himself when he had trouble falling asleep. He also knew that when Sophia crawled out of bed, she would feel like somebody had hit her on top of the head with a hammer.

Elizabeth had decided to let Sophia stay in bed and get up on her own. If she had gotten her out of bed, she wouldn't have been able to do anything. Elizabeth moved around quietly in the mansion, so that she wouldn't disturb Mrs. Miller and Mary, because they too were still in bed. Albert had gone to school. Elizabeth had been moving around as quietly as a mouse, and she knew that she didn't wake her up. However, she had gotten a glimpse of Mary tipping through the house, and on her way to see Sophia. Although Sophia was still asleep, Elizabeth didn't stop her. Later, Elizabeth peeked in and saw that Mary had climbed in bed next to Sophia, and both were asleep.

Mrs. Miller had gotten out of bed, but it was well into the morning. She had noticed that Mary wasn't in her room. Elizabeth told her that she was in bed with Sophia. After she had finished a cup of coffee, Mrs. Miller decided to check on Sophia and Mary. She just eased the door open to the bedroom, and then she closed it.

Later in the afternoon, Sophia was out in the yard with Mary. Elizabeth had finished with the housework, and she had gone outside. She and Sophia walked around in the yard looking at the flowers. When they had come to the rose bush that she had planted for Amanda, Sophia stopped to have a look at it.

Mary was some distance away, but yet, she was close enough for Sophia to keep an eye on her. Elizabeth could tell that Sophia was about as depressed as ever as she stood there looking at the rose bush. She told her that she would have the preacher talk to her next Sunday when they went to the bush harbor. She was sure that it would do her a lot of good, and that it would help ease her mind. Elizabeth told her that when you have problems that you can't handle by yourself, that's when you turn to God.

Sophia told Elizabeth that she wasn't going to church next Sunday or any other Sunday. She wasn't going to talk to the preacher, and she didn't want anyone talking to her about God. She had raised her voice at Elizabeth, and that was something that she had never done before. She had gotten even louder when she said that if God cared about people the way everybody thinks that he does, then he wouldn't let things happen the way that they do. Elizabeth asked her again if she would just please sit down next Sunday and let the preacher talk to her. Sophia said that she had been listening to him talk every Sunday, but she didn't want to hear him anymore.

Elizabeth wondered if Sophia had lost her mind. She was angry, defiant, and she had never questioned God or Christianity. It was like she had become an advocate of Satan and was out campaigning for him. After Sophia had turned to walk away, Elizabeth thought that she had used up all of the zany remarks that she could think of, but she stopped and turned around. She said that she didn't believe that there was a God. He was just something that people had made up, and everybody was just too dumb to know any better. As far as she was concerned, going to church every Sunday had been nothing but a waste of time. She said that she would rather go fishing.

Elizabeth had thought that she couldn't be put any lower than she had been when she and Alfred had to take Sophia home from the bush harbor. That day had been one of the worst days of her life. She had the feeling that she had been put in a place that she had never been before, a place where if she screamed there would be no one to listen. In her mind, she was standing at the doorway to Hell with Sophia at her side.

Elizabeth didn't know how much more she could take, or if she could take anymore at all. If she was being punished for something that she had done, she would like to know. Yet, in spite of it all, there had been but one place that she could turn and that was to God, because she still believed.

Sophia had walked over to where Mary was playing. Elizabeth couldn't sit down; she just wandered around in the yard. She had told Sophia that she needed to talk to the preacher, but then, she was the one that needed the preacher.

All during the week, Sophia's attitude had stayed the same. She would help Albert with his schoolwork, and like always, she would read to the kids before putting them to bed. On the other side, she had been giving Elizabeth a cold shoulder. In the past, they had always sat in the room together, and they would talk until bedtime. In just a few days, Sophia had gone from a loving and caring daughter to a person that her mother hardly knew. Elizabeth wondered if she had lost her forever.

As much as she hated to, Elizabeth had to talk to Mr. and Mrs. Miller. She had to talk, otherwise she would explode. She told them that Sophia doesn't do anything other than sit and stare out the window. After Elizabeth had told them, then she apologized for bothering them, but she said that she didn't know what else to do.

Mrs. Miller said that she would go and have a talk with her. As soon as she had said it, Elizabeth and Mr. Miller both knew that Mrs. Miller was not the right person to go and have a talk with Sophia. They had always hated each other, and then was the wrong time to put them in a room together.

Tactfully, Mr. Miller suggested that maybe he should be the one to do it since he had known her longer, and that he knew her a little better than Mrs. Miller. As soon as he had left the room to go talk to her, Mrs. Miller hoped that he knew what he was doing. She said that what it called for was a woman's touch. However, Elizabeth was glad that Mr. Miller had talked her into letting him do it, because it was impossible for Mrs. Miller to reach out to Sophia.

The door to Sophia's room had been left partly open. Mr. Miller tapped on it, and spoke her name to let her know that it was him. When he walked in, Sophia had gotten up from her seat. He told her that Elizabeth had been concerned about her, and he just wanted to know if she felt alright. Sophia said that she was fine. He had asked her if she needed to see the doctor, but again, she told him that she was fine ... there was nothing wrong.

There hadn't been much dialogue, because like always, Sophia had chosen to keep her responses as brief as possible, then however, they were more brief than ever. He had asked her if she felt like she had been treating her mother with the same respect, and showing her the same love that she had always had for her. Sophia must have known that the answer to that question had to be no, because she never responded. Instead, she just stood there looking at him. He had only spoken a few words, and it had only taken a couple of minutes, but he had left her with a question, one that he hoped would make her think.

Mr. Miller had left the room, and he closed the door on his way out. Mrs. Miller and Elizabeth had been waiting in the parlor. When he had returned, Mrs. Miller told him that she knew that she should have been the one to talk to her. Since he had been gone for such a short time, she had assumed that he had been unable to get through to her. Still, she wanted to know how it went, but he wasn't sure. He said that she didn't have much to say, and that he had ended up doing most of the talking. Elizabeth had decided that however it went, it couldn't have hurt anything.

Elizabeth had gone to her room. When she had opened the door, she saw Sophia standing at the window staring outside. Although she had heard the door open, she never turned around. Elizabeth didn't say anything to her. Sophia just stood there staring outside.

Sunday morning had rolled around, and they were getting dressed for church. Elizabeth had told Sophia that she should hurry, so that they wouldn't be late getting to the bush harbor. Sophia said that she wasn't going. Elizabeth looked at her for a moment, and she almost said something, but then she decided to leave her alone. She had thought—or more than likely she had been hoping—that Sophia may have gotten rid of the hostile thoughts that she had a few days ago, but nothing had changed.

As Elizabeth was about to head off to the bush harbor, Mrs. Miller stopped her, and said that Mary didn't feel well. She wanted Sophia to skip going to the bush harbor, and tend to her. Elizabeth had said that Sophia wasn't going to the bush harbor anyway. Mrs. Miller never asked why, she just gave Mary to Elizabeth and left.

Elizabeth had taken Mary to Sophia. She explained that Mary didn't feel good, and that Mrs. Miller had decided to leave her at home. Before Elizabeth could ask, Sophia said that she would keep her. Elizabeth had felt

Mary's forehead, and she told Sophia that she didn't seem to be running a temperature. Again, Sophia told Elizabeth to go ahead, and that she would take care of Mary.

On her way to the bush harbor, Elizabeth thought about how good she and Sophia used to feel when they made the walk together. In just one week, things had changed. The good feelings had gone away, and for the first time, she walked alone.

When she arrived, Alfred and the preacher met her, and they asked about Sophia. Elizabeth had told them about the sacrilegious attitude that she had. Not knowing what else to say, Alfred said that she'll probably be alright if you just give her a little time—Mrs. Miller's words exactly. The preacher agreed, and said that time can heal a lot of wounds. They had been trying to say the right things to make Elizabeth feel better, but she could only think of the horrible things that Sophia had said.

Sophia had sat down in Elizabeth's rocker, and she watched Mary as she roamed idly around the room. Mary didn't seem to be sick, so Sophia asked what was bothering her. Mary said that nothing was bothering her. Then, Sophia asked her why she didn't go to church. She told Sophia that she had heard her tell Elizabeth that God wasn't real, and going to church was just a waste of time. Sophia had been asking questions, but after Mary had answered her last one, she didn't ask anymore.

Sophia knew that she couldn't tell Mary about Daniel, so she never mentioned the real reason for her anger. She just said that she was sorry that she had spoken those words, and that she was wrong. She also told Mary that she had been cruel to Elizabeth. Mary told her that she had heard her fussing at Elizabeth, and that it wasn't nice. Sophia said that she would get things all straightened out when Elizabeth comes home.

Then, Sophia thought about the question that Mr. Miller had asked, "Do you think that you've been treating your mother with love and respect?" Sophia remembered that she never did respond to the question when it was asked. Then, however, she realized that the answer was no, and that she needed to be with Elizabeth.

Feeling satisfied with her somewhat camouflaged, and less than truthful explanation to Mary, Sophia was still disturbed about the things that she had said to Elizabeth. Furthermore, she was more disturbed about the way that she had said them. After sitting around and doing nothing for a while, she had asked Mary if she would like to go with her to the bush harbor. Mary had said yes, and Sophia told her that she would be ready in a few minutes. Although rushing, Sophia had been mindful enough to leave a note in the mansion to let the Millers know where they had gone in case they returned home first.

Mary had never been to the bush harbor, and she was as happy as Sophia had been when she had gone for the first time. Everybody had been paying attention to the preacher, and Sophia and Mary had almost snuck in unnoticed. They had circled around the back, and were making their way up the other side toward Elizabeth and Alfred. Elizabeth still hadn't noticed them, but Alfred had. He nudged Elizabeth and pointed in their direction, so that she could see who was coming.

Neither Elizabeth nor Alfred knew what to expect from Sophia. Elizabeth hoped that it wouldn't be another one of her outrageous scenes. When they sat down, Sophia and Mary separated Elizabeth from Alfred, because they had sat down between them. Mary sat next to Elizabeth, and Sophia between her and Alfred. Sophia reached across Mary's lap to grasp her mother's hand, and she didn't let go.

The preacher had started to wind things down, but he started up again when he saw Sophia with Elizabeth. Finally, but only after he had been longwinded long enough, he dismissed the congregation and everybody stood up. When they did, Sophia put her arms around Elizabeth and told her that she loved her, and that she was sorry. Mary was standing between them. She had one hand holding onto Sophia, and the other holding onto Elizabeth. The preacher couldn't stay away. He had walked over, and said welcome home child.

The congregation had stood around, and talked for a long time, but not about anything that might be painful. They all knew that Daniel was gone, but there was nothing that they could do about that. Most of them knew exactly how Sophia felt, because they had seen it before, and they had felt the same thing. The unfortunate part about it was that they would no doubt have the misfortune of having to experience it again—it was not uncommon, and it would be just a matter of when and who.

With the crowd dwindling, Elizabeth, Sophia and Mary slowly made their way toward the mansion. Mary walked between them, and held onto Sophia's hand. Sophia had told Elizabeth that Mary never was sick, she had only been pretending. Elizabeth had asked Mary why she would do such a thing. Sophia didn't let Mary respond, instead, she explained to Elizabeth what Mary had said to her.

Elizabeth didn't know what it was that had made Sophia come to her senses. She imagined that it might have been something that Mr. Miller had said, or maybe it had been something that Mary had said. On the other hand, she imagined that it could have been the two of them working together. Whoever it was, or whatever it was, she was thankful that she had her daughter back.

As they got closer to the mansion, they could see that the Millers had returned from church. They had been standing out in the yard. Mrs. Miller was upset, because she expected to come home and find Mary in bed with Sophia watching over her.

Mrs. Miller knew that Sophia had taken Mary to the bush harbor, because she had seen the note. Still, she went ahead and asked where they had been. Elizabeth told her that the three of them had been to the bush harbor. Mrs. Miller snapped back at Elizabeth, and said that she shouldn't have taken her to that bush harbor, because she was sick. She said that's why they didn't take her to church with them; Sophia was supposed to stay at home and take care of her. Mary had been listening to her mother fuss at Elizabeth. She told her mother that she hadn't been sick, and that she didn't want to go to church so that she could stay at home with Sophia.

Being careful not to be too rowdy in front of the children, and really not having a reason to be rowdy at all, Mrs. Miller took Mary by the hand, and walked away. She had left Mr. Miller, Elizabeth, Sophia, and Albert standing in the yard. Mr. Miller asked Elizabeth if Mary liked the bush harbor. She told him that Mary liked it just as much as they did. He had asked Sophia how she was doing, and when she told him that she was doing just fine, that time he believed her.

Mr. Miller had to go inside. He knew that Mrs. Miller would still be upset, and he would have to calm her down. He knew why she was angry, but he felt like she had made too big of an issue of things. She had Mary sitting on the bed, and she was checking to see if she might be running a temperature.

Mr. Miller said that she seemed to be doing just fine, and that it was probably just like Elizabeth had said, she just wanted to be with Sophia. Mrs. Miller had ignored him, and she went ahead and put Mary in bed. She told her that she should take a nap, so that she would feel better.

Again, Mary tried to tell her mother that she was not sick, but Mrs. Miller insisted that she stay in bed. Mr. Miller hadn't left the room. While he was still there, Mary asked if all of them could go to the bush harbor with Elizabeth and Sophia sometimes. Mrs. Miller tucked her in nicely, and said that she would be back later to check on her.

After they had left the room, Mrs. Miller said that Mary should feel better after she wakes up. He agreed, a good nap would make her feel a lot better. Then, Mrs. Miller expressed concern about what the people around town might say if they found out that their daughter had gone to church at a bush harbor with a bunch of slaves. It had only been a few minutes since Mrs. Miller tucked Mary in bed, but she had to go and see if she was alright.

When she returned, she said that it's a wonder that she hadn't been frightened out of her mind, down there stuck in the middle of all that whooping and hollering. Since he had known all along that nothing was wrong with Mary, Mr. Miller couldn't understand why she couldn't see the same thing. It wasn't long before they had both become quiet. They sat on the sofa next to each other. After a while, both had dozed off with her head resting on his shoulder.

They had almost finished their nap, but the noise coming from the backyard had awakened them. Mr. Miller walked over to the window to investigate and he saw Sophia, Albert and Mary chasing after each other. Mrs. Miller had walked over to have a look, and she was surprised to see Mary outside, because she was supposed to be asleep. She watched her playing, and then insisted that she had been right. She said that all she needed was some rest, and now she's just fine. Mary hadn't been asleep. As soon as Mr. and Mrs. Miller had dozed off, she crept from her room, and went outside to play.

Mr. Miller had said that he was glad to see that Sophia was gradually getting back to her normal self after losing her friend Daniel. Mrs. Miller said that she didn't know what she needed him for anyway, and that it was probably a good thing that he's gone. It would be one less thing for them to worry about.

Sophia had put Albert and Mary in bed. Elizabeth had a rag in her hand, and was walking around wiping dust from first one thing and then another. Albert had been talking to Mary about the bush harbor, and it sounded good to him. He had gone to Mary's room, and he had gotten her out of bed. The two of them had a proposal that they wanted to discuss with their mother before turning in for the night.

When they walked into the parlor, Mrs. Miller had assumed that they were there for their usual good-night kiss. Mary didn't beat around the bush, and she presented her question directly to her mother. She had asked once before, but didn't get a response. Albert had talked her into asking again, but she had rephrased the question. She asked Mrs. Miller if she and Albert could start going to church at the bush harbor with Sophia and Elizabeth.

Mrs. Miller would have fallen over had only a gentle breeze been blowing her way. Mary had already asked her that question once, but she realized that the question no longer included her and Mr. Miller, only Mary and Albert. Furthermore, she had assumed that she was through with it since she had ignored it the first time.

The answer to the question would definitely be no, but since it was her children that had asked, she decided that she should use some tact. She had paused for a moment, but just long enough to settle down. When she had gotten it together, she opted to respond to the question by asking a question. Looking at Mary and then at Albert, she asked why would you want to go to an old run down place like that bush harbor rather than go to a nice church like the one that they had in town.

Mary didn't have to pause, or search for any words, and therefore, she had a quick response. She said that going to church with Elizabeth and Sophia was more fun than going to the nice church in town. Mr. Miller didn't say anything, and he sat there waiting to see how his wife was going to get through that one. Mrs. Miller explained how beautiful the church was in town, and she said that all of the people were nice, and that they wore nice clothes. Mary told her that the bush harbor was nice too, and the people were also nice. She told her mother that she couldn't remember what their clothes were like, because she hadn't paid any attention.

Albert had said please, but Mrs. Miller was through with it. She told both of them to go back to bed. With the kids gone, Mrs. Miller asked Mr. Miller if he could believe that they would want to go to that bush harbor. He said that there must have been something about the people and the place that had gotten Mary's attention, and she liked it. Mrs. Miller said that kids never know what they want or what's best for them, and that's why it's important that parents keep a close eye on them.

Mr. Miller asked her if she had ever thought about the fact that Albert and Mary just like being around Elizabeth and Sophia. He said that's probably the reason for the whole thing. She didn't like his attitude regarding the situation. She felt like he should have shown more concern. Finally, she told him to forget about, because she didn't want to talk about it anymore.

The fine wood grain seemed to be showing through the varnish on the post at the bottom of the staircase. It had been assumed that it was probably due to normal wear and tear, mostly from Albert and Mary. Actually, it had been due to Elizabeth, and sometimes Sophia, standing there with a dust rag, and rubbing in the same spot while eavesdropping. Such had been the case with Elizabeth while Albert and Mary tried to coax Mrs. Miller into letting them go to the bush harbor.

Sophia and Elizabeth were in their room, and things had gotten back to being the way they used to be. She had been brushing Elizabeth's hair—just doing something that would put her close to her mother. She still felt terrible about the things that she had said, and being near her was the best way to repair the damage.

Sophia had asked Elizabeth if she thought that she and Alfred would ever get married. Elizabeth didn't want to talk about that, but she did, and she spoke honestly. She didn't know if they would or not, but it didn't seem to her like they ever would. She supposed that they would probably have to be satisfied with the relationship that they had.

It was the first time that Sophia had ever talked to Elizabeth about Alfred, at least regarding marriage. While they were talking about intimate relationships, Elizabeth told Sophia that she was aware of the fact that she had to miss Daniel, and that she was sorry about what had happened to him and to her. She had decided that she should let Sophia know that if she wanted to, she could talk to her about her personal feelings. Sophia said that she did miss him a lot, and the bad part about it was that he was still alive, but gone forever. He would just be someone for her to remember, and wonder about for the rest of her life.

Sophia had sat down next to Elizabeth. She said that it's bad to have to live the way that they do—unable to make any kind of personal plans for the future. She would always be afraid to love someone again the way that she had loved Daniel. It would be living a life filled with fear. The fear being that one of them might be sold, and taken away from the other. She didn't know them, but she wondered how Daniel's family must have felt when he was taken away from them. Elizabeth agreed with her, it had to be a bad feeling, one that you might be able to imagine, but one that you know nothing about until it happens to you.

Sophia swore that she would never again feel the way that she had felt when she lost Daniel. She wouldn't feel that way, because never again would she let herself love anyone the way that she had loved him. She told Elizabeth that loving Daniel had been the best feeling of her life, and then her love for him tortured her. She wished that she could forget that she had ever known him, but it was an impossible wish—she would never be able to forget him.

It was the first time that they had ever expressed their inner feelings so freely with each other, and they felt better after having done so. Sharing their personal thoughts ridded a lot of pressure, especially for Sophia. The nightmarish ordeal that she had experienced pushed her to the outer limits of sanity, but it had also pushed her closer to being a woman.

Mrs. Miller had started having morning sickness. Elizabeth had noticed it for several days, and suggested that she see the doctor. Mrs. Miller brushed it off, and said that it was nothing. She thought that it would all go away soon, but it didn't. Finally, she went to see the doctor without telling Mr. Miller. The doctor confirmed what Elizabeth had already suspected, Mrs. Miller was pregnant.

Mrs. Miller had left the doctor's office, and she had gone to her husband's law office to tell him the news. He immediately started treating her like the baby was due at any time. He had gotten a chair so that she could sit down and take it easy. She said that it was too soon for all of that. She told him to go back to whatever he had been doing, because she was going home.

When Mrs. Miller arrived back at home, she told Elizabeth and Sophia that she was pregnant. Everyone started pampering her, and she had no problem with that. As always, she liked being the center of attention. Still, sometimes she found it to be annoying, because they had been overdoing it, even for her. Whenever Mr. Miller was with her, if he saw her make a move to do something, he would do it for her, and Elizabeth and Sophia had been doing the same thing.

Since Mrs. Miller had become pregnant, Sophia had more concern about her wellbeing. Yet, her feelings toward her were about as cold as ever, they were just less obvious. Mrs. Miller loved the increased attention, even from Sophia, but she didn't let it affect what she thought of her. Mr. Miller and Elizabeth knew that they both preferred being anywhere rather than around each other. They were like enemies, lined up for battle, just waiting for the right time to strike. Elizabeth knew that the only thing that had kept her and Sophia under the same roof was Mr. Miller. Without him, or if his attitude had been like that of Mrs. Miller, Sophia would have been sold a long time ago.

Albert and Mary had found out that there would soon be a new addition to the family. Sitting at the dinner table, Mary brought up the subject of naming the baby. Everyone had started throwing out suggestions—some of Mr. Miller's had been ridiculous, but he had done so just for the fun of it. After a while, they had decided that they would name the baby Charles, should it be a boy, and they would name it Annie, should it be a girl.

On Christmas day, there were lots of gifts under the tree, but the most exciting gift of all was in the bedroom, it was Annie, born on December 25. It was a birthdate that they could never forget. Before day's end, Mrs. Miller was so tired that she could hardly stay awake.

All day long, and far more than necessary, someone would enter her bedroom every few minutes to see if she and the baby were alright, or to see if she needed anything. She kept telling them that she and the baby were doing fine. What she needed most was for them to just leave her alone so that she could sleep.

The watchful eyes kept on watching, even after it had gotten late, and when they all should have been in bed. Mr. Miller had been sleeping in another bedroom just so that he wouldn't squash the baby, but he was up and down all night. Once, while he was up and tipping around, he bumped into Elizabeth, who was up tipping around. Another time, he had met Sophia in the hallway. He told her that they were fine, so that she could go back to bed.

Involved in politics up to his elbows, Mr. Miller still made lots of trips out of town. With the new baby, he felt like he needed to stay at home, but Mrs. Miller had told him that she could get along for a while without him. Mrs. Miller had confided in Elizabeth that he had been hesitant about being away from home since they had Annie. She said that if they had an emergency, he would be more in the way than anything else. Elizabeth had talked to him just to let him know that he didn't have to worry. She had been around lots of newborn babies, and she and Sophia could take care of things.

The State Legislature still devoted a lot of time at each meeting discussing whether or not their State should remain in the Union if that decision had to be made. It was a hot issue, but Mr. Miller felt like the discussions had become redundant, everything that they talked about had already been said. As an elected official, and like it or not, he had to sit there and be part of it. Still, he felt worn, because all across the south, it was the same old thing, and the same old talk, secession, secession .... He had listened to it over and over again.

Every slave holding state in the country had drawn up resolutions, and sent them to Washington—resolutions with regards to states rights versus federal rights. Mr.

Miller's opinion was that the resolutions had probably been placed in some backroom closet at the bottom of a tall stack of things that had been tabled—there to collect dust.

Mr. Miller had supposed that if he was right, their resolution had probably been placed in the closet with the rest of them, because the State of Tennessee had one there somewhere. However, Tennessee's resolution didn't include anything about secession. Still, his opinion had been that managing governmental affairs at the state level was hard enough, and it was even harder in Washington. He had been involved in politics most of his life, he knew the rules, he was one of the players, and he was in the game, therefore, he was seldom surprised at what went on in Nashville or in Washington.

TEN

Austin Miller felt like he had racked up more miles in the last three years than he had in the ten years prior. Operating a plantation in Mississippi and one in Tennessee, managing his law practice, and traveling back and forth to the State House in Nashville had gotten to be stressful. In addition to all of that, he had gotten himself involved with railroads. Mrs. Miller told him that he should have turned them down, but as usual, he had to join in.

He couldn't remember where the time had gone, but they had celebrated the third birthday of his daughter, Annie. He had supposed that he was probably a stranger to her. In addition to that, Mrs. Miller was expecting another child at any time. He had strongly considered that his current term in the legislature could very well be his last. However, since he had been elected, it had to be business as usual.

Mrs. Miller gave birth to their son in July and they named him Charles Austin. They named him Charles because when Annie was born, it would have been her name had she been a boy. The middle name, Austin, had not been considered when Annie was born, and it was a last minute idea when Charles was born.

It was the middle of August and not terribly hot for that time of year. Mrs. Miller felt like she had been caged in long enough, and she wanted to get out of the mansion just to spend a day someplace else. She had been invited to a friend's house, and she decided to take her up on the invitation.

Mr. Miller took care of the travel arrangements. Alfred would drive the carriage, and the trip wouldn't take more than an hour or so each way. Mrs. Miller wanted Mr. Miller to go with her, but as usual, he had some urgent business that he needed to take care of. His decision not to go didn't come as a surprise. She had figured that he would say no even before she had asked him.

On the morning that they left, Alfred had the carriage at the mansion—parked outside and waiting. Mr. Miller had already gone to his office. When they were ready to leave, Mrs. Miller walked out onto the porch and stopped long enough to pay attention to the beautiful morning, and to relish the idea that at last she would be getting out of the house.

With or without her husband, she had decided that she was going to enjoy the day. After she had taken in a deep breath of fresh air, she then strolled toward the carriage with the kids at her side. Elizabeth and Sophia followed her; Elizabeth carried the baby, and Sophia had a basket filled with necessities.

Alfred and Sophia helped Mrs. Miller and the kids climb aboard. When Mrs. Miller had sat down, Elizabeth gave her the baby, and then she waited for Alfred to help her climb aboard. Alfred had paused for a moment, and Elizabeth looked at him, then he assisted her.

Alfred didn't know that Elizabeth would be one of his passengers. Sophia noticed that he had perked up a little when he found out that she was making the trip as well. When they had all found their position and settled in, Mrs. Miller gave the baby back to Elizabeth, and she told Sophia that they would be back before sundown.

Sophia had Magnolia Manor all to herself. She went back into the mansion to finish up with the chores. She would have to do everything all by herself, but she didn't mind. She could take her time, and there would be no one around to interfere. When she had finished tidying things up, she had some free time on her hands. She had gone to Mr. Miller's study to find something to read, anything to while away the time. She had found a newspaper, and decided that it would be just the thing. She could find out what's going on around town, and maybe see what's happening elsewhere.

She felt good sitting in the parlor reading the newspaper. She felt like the place was hers. There on the front page, she had found an article regarding slavery, and she read it very carefully. Several times she had heard Mr. and Mrs. Miller talk about the very things that she had been reading about. However, she had gotten more information from the newspaper than she had gotten from all of the eavesdropping that she had done. She had a lot more information, but she found a lot of it to be mind boggling—she didn't know what some of it meant.

She wondered if slavery would be done away with, and then, if there was a secession of states, would slavery continue. It was a lot for her to think about, and it messed with her mind. It seemed that reading the newspaper had left her with more questions than it had answered. She thought that maybe Elizabeth would be able to make sense of it, so she decided to wait until later and talk about it with her.

The sky had been partly cloudy, and thunder rumbled off in the distance. Sophia kept reading the newspaper. The section advertising ladies apparel had gotten her attention, and she was astounded at the high prices. She thought about all of the beautiful dresses that Mrs. Miller had, and how much they must have cost. She had never had any money, but she sat and daydreamed about what she would buy if she had some.

Sophia kept on reading, and the sound of thunder had gotten closer, and dark clouds had started to roll in. Sophia figured that Alfred and his passengers had made it to their destination by then, and wouldn't be caught in a downpour. She walked through the house just to make sure that the windows were all down in case it did start to rain.

When she had the house secured, she went back to the parlor; once again, she started reading the newspaper. She couldn't believe some of the things that she had read, and the one thing that had gotten her attention the most was an advertisement promoting an upcoming slave auction. The ad described Negroes as being sound, having good teeth, strong and well mannered—to her, the ad was no different from one promoting a livestock sale. She wondered how anyone could be so cruel. She suddenly felt depressed at the idea of one people having control over another to the point that they could buy and sell a person at will.

She wondered how Mr. Miller felt whenever he saw an article in the newspaper like the one that she had read. After thinking about it, she concluded that he must not have felt troubled by the way people treated blacks, or by having slaves since he had so many of his own. To get them, she knew that he had to go to slave sales, or to somebody's farm and purchase them just like every-body else. That was how he had ended up with her and Elizabeth. All of it sounded so cruel, and so wrong to her, so she tried to forget about it.

Sophia was still sitting in the parlor when Mr. Miller walked into the house. He had frightened her, because she didn't hear him enter. Her mind had been completely focused on the newspaper. When she saw him, she laid the paper down and stood up immediately. He could tell that she had been surprised, because she didn't expect him to come home until toward the end of the day. He apologized for the scare, but said that the weather looked kind of bad outside. Therefore, he had decided to close his office and go home.

He felt pretty sure that Alfred would know what to do had they gotten caught out in it. However, due to the time of day, he too had suspected that they would still be at the house of Mrs. Miller's friend. He noticed that Sophia had been reading the newspaper. He said that there's usually more bad news in it than good news. She agreed with him, because she had read some of it.

The weather front had arrived, and it had started to rain. Mr. Miller had sat down on the sofa, and he asked Sophia to have a seat. Ordinarily, she would have come up with a reason as to why she couldn't sit down, but the wind had started to blow, and she had started to feel un-easy. Therefore, she sat down. He looked at the newspa-per that she had been reading. His eyes had been drawn to the article advertising slaves for sale, and he knew that

Sophia had probably read it. He folded the paper, and laid it off to the side.

The rain had started to come down hard, and every now and then, strong gusts of wind hit the mansion, and made it shake. A loud clap of thunder had scared Sophia. Mr. Miller knew that she had always been afraid of storms. He had moved closer, and put his arm around her shoulder. She had been so frightened that she didn't even know that he was holding her.

The storm had lasted for about an hour, and then it passed on through. Mr. Miller didn't go back to his office. He decided to stay at home and work in his study. Late in the afternoon, but well before sundown, Alfred had returned with his passengers. On the way back, and as they got closer to home, it was obvious that it had rained, but not a single drop had fallen on them. When they pulled in at the mansion, Sophia told Mr. Miller that they had made it back. He had gone out to meet them, and to see if they were alright. He was surprised when Alfred told him that they didn't get any rain.

Sophia had been busy cooking. She told Mrs. Miller that the food would be ready shortly. The baby had been asleep, and Elizabeth had placed him in his crib. Mrs. Miller was glad to be back at home, so that she could move around some after sitting for so long.

Mr. and Mrs. Miller were both hungry, but they were not looking forward to eating. They had eaten Sophia's cooking before, and they knew that it was nothing to look forward to. When everyone had finished eating, and the chores had been done, Elizabeth and Sophia went to their room.

Elizabeth asked Sophia about the storm. Sophia told her that it was scary, but she wasn't sure about how long it had lasted. Sophia had said that the storm was scary, but Elizabeth didn't pay much attention to her description. She knew that a strong whirlwind would almost generate the same amount of concern from Sophia.

Mr. and Mrs. Miller sat on the porch. She was glad that they didn't get caught out in the wind and rain. Then she said that supper had been alright, but she could tell that it was Sophia that did the cooking. Mr. Miller agreed, but he said that it wasn't that bad. She let him know that she didn't say that it was bad, she said that she could tell that it wasn't Elizabeth's cooking.

Elizabeth and Sophia had attended church at the bush harbor up until the weather forced them back to the church in town. Every Sunday, Sophia would sit next to Elizabeth. It had gotten close to Christmas, and Elizabeth had noticed that Sophia's appetite had increased. In fact, she would even get out of bed at night, and find something to munch on—something like a slice from one of the cakes or pies that Elizabeth had baked.

Elizabeth didn't pay much attention, but it was unusual, because it was something that she had never done before. Sophia had even gotten to the point where some of her dresses didn't fit the way they used to. Elizabeth told her that she needed to stop eating so much before she got overweight. Sophia said that she would cut back, but she didn't, and she kept getting bigger, but mostly in the middle.

Elizabeth's suspicions had finally gotten the best of her. It was cold outside, and they were sitting in their room near the fireplace. Elizabeth had her sewing kit out doing some stitching. Without looking up, she asked Sophia if she was pregnant. Sophia had heard her, but she didn't say anything, she just sat there with her head down. Elizabeth didn't ask the question again, because Sophia's silence had been so loud that the answer to the question had to be yes.

Elizabeth kept on sewing. When she did look up, she saw that Sophia had her head down, and she was softly crying. Sophia raised her head, looked at Elizabeth and said that she was sorry. Elizabeth had asked her about the father. Again, Sophia didn't say anything. Sophia had never been away from the mansion unless Elizabeth was with her. Therefore, it didn't take long for Elizabeth to figure out that it had to be Mr. Miller.

Elizabeth never stopped sewing. Sophia had been sitting next to her, and she stared at the flickering flames in the fireplace. It was completely quiet in their room, because neither of them spoke. Elizabeth was not about to rake her daughter over the coals because of what had happened. Even though Sophia had not told her, she knew exactly how it had happened. She knew her daughter, and she knew that she would submit to such a thing only because she had no other choice.

Sophia sniffled, and she kept watching the flames dance in the fireplace. After a while, she spoke, but her words were broken, trying to speak and trying not to cry all at the same time. She said that she didn't know what to do, so she just laid there and cried, with him on top of her. Elizabeth had put her sewing aside, and she knelt down on the floor beside her. Neither of them said anything. Instead, they had their arms around each other. Elizabeth was on her knees with her head against Sophia's chest—listening to her cry.

Sophia had asked Elizabeth if she was mad at her. Elizabeth said that she was not, and she said that she wouldn't ask what happened, because she already knew.

Elizabeth had stood up, and she took Sophia by the hand to help her to her feet. She then told her to put her night clothes on so that she could go to bed.

With Sophia in bed, Elizabeth sat down beside her, but they didn't talk. Elizabeth just wanted her to know that she understood. Elizabeth knew exactly how her daughter felt, because the same thing had happened to her. After Sophia had fallen asleep, Elizabeth went back to her rocking chair. Then, it was she that sat and cried, while staring at the flickering flames in the fireplace.

Elizabeth had a big problem, one that she didn't know how to handle. The problem was Mrs. Miller. What would be her reaction when she found out about Mr. Miller and Sophia? She would certainly find out one way or another, because it was something that they couldn't hide.

Elizabeth didn't know whether she should tell Mrs. Miller, or if she should just wait, and let her find out on her own. She wondered if she should say anything to Mr. Miller, and let him take care of Mrs. Miller. Regardless of how Mrs. Miller found out, hell was going to break loose, and things were going to get ugly around Magnolia Manor; they were going to get uglier than ever before.

After thinking about the problem, Elizabeth had come to the conclusion that it would be a lot easier for her to talk to Mr. Miller rather than to Mrs. Miller. He should be the one to tell his wife. Elizabeth felt like he should be the one to tell her, because he was the one that had created the big mess that they were in. Since he created it, let him be the one to deal with it.

Elizabeth waited for the right time, a time when there would be no one else around, just her and Mr. Miller. When the opportunity presented itself, Elizabeth told him that Sophia was pregnant. He didn't act surprised at all, instead, he was rather passive. For a few seconds, he didn't say anything, and then he said that he thought that she might be, because she had been gaining weight. Elizabeth asked him what he intended to do about Mrs. Miller. He guessed that he would have to tell her, because she would find out sooner or later anyway.

Elizabeth had been outraged from the moment that Sophia told her about what he had done, and she hated him for it. Yet, she knew that from where she stood, there was nothing else that she could do other than hate him. How, when, where, and why didn't matter—none of it made any difference—because Elizabeth was in no position to say anything that might be interpreted as contempt for what he had done to her daughter.

Elizabeth had noticed that Mr. Miller didn't talk quite as much as he normally did. Several weeks had passed, but he still hadn't said anything to Mrs. Miller about Sophia being pregnant. Elizabeth knew that he hadn't said anything to her, because if he had, Mrs. Miller would have been head-to-head with everybody in the house.

Meanwhile, Sophia's pregnancy had become obvious. Obvious to the point that one evening while having supper, Mrs. Miller asked her if she was pregnant. The entire family had been seated at the table. When Sophia didn't respond, Mrs. Miller knew that there had to be a dead cat on the line somewhere. She told Albert and Mary to go outside. The children told her that they hadn't finished eating. They had also said that it was too cold outside. Mrs. Miller stood up and shouted at them. Again, she used the same words that she had spoken before. She said, "Go outside." Albert and Mary didn't have to be told again, they got up from the table, and quickly found the door.

With Albert and Mary gone, Mrs. Miller asked Sophia again if she was pregnant. Still, Sophia didn't say anything. At that moment, Elizabeth and Sophia had been standing and looking at Mr. Miller, wishing and hoping that he would go ahead and tell her. Mrs. Miller had noticed that all eyes were on her husband, so she cast hers' on him as well.

Elizabeth felt like at that moment, the only thing that kept Mr. Miller alive was the fact that Mrs. Miller didn't have a weapon of sorts to kill him with. Mr. Miller was still seated at the table, but Mrs. Miller had stood up. She looked at him, and called him a shameful bastard. He never did get up from his seat, and he never said a word.

Mrs. Miller had left the dining room. Suddenly, Mr. Miller had lost his appetite, and he had gotten up from the table. He, Sophia and Elizabeth were all standing in the dining room together. Elizabeth told him that he should have told her before it got so far. Elizabeth wondered if he could still talk, because he still hadn't said a single word. Instead, he left the dining room, and went to his study.

Sophia had gone outside to tell Albert and Mary that they could come back inside and finish eating. They were standing on the porch shivering, partly due to the cold, and partly due to the scare that Mrs. Miller had put in them. Elizabeth had started cleaning, and putting things away. When the kids had finished eating, Elizabeth told Sophia to take them upstairs while she finished up in the kitchen. She knew that things were probably going to get loud downstairs. When Elizabeth had finished in the kitchen, she found a rag and started walking around knocking the dust off of some things, and maybe to do a little scouting around to see what was going on.

Mrs. Miller had been in the parlor, but when Elizabeth started in, Mrs. Miller bumped into her. They had met each other in the entryway. She didn't say anything to Elizabeth. She was looking for her husband, and she knew where to find him. After she had entered his study, she closed the door. Elizabeth could hear them, but mostly she heard Mrs. Miller.

Elizabeth had been caught up in a similar mess when she had gotten pregnant with Sophia, and she was caught in it again. It was the same thing—like a big wheel rolling downhill, getting faster by the second with no way to stop it. Trapped in the middle was her daughter, an innocent nineteen year old girl—scarred forever.

Elizabeth kept finding things to do in the mansion, so that she could listen in on what was going on in the study. Sophia had the kids upstairs, so that they wouldn't know what was going on downstairs. Still, Albert and Mary knew that something was off center, because they had asked Sophia why their parents were mad at each other. Sophia said that it was nothing that they had to worry about. She was right, it wasn't anything for the kids to worry about, but for everybody else in the house, it was a different story. It was like a horrible nightmare getting worse by the minute.

Mr. and Mrs. Miller had finally quieted down. It was time for Elizabeth and Sophia to get the kids ready for bed. Once they were all tucked in, Elizabeth attended to Charles. She had taken him to her room, and she held him in her arms until he had fallen asleep. Then, she took the baby to Mrs. Miller's room, and placed him in his crib. Mrs. Miller had been sitting on the side of her bed, and she watched as Elizabeth pulled the covers up over the baby.

She asked Elizabeth how long she had known that Sophia was pregnant. Elizabeth said that she became suspicions a few weeks ago when she had noticed Sophia getting bigger in the middle. She said that at first she thought that she was just eating too much, and a few weeks later she knew that she had to be pregnant. Elizabeth said that when she asked her who the father was, she didn't say anything, she just started crying. Since Sophia never went anywhere, she figured that it had to be Mr. Miller's child.

Mrs. Miller asked Elizabeth if Sophia had told her about how it happened. Elizabeth said that she didn't tell her, and that she had never asked. Mrs. Miller kept sitting on the side of her bed, and staring out the window. She told Elizabeth that she didn't know what to do. She said that it was a common thing for slave owners to have children by slave women, but she had never thought that her husband would be one of them. She said that Sophia was attractive, and if she could see her that way, then she supposed that her husband had to see the same thing.

Elizabeth stayed in the bedroom with Mrs. Miller for a while. She stayed because she knew that if Mrs. Miller needed to talk to someone—and she did—then more than likely, that person had to be her. Mrs. Miller didn't have a lot of people with whom she could share her personal thoughts. She had never considered Elizabeth to be a friend, simply because she was a slave. Yet, she knew her well enough to know that she could talk to her, and whatever they talked about would stay at home. Elizabeth didn't have to say much, Mrs. Miller just needed someone to listen—even if it had to be Elizabeth.

Elizabeth was cognizant of the fact that through the years, Mr. Miller had been an ally for her and Sophia.

She knew that without him, Sophia would probably be gone just like Daniel. Although he had gotten Sophia pregnant, Elizabeth still knew that it was in her best interest to work both sides of the fence, and maintain a neutral position. She was as angry at him as Mrs. Miller, because of what he had done to Sophia. Yet, she and Sophia still needed him on their side, and then more than ever.

As far as Elizabeth was concerned, what was done was done, and there was nothing that anyone could do to change things. One thing was for sure, she didn't want to choose sides, or lean too far in either direction. Elizabeth had listened to Mrs. Miller until she decided that she would go to bed. Before leaving the room, she had asked if there was anything else that she needed her to do. Mrs. Miller said that if she didn't have any children, she would shoot the son of a bitch that she was married to, and then shoot herself.

Elizabeth had left Mrs. Miller's room, and she was going to her room when she heard footsteps. She looked back and saw Mrs. Miller. She had stopped to ask if she needed something. Mrs. Miller said that she wanted some of whatever that stuff was that she brewed up to make you sleep.

They had gone to the kitchen, and Elizabeth asked her to have a seat; she would have it ready in just a few minutes. Elizabeth told her that she could keep the baby in the room with her during the night. Mrs. Miller knew that Elizabeth would have to keep the baby, because after a cup of that stuff that Elizabeth made, she wouldn't be able to. She didn't know what was in it, and she didn't care. She had told Elizabeth to make sure that she got it strong enough.

Elizabeth had filled a cup, and she slid it over in front of Mrs. Miller. She said that she was going to sit there and sip on whatever it was that she had in her cup, and do nothing. When she got to the point where she couldn't stay awake, that's when she would go to bed.

It had passed his bedtime, but Mr. Miller was still in his study. He was in no hurry to turn in for the night. He wanted to make sure that Mrs. Miller was sound asleep before he entered the bedroom. He had even thought about sleeping in a separate room, but he decided that nothing would become of that, nothing positive anyway. When he did go to bed, Mrs. Miller was sound asleep.

The next morning, Mr. Miller had gotten up unusually early, just him and Elizabeth. Elizabeth had put Mrs. Miller's baby in the bed with Sophia. Once he was dressed, Mr. Miller had just one cup of coffee. He had told Elizabeth that he didn't care for breakfast. He and Elizabeth didn't have much to say to each other. It had to be clear to him that everyone in the house probably hated the ground that he walked on. He had left his empty coffee cup in his study. After stuffing a bunch of papers in his satchel, he left the mansion.

Mrs. Miller had slept well into the morning—even longer than usual. It was due to the tranquilizing effects of that downer that Elizabeth had conjured up just before she had gone to bed. It was quiet around the house with Albert and Mary both in school, and Annie still asleep. Elizabeth didn't have much to do since she had to wait until Mrs. Miller and Annie were up before she could tidy up in their bedrooms. She checked on Sophia; she and Mrs. Miller's baby were still asleep.

Elizabeth could hear Mrs. Miller. She wasn't sure if she was fumbling around, or stumbling around, but she had to go and check on her. Mrs. Miller said that she needed some coffee. That cup of whatever it was that Elizabeth had brewed up for her tasted alright going down, but the after effects had her wondering if perhaps she could have gotten along without it, or maybe replaced it with a few shots of bourbon.

Referring to her husband, Mrs. Miller assumed that he had slept in bed with her last night, but she couldn't say for sure. She said that the only indication that he probably did was that the covers had been turned back on his side of the bed. Elizabeth said that he had one cup of coffee, and before she realized it, he had gone. Mrs. Miller said that she didn't give a damn, and as far as she was concerned, he could keep going all the way to Hell.

Mrs. Miller talked and Elizabeth listened while she fumbled around with this and that. Mrs. Miller had decided that she was not going to die, at least not over what her husband had done. Then she asked about the baby. Elizabeth told her that he was in the bed with Sophia, and that they were still asleep. She had pushed her empty coffee cup toward the edge of the table for a refill.

Thinking out loud, Mrs. Miller wondered if she should forgive him, or if she should just leave it alone, and let him think about it forever. On the other hand, she considered that if she did forgive him, it wouldn't be soon. She wanted him to know what it felt like to be disregarded and betrayed.

Eventually, Mrs. Miller got around to asking Elizabeth if he had ever tried to do to her what he had done to Sophia. Emphatically, Elizabeth said that he had never tried to lay a hand on her. Mrs. Miller said that she was surprised. After what he had done to Sophia, she didn't know why he had passed up on Elizabeth.

Elizabeth had been listening and talking to Mrs. Miller, but she still didn't know what she had in mind for Sophia. She had always thought that it would be Sophia's attitude that would get her in trouble, and she had never thought that it would be because Mr. Miller would get her pregnant. She had been trying to comfort Mrs. Miller with the idea that maybe she would have enough sympathy for her not to get rid of her daughter. At the same time, she realized that Mrs. Miller had never wanted anything more than a good reason to make her husband get rid of what she had always referred to as that pest around the house.

Elizabeth had started taking care of the chores. She had noticed that her hands were not as steady as they should be, but she knew why. It hadn't been long ago since Daniel was sold. She remembered thinking about how his parents must have felt when he was being taken away. Then she felt like maybe she did know—she was afraid that her daughter was about to go the way of Daniel. Yet, she still had Sophia, she just didn't know for how long.

Mrs. Miller had decided that it was time to talk to Sophia. Elizabeth saw her as she was making her way to the bedroom. Through the years she had done a lot of eavesdropping around the house just to stay informed, but not on that day—she didn't want to listen. The door to Sophia's room was closed; Mrs. Miller had tapped on it lightly—very unusual for her—then she entered. She found Sophia sitting on the side of the bed holding the baby. She asked if he was awake, and Sophia said that he was. Sophia was afraid, and her fear was obvious to Mrs. Miller.

Sophia had been thinking that her time at Magnolia Manor was about to come to an end. She hadn't slept much during the night. While in bed, she had thoughts about the options that Mrs. Miller had to get back at her. If she was going to be punished, a verbal thrashing would be more than welcomed—she could easily stand there and listen to whatever Mrs. Miller had to say, and be an obedient servant while doing it. She had decided that she could tolerate as many lashes across her naked back as might be handed down ... anything except selling her to somebody else.

She was sure that things had shifted so much in Mrs. Miller's favor that she had the leverage that she needed to force her husband to do whatever she wanted. Anything that she demanded of him would probably be granted. Sophia was sure that her first mandate would be for him to get rid of her.

Sophia was aware of the fact that since his marriage, Mr. Miller had always stood between her and Mrs. Miller. Had it not been for him, she would have been gone. Yet, she had considered that she and Mr. Miller were in the same position; both had been backed into a corner with Mrs. Miller standing in front of them—he couldn't help her anymore.

Sophia had thought about the fact that if he really wanted to, Mr. Miller could still exercise his authority, and keep Mrs. Miller at bay. However, he had literally been caught with his pants down, and being meek would by far be a better option for him than fighting back. Therefore, she was sure that she had been left to stand alone. With her gone, along with the child that she was carrying, there would be no long time reminders of what had happened, and there would be no gossip from the blabbermouths around town.

Sophia was still sitting on the side of the bed, but she couldn't look Mrs. Miller in the eye. She sat there with her head down, quietly waiting to hear what her fate might be. As she waited, tears rolled down her cheeks. When Mrs. Miller didn't say anything, Sophia decided to plead on her own behalf before Mrs. Miller handed down her sentence. She had said that she was sorry, that she didn't want to do it, and that she was scared. Never before in her life had it been necessary for her to beg for anything, but then, she felt like she had no other choice.

Still holding Mrs. Miller's baby, Sophia had started pleading with her ... please don't sell me, don't take me away from my mama. Mrs. Miller tried to speak to her, but Sophia wouldn't let her. She didn't want to hear what she had already imagined that Mrs. Miller was going to say. Mrs. Miller spoke her name, and Sophia looked up at her. When their eyes had met, Sophia said that she would do anything, but she didn't want to be sold. Every time that Mrs. Miller tried to speak, Sophia would interrupt.

Mrs. Miller had placed her hands on Sophia's shoulder, and she shook her—she shook her hard. She had to in order to get her attention. When Sophia had stopped talking, Mrs. Miller told her that she was not angry with her. She said that only her husband was to blame for what had happened. Again, Sophia asked Mrs. Miller if she was going to sell her.

Even though Sophia was not her favorite person, Sophia's question had caused Mrs. Miller to have second thoughts about the way things were, and the way they had been for so long. Maybe she had never thought about it before, or maybe it was the first time that she had been so close to it. Nonetheless, listening to a person begging not to be sold didn't sound right, not even to Mrs. Miller.

Although Mrs. Miller had been hurt because of what her husband had done, she felt like Sophia had been hurt much more than she had. As much as she disliked Sophia, she felt sorry for her. Starting with the first day that they had met, she had wished that Sophia was not around, and she probably still had the same wish. She had even told Mr. Miller that they should sell her. Whether she meant it or not, she told Sophia that she should know that they wouldn't take her away from Elizabeth.

Mrs. Miller told Sophia that she hated Austin as much as she did, but she guessed that they would someday get over what he had done. It would just take some time. Although she had supposed that they would get over it, she was absolutely sure that it would be impossible to ever forget.

Sophia hadn't stopped crying. Still sitting on the side of the bed, tears from her eyes fell onto the face of Mrs. Miller's baby that she was still holding in her arms. Mrs. Miller had to wrestle with her herself to hide her own feelings after seeing and listening to Sophia. She had forced herself not to shed any tears, but she had come close.

Mrs. Miller had left Sophia sitting on the bed. When she saw Elizabeth, she sat down. Elizabeth didn't know what had happened upstairs, and she was afraid to ask. Mrs. Miller was quiet and Elizabeth was too—both had been shaken, Elizabeth, because she didn't know if she would be able to keep her daughter, and Mrs. Miller because Sophia had been so afraid that she would be put on the auction block and sold.

When Mrs. Miller spoke, she told Elizabeth that she had left Sophia sitting on the bed crying, because she had been thinking that they were going to sell her. Then Elizabeth started crying, because she had been thinking that they would. Mrs. Miller had told Elizabeth to go and talk to her. She said that she was going for a walk.

Sophia had been crying out loud. Elizabeth could hear her before she had made it to the room. Sitting on the bed, Elizabeth put her arms around her while she held onto the baby, and they both cried together. After Elizabeth had left Sophia, she walked to the window and looked down the street, but she didn't see Mrs. Miller. When she went to the back porch, she saw her. She had walked down that gentle grade that led to the bush harbor, and she was sitting on one of the makeshift benches.

Mr. Miller returned home after a longer than usual day at his office. When she felt like talking to him, Mrs. Miller told him that she had spoken to Sophia just to let her know that she was not angry with her. Mr. Miller didn't say anything. There wasn't much that he could say anyway.

Mrs. Miller told him about how Sophia had reacted, and that she had never seen a person be so afraid before. He didn't ask what it was that had her so afraid, but she told him. She said that Sophia had been thinking that they were going to sell her, and that she was almost out of her mind.

Mr. Miller didn't say that he would talk to her, or anything like that, and Mrs. Miller probably didn't expect him to. Furthermore, Sophia didn't want to have to listen to him anyway, because nothing that he could say would erase what he had done to her. What Mrs. Miller had said earlier was right, Sophia hated him.

Mrs. Miller had been very calm while talking to her unfaithful husband. She said that she had a weird feeling while talking to Sophia, and she had been wondering why. She told him that Sophia was crying and begging for them not to sell her; it was like she was begging for her life. She then supposed that in a way, she probably had been doing just that.

She wondered aloud if Heaven was for people like them. They had been in Mr. Miller's study all while they were talking. After they had stopped talking, they both kept sitting there—just briefly—neither knowing what the other might be thinking, but for sure wondering.

Sophia hadn't been to the bush harbor with Elizabeth for several weeks. She didn't want anyone to see that she was pregnant. However, Elizabeth did tell Alfred. Mr. and Mrs. Miller didn't miss a single Sunday at church, walking arm and arm, and smiling like nothing was wrong. No one at church or any of their friends knew anything about the stressful conditions brought on by Mr. Miller's infidelity. Mrs. Miller usually left the baby at home with Sophia on Sunday's and sometimes, the other kids stayed with Sophia as well.

Mrs. Miller had been downstairs, just she and Sophia. She had asked Sophia where was she and Elizabeth when Austin raped her. Sophia didn't want to talk about it, and Mrs. Miller could see that she didn't. Mrs. Miller said that she just wanted to know. Sophia told her that it was the same day that Alfred took her to visit her friend, and they had the storm. Mrs. Miller remembered the day, but she also remembered that Mr. Miller had gone to his office before they left home. Sophia told her that he came home when he saw that the weather might get bad.

Mrs. Miller asked if he did it in her bedroom. Sophia explained what happened, at least what she could remember. She said that she had been sitting in the parlor reading the newspaper, and listening to the wind and thunder. She didn't hear him come in, and he was standing in the doorway to the parlor when she saw him. For just a moment he had scared her, because she didn't expect to see him until later in the day.

When the wind started blowing hard, she said that she became very frightened and he put his arms around her; he had told her not to be afraid. She remembered crying when he told her to lie down on the sofa. That was all that she could remember. When she stopped crying, she said that she was still on the sofa, but she didn't know how long it had been since he had left the room. Mrs. Miller told her that she was probably tired, and that she should go and lie down for a while.

The lack of respect for Mr. Miller was evident by the quietness around the house. Other than the children, no one else in the house cared to be around him. Sophia never had talked to him much, but she talked to him even less. Elizabeth had always fussed at him about not sitting down and eating breakfast, but she had stopped—after what he had done, she didn't care whether he ate or not. She was his slave, but Elizabeth had trusted him, and she had always thought of him as being different from other slave owners. After what he had done, her opinion of him had changed. She supposed that all slave owners were alike; some just wore sheep's clothing ... like Austin Miller.

If he could have gone back and changed things, he probably would have. He hoped that temperaments would get better with time, but there would always be that permanent reminder, his black child by Sophia. Even so, the makings had been his, and like it or not, he had to live with it. He would have to live with it forever.

After a while, Sophia started looking and feeling like she might be ready to give birth at any time. She didn't do much around the house anymore. In fact, there was nothing much that she could do. When she was sitting, she could use some help with getting on her feet, and when she was on her feet, she could use some help with sitting down. That being the case, mostly she sat, and she was waited on just like Mrs. Miller had been when she was pregnant.

Eventually, Albert and Mary noticed that Sophia had gotten to the point where she had become pretty much helpless, but they had already stepped in to help. It was Sophia that had always taken care of them, but then, it was their time to take care of her. If she needed anything, and if it was something that they could do, they would.

Understandably, the children had been the last to know that Sophia was going to have a baby. When they found out, it was fine with them. They didn't know who the father was, nor did they ask, probably because it didn't matter. Being kids, they may have thought that when it was time, she would just have a baby—maybe even find one in the cabbage patch.

At the end of the day, Sophia still had to read to Albert and Mary. However, she had all but given them the responsibility of reading while she listened. Once when Sophia had finished reading, Mary wanted to know if she had decided on a name for the baby. Sophia said that she hadn't thought about that. Then, Albert and Mary started coming up with possibilities, and finally, they had all settled on one.

Albert and Mary ran through the mansion searching for their mother and Elizabeth, and making far too much noise for Mrs. Miller. She wanted to know what the commotion was all about. Mary and Albert were both talking at the same time; they had decided on a name for Sophia's baby. If it's a girl, they were going to name her Katie, and if it's a boy, they were going to name him Richard.

Mrs. Miller had said that those were good names, and that it's good to have a name for a boy, and one for a girl. When she had said that you don't know if it's going to be a boy or a girl until they get that first spanking, she wished that she hadn't said it. Mary wondered why anyone would spank the baby. Mrs. Miller didn't try to explain; she started talking about something else.

Mr. Miller had started spending even more time at his office in town, simply because he felt uncomfortable at home. Not only was he uncomfortable, he was pretty much unwanted as well. He didn't dread those out of town business trips nearly as much as he once had. Surely, he had noticed that when he had to leave home for a few days, there was no one standing on the porch waving goodbye when he left.

In early spring, the weather had started to turn warm. Mr. Miller decided that it would be a good time for him to check on things at his plantation in Mississippi. He told Mrs. Miller that he would be gone for a few days, but she didn't seem to care what his plans were anymore. In fact, she had already told him that he didn't have to tell her where he was going; and she didn't care if he fell off the edge of something, and ended up at the bottom of nowhere.

He had packed his bags, and Alfred took him to the train station. After he had gone, Elizabeth asked Mrs. Miller if she didn't think that she had been a little hard on him. She said that all of it was her way of letting him know that it's going to be a while, and it's going to take some doing before things got back close to being right again.

Mrs. Miller seemed pleased that Mr. Miller was out of her hair for a while. At least, it appeared that way to Elizabeth. She wanted them to strike an accord of some sort, because there had been so much tension between them whenever they were both at home. The stressful conditions affected everybody in the house, right on down to the children. Even they could tell that things weren't right, but they had no clue as to what was wrong. No one dared to tell them, because they were too young.

What at one time had been an almost well balanced household had become a camouflaged backdrop, filled with ill will, and sharp quips—raw feelings and cutting remarks, most of which had come from Mrs. Miller, and slung at her husband.

Mr. Miller had been gone only two days when Sophia went into labor. Neither Elizabeth nor Mrs. Miller knew much about that sort of thing. When things started to happen, it seemed like it was all at once. Elizabeth knew of a nearby black woman that was a midwife. She told Mrs. Miller about her, and said that Alfred could go and get her. Mrs. Miller decided that she should write a note for Alfred to give to the woman's owner to explain things. While Mrs. Miller was writing the note, Elizabeth had called for Alfred to come inside quickly.

Alfred had been working in the yard. He didn't know what was going on, but he stopped and ran inside. He ran because when Elizabeth called him, it sounded urgent. Elizabeth had told him that Sophia was ready to have that baby, and they needed Louisa. Alfred knew Louisa, and he knew where she lived. Mrs. Miller gave him the note; she told him what it was for; and then she told him to go.

With Alfred gone, Mrs. Miller and Elizabeth had gone to be with Sophia. The only thing that they could do was to try and make her comfortable, but making her comfortable had been next to impossible. Sophia had been screaming, and so had the kids. It may have been Mrs. Miller's busiest day ever. Never before had she made so many trips up and down the stairs—not in the same day. She had to keep an eye on Annie and Charles, she kept looking down the street for Alfred and Louisa, and she had to help Elizabeth with Sophia—all at the same time.

Mrs. Miller and Elizabeth felt like Alfred had been gone for a long time, but he hadn't. It just seemed that way. Alfred returned with Louisa, but none too soon. It was Sophia's first child, but it went fast, and without any glitches. Mrs. Miller and Elizabeth watched as Louisa went about it with the confidence of a seasoned medical doctor, one that had graduated at the top of his class. When she had him in her hands, Louisa slapped Sophia's son on the bottom, and he responded with that familiar scream, letting them know that it hurt, but yet, he was alright. Elizabeth and Mrs. Miller had been standing there watching when he came into the world.

Alfred had been on standby just outside. He stuck his head in and asked if everything was alright. Mrs. Miller told him that he could come in. Louisa had cleaned the baby up, and she placed him in the bed next to Sophia. Mrs. Miller was the first to speak his name when she said that there's Richard. When she did, Sophia managed a smile. Elizabeth told Alfred that when he left to go get Louisa, he had been gone so long that they thought he had run away.

Louisa said that she would stay with Sophia for a while just to make sure that everything was alright. She said that she had delivered a baby once, and then she had to go back and do it again, because the mama had twins.

Alfred looked at the baby, and told Sophia that she had a good looking son. He then told Mrs. Miller that he would be working in the yard, and that he would take Louisa home whenever she was ready to go.

Mrs. Miller and Elizabeth stood near the bed looking at the baby. When Mrs. Miller had said that he looked a lot like Charles, Elizabeth didn't say anything, because she didn't want to say yes he does. However, yes he does would have been the correct response.

After a while, Sophia was about to fall asleep with Louisa sitting at her bedside. When Albert and Mary had come home from school, Mrs. Miller told them about Sophia's baby. They wanted to go and see, but Mrs. Miller had told them that they would have to wait. Mrs. Miller did tell them that it was a boy. When she did, they knew that his name was Richard.

Elizabeth had started cooking, and at the same time, she had to keep an eye on Albert and Mary. They wanted to see Sophia and the baby. Mrs. Miller had noticed how insistent they were, so she told them to go and do their homework for school. Then, maybe they could see Sophia and the baby. Mary said that she couldn't do her homework, because Sophia had to help her. Mrs. Miller explained that it would be several days before Sophia would feel like doing that again.

Mrs. Miller told Albert and Mary that she would help them with their homework, and then they would have lots of time to spend with Sophia and the baby later on. Mary said that she would get behind in school if Sophia didn't help her. Again, Mrs. Miller told her that she would help her. Mary told Mrs. Miller that she couldn't teach her as good as Sophia.

Elizabeth pretended that she hadn't heard Mary, but she did look to see what Mrs. Miller's reaction might be. She had been somewhat surprised when she saw that there was no reaction. She felt like Mrs. Miller must have already been bent out of shape enough, and therefore, she didn't want to be bent anymore.

Mrs. Miller had won the argument, and she helped Albert and Mary with their homework. Louisa was ready to go, and Alfred had brought the buggy around to take her home. Mrs. Miller and Elizabeth had walked out onto the porch. Louisa had said that Sophia didn't have twins, but she needed to stay in bed for a few days.

Again, Albert and Mary asked if they could see Sophia and the baby. Seeing that they wouldn't be satisfied until they did, Mrs. Miller took them to see the baby. Standing at Sophia's bedside, Mary asked if she could hold the baby. Mrs. Miller said that it's best to leave him in bed for now. Albert and Mary had been all over Sophia when Mrs. Miller pulled them back.

While Mr. Miller had been gone, Mrs. Miller had time to think about things, and she wondered whether or not she had made her husband miserable long enough. She had considered the fact that it was impossible to be angry for the rest of her life. On the other hand, she knew that his child by Sophia was there to stay, and she may as well get used to the idea of having him around. Yet, she wanted her husband to always remember that there was nothing that could justify the unmitigated lack of respect that he had for her and his family, Sophia and Elizabeth include.

Sophia was their slave, and a slave that had always clashed with Mrs. Miller, but Mrs. Miller expressed her compassion for Sophia. She had told Elizabeth that her husband was the first man that Sophia had ever been with; if she had seen Sophia shoot him, and then had to testify in court, she said that she would lay her hand on the bible, and then swear that she had seen the whole thing, and it was an accident. She was walking down the hallway, talking as she moved along. She had said that a few subtle hints suggesting fidelity and respect scattered about from time to time might keep his pants up, and keep him on the right side of the fence.

Mr. Miller had been gone all week. When he returned and walked into the mansion, Mrs. Miller pretended to be surprised, but she wasn't. She had seen him when he was coming down the street. She asked him how the trip had been, and he told her. Actually, she couldn't have cared less about how it had gone. She was just saying something to create conversation, letting him know that maybe she was willing to talk to him again.

Albert and Mary had told him that Sophia had a baby. Mrs. Miller had avoided telling him just to send the message that she had not been all that excited about her stepson. Mary had taken Mr. Miller by the hand, and insisted that he go see the baby. Rather timidly, he looked at Mrs. Miller. She had said that it would be as good a time as any, because they would both probably be awake. He went with Mary and Albert, but he wasn't sure if he should or shouldn't. He had noticed that his welcome home was not quite as cold as the send-off when he had left.

Mr. Miller had knocked on the door to Sophia's room, but as soon as he started to knock, Albert and Mary just opened the door and walked in. He had stopped short of the bed, and asked Sophia how she was feeling. She told him that she and the baby were both alright. Albert told him that the baby's name was Richard. He said that he liked that name. He was standing there looking, but he didn't have much to say, because he was too aware of what he had done that had him standing there in the first place.

He took a step closer to the bed. Sophia had pulled the blanket down a little, so that he could have a better look at his new son. Every few seconds, his eyes would drift to Sophia, but whenever he noticed that she was about to look at him, his would go back to the baby. He was in a very awkward position, but he had put himself there. He hadn't said much, but he must have felt like more was needed. Maybe that's what triggered his mind, and made him recall those universal words of praise that had always been appropriate for any newborn. He said that he certainly looked healthy enough.

No doubt feeling like he was somewhere that he didn't belong, he took Albert and Mary by the hand, and said that they should go, and let them rest. In the past, it had always been Sophia that said as few words as possible, and then walked away. That time, however, he was the one that didn't have much to say, and was in a hurry to leave.

Elizabeth had supper on the table, and they had sat down to eat. Albert and Mary had been going on and on telling Mr. Miller about Sophia's baby. He hadn't experienced so much uneasiness since his first day in court. Mrs. Miller pretended not to notice, but she could see the anxiety, and she knew that he would rather walk away from the table, but he couldn't. Elizabeth was still Elizabeth, on the outside that is. Inside, she was as angry at him as Mrs. Miller.

Later, Mrs. Miller asked Elizabeth if she could see how tensed he had been. Elizabeth sort of smiled, but she didn't say anything. Mrs. Miller had said that if she thought that they could escape the legal ramifications, the two of them could do him in, and have Alfred bury him somewhere out back. Elizabeth had to laugh, but she told Mrs. Miller that she should stop talking like that.

Mr. Miller had gotten his newspaper, and he sat in the parlor reading. Elizabeth didn't think that he had really been interested in the newspaper. She felt like he was just trying to figure out where his place was around the house. A few minutes later, Mrs. Miller walked into the parlor. She had sat down on the sofa—not next to him, but close enough to suggest that maybe he could, and yet, far enough away to make him wonder.

She knew that he didn't want to talk about Sophia and her baby, or rather, their baby. However, she had a stranglehold on him, and she decided to choke him a little, if for no other reason, just because she could. She had asked him what he thought about the baby. After she had asked the question, she then stared right into his eyes just to intimidate him. He stared back, certainly not to be arrogant, but because he had been dumbfounded. Then he supposed that the baby looked alright, and once again, those universal words of praise had come to mind—they had worked once, he could use them again. He said that he certainly seemed to be ....

He perhaps felt that he had been a rather tactful response—safe enough to keep him from sinking any deeper—but Mrs. Miller hadn't finished. She said that she thought that the baby looked a lot like Charles. He had the perfect response for that comment. He simply said that all babies seemed to look alike. She said maybe so, but that you could certainly tell that he's a Miller.

Mrs. Miller was sure that her husband probably felt like he had been sitting on a hot stove. Still, he didn't want her to see him squirming around. He was an attorney, but his had been a difficult case to argue, he couldn't say I object, and he couldn't cross examine. He was pretty much at the mercy of the court, and Mrs. Miller was on the bench.

After a while, Mrs. Miller decided that she had thrust the dagger all the way to the hilt, she had twisted it a little, and it was time to let him lick his wounds. She had said that she was going outside, and cut some flowers to freshen up her bedroom. Even those words had made him wonder. He didn't know if her remark about freshening up the bedroom had been directed at him, or if she really did mean to freshen up the bedroom. If it was or wasn't, he didn't say anything, and he was relieved that she had finished with her questioning.

Mr. Miller wanted to be near his wife, but it seemed to him that she had been sending mixed signals. Her words and her actions had him confused, and he didn't know what to do. Mrs. Miller felt like she had accomplished exactly what she had set out to do, make him feel uncomfortable and not terribly wanted.

When Mrs. Miller had gone outside, she saw Alfred working in the yard, and she walked over to him. She said that she wanted some fresh flowers for the house, and he showed her where to find them. The grounds around the mansion were a little foreign to her, because she had never spent much time out there.

Elizabeth had seen her outside, so she had gone out to see what she was doing. Mrs. Miller told her that she was just getting some fresh flowers for her bedroom. Elizabeth said that she could have done that. Since she was just doing something to get outside, Mrs. Miller said that she didn't mind. Still, Elizabeth walked around in the yard with her, stopping here and there to select an assortment of flowers for her floral arrangement. They talked, but not about the recent goings on around the mansion—just trivial things, something to do to help while away the time.

They walked up to the rose bush that Sophia had transplanted in memory of her friend, Amanda. Mrs. Miller looked at, and said that she must have been a nice girl. Elizabeth said that she was as sweet as she could be. Mrs. Miller had bent over to pick some flowers from the rose bush, and then she changed her mind. She said that she would leave them there, they were for looking at.

Eventually, Sophia got out of bed and was back on her feet. Elizabeth could remember when there had only been three around the house, she and Sophia along with Mr. Miller. Now, there were four adults and five kids, and the workload had increased along with the head count. Albert and Mary were old enough to pretty much take care of themselves, but Annie, Charles and Richard knew how to wear them down.

When Richard was old enough to crawl around, Sophia could turn him and Charles loose in the backyard, and keep one eye on them and the other eye on Albert, Mary and Annie. On Sunday's, Albert, Mary and Annie went to church with Mr. and Mrs. Miller. Elizabeth and Sophia took turns on going to church, whether at the bush harbor, or at church with Mr. and Mrs. Miller. They alternated because one had to stay at home and take care of Charles and Richard.

Elizabeth had given Alfred the assignment of keeping an eye on Sophia whenever it was her turn to go to the bush harbor. Elizabeth just felt better knowing that she was with him. Alfred knew their schedule, and he always waited and watched for Sophia's arrival, just as he did when waiting for Elizabeth. Sophia always sat up front with him. Sitting up front had become a conscious effort, because she remembered how she and Daniel had sat in the back, and then, fell in love. She didn't want that to ever happen again, at least, no time soon.

ELEVEN

It took some doing, but Mr. and Mrs. Miller had rekindled their relationship, and things eventually got back to where they used to be. Any animosity regarding the fact that Annie and Charles had a half-brother that was black, and also a slave, was not something that was often talked about. Richard had become part of the family, and like it or not, they couldn't just toss him outside, and think that he would go away.

Elizabeth had been busy in the mansion, and Mr. and Mrs. Miller sat on the back porch watching the children play in the backyard. Sophia was in the midst of them having just as much fun as they were. Mrs. Miller wondered how she had the energy to run with them the way that she did. Mr. Miller said that she's young and young people just have lots of energy. He told her that she had probably done the same thing when she was that age. She said that she wasn't that old; she could still run and play if she wanted to.

Speaking about her husband, Mrs. Miller had once said to Elizabeth that around the house, he always seemed to have simple answers for everything. She didn't know if it was because he saw things around the house as being simple, or maybe he just didn't think much about the simple things.

While watching the kids play, Mrs. Miller said that when you look at them, you can't tell the white ones from the black one. Mr. Miller didn't say anything, no doubt thinking that if he did, the tranquil atmosphere of sitting on the porch relaxing with his wife might come to an end. They had gotten back on good terms with each other, and he wanted to keep it that way.

Mrs. Miller had asked him if he knew Sophia's father, and he said yes. He told her that he was from North Carolina, and that's where Elizabeth and Sophia had been born. Then Mrs. Miller guessed that the man that he had bought them from was Sophia's father. He told her that she was correct. After that, they sat there quietly.

Even though Sophia had Richard in bed with her at night, there were still times when she had to scoot over, and make room for Mary. Mrs. Miller didn't seem to mind, and she had come to understand the reason why. She had even admitted to Elizabeth that sometimes she felt jealous, because of Mary's love for Sophia.

When Richard had learned to walk, he was always following in Charles' footsteps. Since they were brothers, it was exactly what they had expected. With Richard around, Mrs. Miller had a better understanding of how Sophia had grown up, and why Mr. Miller had let her be so free with Amanda, Caroline and Emily. She had a better understanding, because she could see the same thing happening again, but it was happening closer to her.

There was nothing to keep Richard, Charles, Albert and Mary from not being Sophia, Amanda, Caroline and Emily all over again. She said that she had often wondered what their relationship might be like when they become adults. After wondering, she said that it was a question without an answer, and the only thing that she could do would be to wait and see.

Mrs. Miller had a humorous side, but it had always stayed pretty rusty, because she didn't use it a lot. Once, she and Mr. Miller had gone to town, and since they had been gone so long, Elizabeth let the children go ahead and eat. When Mr. and Mrs. Miller returned, just the two of them sat at the table, and they ate together.

They had been laughing and talking, and then teasingly, Mrs. Miller had asked him if he thought that Richard was going to call him daddy when he got older. Mr. Miller looked at her, and she had bent over the table laughing. In a few seconds, he had started laughing with her. Elizabeth stood back and watched the two of them have fun with each other ... again. Mr. Miller didn't answer her question. He just kept on laughing with her.

Elizabeth told them that they didn't have to wait until he got older, because he had already started calling Mr. Miller daddy. She told Mrs. Miller that he referred to her as mama—Mrs. Miller still hadn't stopped laughing. Richard had come to know that he was Sophia's son, but to him, she was Sophia.

Elizabeth said that Richard would use the same names around the house that the other kids used, and that it would be hard to get him used to saying anything else. Mr. and Mrs. Miller were still laughing, but they agreed that they would think of something.

When they started, Elizabeth had thought that Mrs. Miller shouldn't have brought the subject up. However, in the end, she had decided that it was probably good that they had talked about it, especially since they could do it and laugh. Still, Elizabeth questioned what it would look like with Richard calling Mr. and Mrs. Miller daddy and mama. She wondered if Mrs. Miller would laugh if it happened in front of some of her house guests.

The anger had gone, however, there had to be times when Mr. Miller walked into his own home and was reminded of the fact that he had faltered. Surely, he had to know the he had lost at least some of the confidence and respect of those that had trusted him—even if it did seem like they had forgotten about it. Since he felt like he had gotten back some of that trust, he hoped that he would be forgiven for the things that couldn't be erased.

TWELVE

Elizabeth felt like the years had been piling up behind her too fast. Now and then she would recall when Sophia, Amanda, Caroline and Emily were all little girls, romping around out back while she kept watch on them. Sometimes it seemed to her like she had turned her back for just a short while, and then they had all grown up. Sophia had become a woman with a little one of her own.

It didn't seem like it, but it had been five years since Mrs. Miller had joked about doing away with her husband, and letting Alfred bury him somewhere out back. She had supposed that the day would come when she would look back at her own life, go back to the yesteryears of when she had been a little girl, and then it would seem like a time that had been so short. Then, when she turns back around, she would see her real self in real time, an old woman bent over and leaning against a cane.

Mr. Miller was well aware that through the years, he had let himself get involved in more things than perhaps he should have. Mrs. Miller had told him time and again that he should step aside and let someone else do it. She felt like he had the attitude that if he did step aside, the one that stepped in might not do it right. To her, it seemed like he had spent half of his married life away from home. Yet, she supposed that it had been no more than he wanted.

Mrs. Miller felt like he had always set his goals higher than he could ever reach, and that he had done it intentionally. To her, his philosophy seemed to be, although it's out of reach, if he could see it, he might be able to grab on to it. The only thing that he had to do was to keep on trying.

Mr. Miller had to attend the Democratic National Convention in Cincinnati, Ohio. He would be staying at one of his favorite hotels, the Gibson House. When he arrived, he had never seen the place so crowded before.

People, mostly politicians, were standing around everywhere, just talking. He could hardly make his way to the clerk's desk to check in. He knew that he had to get up early the next morning, so he had planned to go to his room, relax for a while, do a bit of reading, and then turn in early. Shortly, after making it to his room, he was quickly aware that the possibility of relaxing would be next to impossible. Noise from the hallway sounded like the continuous clatter of steel wheeled wagons going down a street paved with bricks.

He had been in situations like that before, and he knew how to deal with the problem. He decided that he would go downstairs, and have a stiff shot of bourbon, which he did. The first shot had been a smooth one, and it had gone down so easily, that he decided to have another—one to sip on for a few minutes. While he had been sipping on the second shot, he wished that he had finished the first one, and fled to his room.

Several of his old friends had arrived early, and it was obvious that they had been drinking for a while. To his dismay, they had spotted him standing at the bar, and they had to go over and say hello. When they had first shook hands, it was about six o'clock in the evening, and when they said goodnight, it had gotten close to midnight. During the course of events that evening, his second shot of bourbon had turned into more shots than he could remember. When he did make it back to his room, he had no trouble falling asleep, and he didn't do any reading.

The next morning after he had awakened, he looked at his watch, and it told him that the meeting had already started. While getting dressed, he thought about that potion that Elizabeth had doled out from time to time. He considered that it and bourbon might be close kin. He thought about it, because the after effects of that stuff that Elizabeth made and that of bourbon were about the same.

He had dressed in a hurry, and rushed off to the meeting. When he arrived, he eased in with a style that no one could detect as being late. He had found a seat amongst the masses, and slid in so smoothly that no one suspected that he had just walked in.

When the convention ended, they had nominated James Buchanan for the office of President, and then he had gone on to win the election. Buchanan opposed slavery, but he had insisted that the right to own slaves was protected by the Constitution. They wished that he had been proslavery, but still, he whistled part of Dixie.

The President's interpretation of the Constitution was the same as theirs. It was just what southern slave owners had been wanting. At last, they could rest easy. Southern agriculture was booming. The driving force behind it had been slave labor, and they had the legal right to own slaves—the President had said so.

Railroad lines were beginning to link the nation, and trains were quickly becoming the primary means of travel, and transport. The nation had been experiencing great economic growth. As a result, many southern planters had become wealthy, and Austin Miller was one them. He was amongst those that could breathe a sigh of relief. His relationship with the people that had elected him had gotten back to where it used to be. He no longer had to go the other way when he saw a gathering on the street. He could walk through the crowd, and once again feel that familiar slap on the back by well-wishers.

The atmosphere at Magnolia Manor had gotten back to where it was pretty much like old times. Still, there had to be a few negative thoughts that cropped up from time to time, especially when some looked at the family tree. It was quiet and comfortable outside. Mrs. Miller had found a seat on the porch, and she had been watching Richard and Charles play in the backyard. They were still little tots, but it wasn't necessary that someone be on their heels every time they made a turn.

Sophia had been inside helping Elizabeth. After a while, Richard had left Charles in the yard, and made his way onto the porch. He had roamed around for a few minutes, and then he walked over to Mrs. Miller, and placed his head on her lap—it was quiet, and they were alone. She looked down at him, and without saying anything, she ran her fingers through his long straight hair.

He rubbed his eyes, and she could tell that he had gotten sleepy. She picked him up, and held him in her arms. It wasn't long before he had fallen asleep.

She noticed how much he resembled his brother Charles. Their skin and eyes were the same color, and both had the same color of hair. Charles was older, but if a mix-up at birth had been possible, she wondered if she would have been able to tell which one was hers. She pulled him closer to her chest, and started humming a lullaby to keep him pacified, and maybe to pacify herself as well.

Elizabeth saw her holding Richard, and she noticed that he had fallen asleep. She bent over to take him from Mrs. Miller, so that she could put him to bed. Mrs. Miller told her to leave him alone; she would just sit there and hold him for a while. Elizabeth had turned to go back inside. She stopped when Mrs. Miller said that she wondered if her sentiments had been changing like the clock on the wall, or if she had simply gotten caught up somewhere in between with no way out.

Elizabeth had been standing slightly behind Mrs. Miller, and she was thinking about what she had just said. She wondered if Mrs. Miller really expected her to say something, if she did, Elizabeth didn't know what it would be. After thinking about what she had said, Elizabeth came to the conclusion that it all sounded crazy. She had no idea as to what Mrs. Miller was talking about. Finally, she eased the door open, and went back inside.

Mrs. Miller didn't know that Mr. Miller had made it home. After placing his satchel on the desk in his study, he walked through the mansion to the back porch where she had been. When he had made it to the door, he saw her holding Richard, and still humming a tune—she didn't know that he was behind her. He had eased the door open, and sat down in the chair next to her. For a few seconds, they didn't talk, and then he asked her what it was that she had been thinking about. Casually, she said that she didn't know. Then she asked him if he thought that they would go to Heaven when they die, or would they end up in Hell.

She kept on rocking the baby, and she never looked up as if she had been waiting on him to say anything. Then, Mr. Miller's thoughts were about the same as those that Elizabeth had a few minutes earlier when she had offered to put Richard in bed. He wondered what she had been thinking about to make her ask such a question.

They sat quietly on the porch. After a while, she took Richard inside, and gently tucked him in bed. When she returned to the porch, Mr. Miller had gone back inside, but she sat back down. Charles was still in the yard playing, but he was out there by himself. Mrs. Miller kept an eye on him, but seemingly, with a blank stare. It was quiet, and she seemed to be where she wanted to be, alone with her thoughts—asking questions of herself and then answering them, no one else had to listen or reply.

Charles was a few months older than Richard, and they were always together. Since Charles was the oldest, he had a few more words in his vocabulary than Richard. Therefore, Richard learned by listening to, and emulating his brother. When Richard had first learned how to talk, he referred to his father as daddy, and he had kept it up. It happened just like Elizabeth had predicted.

In the beginning, Elizabeth felt like Mr. Miller may have been a little apprehensive about Richard calling him daddy, but it had happened so frequently that he got to the point where he didn't pay any attention to it anymore. There wasn't much that he could do about it anyway, except maybe gag the boy, and he didn't want to do that. Therefore, he and everybody else around the house had accepted the fact that Richard was going to refer to him as daddy, and they had left it at that.

Whenever Charles wanted his mother's attention, he called her mama, and he referred to Sophia by her given name, Sophia. Whenever Richard wanted their attention, he did the same as Charles. Richard referred to Mrs. Miller as mama, and he referred to his mother as Sophia.

Mrs. Miller had a different attitude than Mr. Miller. She didn't want Richard referring to her as mama. In fact, she didn't like it at all. She had gotten to where she could be warm with him—like holding him in her arms while he slept—but she didn't want him calling her mama, and she didn't want him thinking of her as his stepmother. She had tried to teach him that Sophia was his mama, but it didn't sink in very fast. As Richard got older, and with some help from Sophia and Elizabeth, he finally started calling Sophia mama. Still, there were times when Mrs. Miller was mama.

Elizabeth had noticed that Mrs. Miller was gaining weight. When they were alone, Elizabeth asked her if she was pregnant, and the answer was yes. She had decided that it would be the last time for her. Mrs. Miller felt like being pregnant was too confining, she would much rather be out doing things, mingling with society's upper crust, and entertaining. Sitting around the house and waiting for a baby to be born was like being chained down.

She hadn't told Mr. Miller that she was pregnant, but she said that she would tell him when he came home.

She said that they didn't need any more kids around the house. She was thirty five years old, and he was fifty seven. She said that he would die from old age, and then she would be left with them all by herself.

Sophia had gotten a letter from Emily. Mrs. Miller gave it to her, and she didn't seem to have any resentment about Sophia receiving the letter. If she did, she didn't say anything about it. Sophia remembered that not so long ago, Mrs. Miller thought that such a thing was completely out of line, but maybe she had softened a bit.

Sophia took the letter to her room and read it. Emily stated in her letter that she had married, and that she had a baby. She said that she had not heard from Caroline in quite some time, but she had sent her a letter a few days ago.

At the end of the day, Sophia responded to Emily's letter. She congratulated her on being married and on being a mother. She also told her that she had a son of her own. She had been reluctant to let her know that Mr. Miller was her baby's father. After thinking about it, she decided to go ahead and tell her—there had never been any secrets between them. While she was telling, she also let her know that he had forced himself on her.

In the letter, she told Emily about how frighten she had been, but in spite of how it happened, she told her how much she loved her son. Sophia placed her letter on Mr. Miller's desk so that he could drop it in the mail. In the past, he had always mailed her letters without being nosy enough to open and read them first. She hoped that he would still do the same.

Mrs. Miller had been wishing that time could speed up so that she could hurry and give birth to the baby—the one that she had said would be her last. She remembered the first time that she had told Elizabeth that it would be her last one, but since then, she had said it more times than she could remember—she didn't want any more children.

Mr. Miller was out of town, but there had been nothing unusual about that. She had been sitting in the parlor when she called for Elizabeth. When Elizabeth walked in, Mrs. Miller was laid back on the sofa. She told Elizabeth that it was time. Elizabeth asked if she was sure, because it was too early. Mrs. Miller said that it might be early, but that she had been through it enough to know what it feels like when it's time. Elizabeth helped her to her feet, and took her to the bedroom.

Mrs. Miller said that she hadn't been feeling good all day, but she didn't think that it was because of the baby. She said that somebody had to go get the doctor. Elizabeth said that she would send Albert. Since it had gotten late in the day, she told Albert that he would have to go to the doctor's house, because his office would be closed.

Sophia and the kids had heard Elizabeth when she told Albert to fetch the doctor. Elizabeth had gone back to be with Mrs. Miller. Shortly afterwards, standing in the doorway to the bedroom was Sophia and the kids. Sophia asked what was wrong, and Elizabeth told her. When Sophia asked if there was anything that she could do, Elizabeth said yes. She told her to get those children out, and keep them out.

Mrs. Miller had said that babies always seem to be born at the most inconvenient time. Elizabeth said that they are born when it's time to be born. Albert had returned with the doctor, and he showed him to the bedroom. He then waited in the parlor. After an hour or so, and after the baby had been spanked, Elizabeth told Albert that it was a girl.

Sophia had been trying to entertain the kids when Albert told her about the new baby. Mrs. Miller and the baby were fine and the doctor had gone home. Elizabeth had placed Mrs. Miller's small bell—the one that she used to summon her house servants—near her bed. She could use the bell to get Elizabeth's attention if she needed her during the night. Although crammed together, Annie, Charles and Richard spent the night in bed with Sophia. It would be four more days before Mr. Miller returned home.

The next morning, Mrs. Miller told Elizabeth that she felt like she had been flogged all night. She was tired, and felt like she could sleep all day, even though she had just opened her eyes. Elizabeth told her that she would cook something for her to eat. Mrs. Miller said that she was going to sleep, and that she would eat later.

Getting back and forth with out of town trips had gotten to be better. The railroad had come through, and the town had a train station. Mr. Miller could have someone take him there in a matter of minutes.

It was mid-afternoon when Mr. Miller returned home. He had no way of knowing that Mrs. Miller had given birth to their daughter until the kids had met him at the door. He dropped whatever he had in his hands, and went straight to the bedroom. He had asked Mrs. Miller if she was alright, how is the baby, what's his name, all of it in the same breath. She told him to slow down. Then she said that she was doing fine, the baby is a she and not a he, and that the kids had named her Mary. He said that they already had a Mary. She said that they now have two, Mary McNeal and Mary Miller.

Mrs. Miller told him about how busy it had been the night that the baby was born. Albert had to go to the doctor's house to get him, because his office was closed, and Sophia had to keep the kids calm. She said that she felt like Elizabeth was going to have to stick a rag in her mouth, so that the people down the street wouldn't hear her scream.

Elizabeth had told Mr. Miller that it seemed like he was always gone somewhere whenever they really needed him. He said that it seemed like that, and he apologized. While he was putting his luggage away, Elizabeth told Mrs. Miller that she had only told him that to make him feel good—had he been there, he couldn't have done anything other than what Albert had done, fetch the doctor.

Mrs. Miller stayed in bed several days just because the doctor had told her to. Elizabeth would help her up, so that she could sit on the side of the bed while eating. Elizabeth had been tidying up the room while listening to her talk.

Mrs. Miller said that her husband must live to work, and that he operated on both sides of the fence, in Mississippi and in Tennessee. She had supposed that he was on top of the fence when he had to go to Washington. She felt like operating two plantations, and being involved in politics would be too much for anybody. Yet, he had been doing it for a long time. She didn't really expect him to change, and she figured that he would keep on doing it as long as he could get it done.

THIRTEEN

It had been a while since Elizabeth and Sophia had been to the bush harbor. Richard was five years. Almost everyone at the bush harbor knew that Sophia had a little boy, but after all that time, they had never seen him. The weather had been beautiful, and Mr. and Mrs. Miller had taken all of the kids to church with them. Elizabeth and Sophia were going to the bush harbor, and Richard was going with them.

When they arrived, Elizabeth, Sophia and Richard found a place to sit near Alfred. Richard had been excited about going, but when he got there, he was uneasy about being around so many people. When the preacher started preaching, and the people had gotten loud, Elizabeth could see that Richard would rather be at home than to be where he was. Sophia agreed, because Richard had been squirming around from the moment that they sat down. When it ended, Richard was glad to get away, and he didn't care if he never went back.

Elizabeth remembered what Mrs. Miller had said when Sophia took Mary to the bush harbor, "She had probably been scared out of her mind listening to all of that whooping and hollering that they did down there." When Elizabeth thought about it, she had to agree with Mrs. Miller, because they didn't hold back at the bush harbor.

While mingling around at church, Mrs. Miller had heard talk about some of the states banding together, and forming their own government. The issue had started getting increased attention because President Buchanan's term in office was about to come to an end, and Abraham Lincoln would be the next President.

Mrs. Miller had asked Mr. Miller if he thought that the states might separate. His opinion had been that they could go through the process of separation, but he didn't think that Washington would sit by and let it happen. Mrs. Miller said that it was all about slavery. Then she asked him if he thought that it was wrong to have slaves.

He had given her one of his simple answers again, and she recognized it as being such. He had said that it depends on which side of the fence you're on. Mrs. Miller said that she couldn't see what difference it made as to where you were standing. She said that it's either right or it's wrong. She said that some people were even talking about the possibility of war. For whatever reason, he didn't want to talk about it much, and she just let it be. She didn't want to have to listen again to one of his oversimplified answers to what had seemed to her as being legitimate concerns.

Sophia had been in and out of the dining room, and she had been listening to them talk. Instead of being satisfied with eavesdropping, she asked Mr. Miller if they started a war, would that mean that soldiers would be all around town shooting and killing people. His response to Sophia's question had been very brief—another one of his simple answers. He said that he didn't expect it to come to that. Mrs. Miller told him that she wished that he would stop being so naïve, and stop treating everybody like they were too dumb to understand—he had no idea as to what she was talking about.

Later that night when Elizabeth and Sophia were alone, Sophia told Elizabeth about Mr. and Mrs. Miller's conversation. She said that Mrs. Miller had asked him if he thought that it was wrong to have slaves, and he had said that it depends on which side of the fence you're on. Elizabeth said that he knows the answer to that question as well as anybody, and where the fence is doesn't have anything to do with it.

President Buchanan had done little or nothing to cool things down between the North and South—if anything, he had fueled the flames. Before he had left office, several slave states had already declared that they were no longer part of the Union. He had let several forts and arsenals be taken over by slave states that had seceded.

Abraham Lincoln had been seated—the sixteenth President of the United States. Shortly after he had taken office, South Carolina fired on Fort Sumter. All of the speeches and resolutions, and hopes of peacefully settling their differences had failed. The weapons of war had been made ready to do what, supposedly, civilized people couldn't do. Then, rules of order had been cast aside in exchange for ball and musket.

The Tennessee Legislature had always maintained that the States should exist as a Union, and therefore, all

States should be represented under one flag. Tennessee had maintained that position up until the very end, therefore, being the last state to secede from the Union. Siding with the Confederate States of America, Tennesseans were not willing to put at risk a lifestyle that had been theirs from the beginning.

For years, Austin Miller had shouted as loudly as anyone that the Union of States must be preserved, but he had crossed the line, and was then standing with the faction that he had once so vehemently opposed. His voice rang out with that of his southern comrades, urging all able bodied men to take up arms in defense of their homeland. The South and its heritage must be preserved, even at the cost of civil war.

The call to arms brought in want-to-be soldiers that spanned the gamut of capability and willingness to serve. The hale and hardy as well as the weak and lame stood together, eager to write their name, or make their mark on the roster of volunteers. There were boys that were too young, and men that were too old, but both extremes were willing and ready.

Mrs. Miller's son, Albert, had been amongst the first to volunteer. After he had told his mother of his intentions, she became furious, but fury wouldn't be enough to keep him from doing what he thought was right. Elizabeth and Sophia had sided with Mrs. Miller, but Albert had already committed himself, and nothing that they could say would change his mind. It would be a few days before they had enough enlistees to leave town. Mrs. Miller had considered that during the interim, maybe her husband would be able to talk some sense into him.

All day, Mr. Miller had been in town, stirring the crowd with words of encouragement. Everybody had been assured that there would be some skirmishes, but it wouldn't last long. After which, their husbands and sons would be returning home. Those that had been able to enlist were keyed up. Mrs. Miller had recognized their enthusiasm as being no different than if they were getting ready to go on a Sunday picnic. They had made jokes about how they would kick those Yankees back to where they had come from, and be through with them once and for all.

Mr. Miller had gotten tired; it was almost sundown, and he had started home. The only business establishment in town that had done any business that day was the saloon. It was obvious that liquor sales had been good, as he slowly picked his way along the crowded streets of drunken fools.

When he had made it home, Mrs. Miller was already standing at the door waiting for him. Anxious and frightened, she told him that Albert wanted to enlist in the army. She wanted him to see if he could talk some sense into him. He told her that he had talked to Albert in town, and that he knew all about his plans. He said that Albert had already enlisted, and that he was a soldier in the army of the Confederate States of America.

Mrs. Miller was infuriated. She told him that he should have stopped him. He said that he didn't try to stop him, and that it was a decision that Albert had made. Mrs. Miller had said that he was only a teenager, but Mr. Miller said that he was a young man, and that he had to decide for himself. He told her that she had to let him go. Otherwise, he would always feel like he had hidden under a rock while others had met the enemy; for the rest of his life, he would suffer from the agony of wondering if he had been a coward.

Sophia didn't seem to be so concerned about what was happening. She had been standing at the window watching the ruckus that was going on in the streets. She had told Elizabeth that she should settle down, and stop worrying so much. Elizabeth told her that she was just like those other young fools in the streets, and that she didn't have any idea about what war could be like.

Sophia believed that Mr. Miller had been right about the war not lasting long. Elizabeth said that Mr. Miller didn't know any more about how long it would last than she did. Sophia had let her curiosity take her outside, so that she could get a better view of what was going on in town. She stayed on the front porch watching until Elizabeth told her to get inside, so that she could help with supper.

Everybody had been sitting at the table eating. It was dark outside, and they could still hear the noise from the rally in town. Mrs. Miller had questioned whether or not they knew what they were getting into. Again, Mr. Miller told her that she shouldn't worry, everything would be alright. Considering what was going on in town, she couldn't understand how he could even think that things would be alright. After they had finished eating, they sat on the front porch, and watch the chaotic goings-on in town.

From the porch, they could see the crowd, and hear the hoopla. After a while, they heard gun shots, and Mrs. Miller became more frightened. Elizabeth had been inside, but she had rushed to the door to see what was going on. Mrs. Miller had said that they're up there shooting, and carrying on like they've gone wild. Mr. Miller figured that it was probably some of that bunch that had gotten plastered in the saloon. Nonetheless, they had all decided to go back inside to avoid being the ill-fated target of some careless drunk.

When they were getting ready for bed, things were still wild in town. Mrs. Miller said that she might need something to help her sleep. Mr. Miller agreed, and he had just the thing that they needed. He stepped out of the room for a few minutes. Mrs. Miller knew exactly what he had in mind. When he returned, he had two glasses, each containing an oversized shot of brandy, his being a little taller than hers.

They sat in the parlor, and slowly sipped on their nighttime sedative. Mrs. Miller looked at the glass that he had given to her. She could see that it had more in it than she really wanted, but she had decided that it wasn't too much. She said that she would feel better the next morning after having an oversized shot of brandy, rather than a shot of that stuff that Elizabeth makes. They didn't know how long things lasted in town, because they were still at it after they had fallen asleep.

Sophia had been back and forth from one window to the other—searching for the best vantage point to see the streets in town. It had passed their usual bedtime, but Elizabeth was wide awake. The commotion in the streets still had her nervous. Sophia couldn't sleep because she had been too nosy, and she didn't want to miss anything. She had watched the crowd from the window until Elizabeth told her to go to bed.

Several days had passed. Meanwhile, the list of volunteers continued to get longer. They were a ragtag shoddy looking outfit. Some didn't know their right foot from their left, let alone be able to form a column and march in unison. Yet, they were ready for war, or at least, they had thought that they were.

On the day that they left town, everyone that didn't go, or couldn't go, had lined the streets to see them off. None of the well-wishers seemed to realize that they were looking at many of them for the very last time. They didn't seem to realize that many would return home permanently disfigured and barely recognizable by their own families.

After the troops had left, things settled down in town. The hustle and bustle that had once been common had given way to emptiness and despair. All of the young able bodied men had gone. The town had become a place where mostly old men gathered and sat around all day, whittling on sticks of cedar, and swapping here says about what was going on around the country. Every day, Mr. Miller would go to his law office, but it was more from habit than the need of doing business, because business had come to a halt.

As the war progressed, Union troops continued making their way further and further south. Getting word that they were headed toward Bolivar, Austin Miller had to consider whether or not he should leave town or stay. He had a legitimate concern, because being a member of the Tennessee Legislature meant that he had played an active role in the secession movement.

When the motion to secede from the Union had been made, and properly seconded, he too had stood up and said aye. When he said it, he became a traitor to his country—a charge with severe consequences. If taken prisoner, with some luck he would have been thrown in prison. Without any luck, he could have been placed against a wall and shot for treason.

He didn't have a lot of time to think about it, but he still hadn't made up his mind as to whether he should stay or leave. Mrs. Miller kept telling him to head south, but he kept saying that he had to stay at home, so that he could take care of his family. She told him that he wouldn't be able to take care of his family if he became a prisoner. It would only be a matter of hours before the town would be occupied by Union troops. Finally, he had made the decision to leave. He packed some things, and decided to travel south with a unit of Confederate troops that were leaving town for the same reason that he was leaving.

Before leaving, he said that he had made a lot of trips out of town when he really didn't want to go, but the one that he was about to make would be the one that he dreaded most. His biggest concern had been that he was deserting his family in a time of crisis. Mrs. Miller assured him that they would be able to take care of themselves.

Before leaving, he kissed his wife and children good-bye, Richard included. He had been talking to Elizabeth and Sophia while Mrs. Miller had been trying to get him moving toward the door. That time, however, her only reason was so that he could hurry and be on his way. Elizabeth had told him not to worry, and that they would take care of things at home.

When he had left, Mrs. Miller told Elizabeth that leaving was the best thing for him to do, but she couldn't help but feel like they had all been abandoned. She could then understand why her husband felt like he had deserted them. Elizabeth sympathized with Mrs. Miller, because everything had been thrown at her all at once, she didn't have time to prepare, and she didn't know what to do.

Eventually, the stores in town had run short on supplies and after a while, the shelves were empty. Supply lines had been cut off, nothing coming into town, and nothing going out—nothing but Union troops. Elizabeth, perhaps being more level headed than Mrs. Miller, had suggested that they start being more conservative with their food supplies. Mrs. Miller agreed, but being conservative was something that she had never had to do.

In Mrs. Miller's mind, people were conservative because of limited funds. She had the funds, but it had gotten to the point where funds were not much of an asset, because there wasn't much that could be bought. Never before had she been in a position where she couldn't get what she wanted. She had told Elizabeth that she was afraid, and that she didn't know what she would do without her.

Mrs. Miller had started having bouts with depression, more so by the absence of her husband and son, than by the Union troops that had taken over the town. She said that she had been trying to deal with something that she didn't know anything about; it had all been so new to her.

Elizabeth had started spending more time with Mrs. Miller. She felt like it had become necessary in order to help her stay sane. Whenever she spoke about her husband, which was quite often, Elizabeth would tell her that he was fine wherever he might be. Yet, that was part of Mrs. Miller's problem. She had no idea as to where he might be, but Elizabeth kept trying to say the right things just to keep her feeling confident.

When Mrs. Miller expressed concern about their food supplies, Elizabeth told her that she knew how to stretch things so that they could make it on what they had. With the wealth of Magnolia Manor, dining had gotten to the point where it was something less than what it had been, but they still ate. They just didn't eat as high on the hog as they once had, and there were no leftovers to throw away from the day before.

Alfred had been taking care of the grounds around the mansion, not that it mattered much anymore. Mrs. Miller told Elizabeth that she was glad that he hadn't walked away like most of the other slaves. She said that if Alfred hadn't stayed, she didn't know what they would do for wood to keep warm during the winter. She had guessed that she, Elizabeth and Sophia would have to learn how to pull a cross cut saw, and how to swing an ax.

Mrs. Miller had come to the conclusion that Elizabeth was the reason why Alfred hadn't left. Things were tough enough with him around, and they would have been even tougher without him. He stayed in a log cabin down the way, but Elizabeth saw to it that he ate every day—he had let himself be part of the struggle to help the residents of Magnolia Manor survive what had become hard times.

FOURTEEN

The town had been occupied by Union troops since the day that Mr. Miller left. Soldiers came in and stayed for a while, and then moved out, only to be replaced by a different group. The town had been occupied by General McPherson's troops. More troops had been occupying the town of Jackson, Tennessee.

For whatever reason, the top brass in Jackson had the need to review General McPherson's troops in Bolivar. Consequently, they had left Jackson and headed south toward Bolivar, a distance of about thirty five miles. Well before arriving in Bolivar, a small detachment had been sent ahead to secure adequate housing accommodations for the top commanding officers.

Magnolia Manor was on the approach into town, and it had caught their eye. They had decided that the mansion would be more than adequate. When the detachment rode onto the grounds of the mansion, they were fired upon by two young soldiers with their make believe rifles. It was Charles and Richard, determined to hold their fortress at all costs. One of the Union soldiers had shouted at them, as they retreated and found refuge behind some shrubs.

No one in the mansion knew that the soldiers were outside until one of them had knocked on the door. Elizabeth was closest, so she responded to the knock. When she opened the door, she was surprised to see the Union soldier. He had asked if he could come inside, and Elizabeth let him in. She didn't ask him to be seated, she told him to wait while she went to get Mrs. Miller.

Mrs. Miller had been in her bedroom, and she didn't know what to think when Elizabeth told her that there was a Union soldier wanting to speak to her. She wondered out loud what he could possibly want. Suddenly, depressing possibilities had cropped up in her head. Did they have her husband as a prisoner, was he injured, was he dead, she had to know.

She went to the front door where the soldier had been waiting. He was polite enough to remove his cap when he saw Mrs. Miller. The soldier stated that three Union officers would be arriving in town within three or four hours, and that they need housing accommodations during their stay. Mrs. Miller was also informed that another Union officer that was already in the area would be joining them as well.

Mrs. Miller could think of only one question to ask. She said, "What does that have to do with me?" The soldier told her that the mansion would meet their needs, and it would be necessary for her to make other housing arrangements. Having stated his purpose, the soldier turned and walked away. Once he was at the bottom of the steps, he stopped, and turned around. He reiterated that the officers would arrive within the next three or four hours. Mrs. Miller asked the soldier, "Are you telling me that I have three or four hours to get out of my own house?" He simply replied, "Yes, three or four hours," and then he left.

Elizabeth and Sophia had been standing in the hallway and they heard the soldier's order. With everything that had happened at Magnolia Manor, Elizabeth felt like Mrs. Miller had been angered more at that moment, than ever before. She said that she had never heard such a bold contemptible request before in her entire life. Elizabeth said that she didn't know what to do. Mrs. Miller had said that she wasn't going to do anything; she wasn't going anywhere; and that she intended to be sitting in Magnolia Manor when they arrived. She had gone to her bedroom, flung herself across the bed, and put her head underneath a pillow.

Elizabeth and Sophia had stayed on the porch, and they watched as the small detachment rode away. When they went back into the mansion, they found Mrs. Miller lying across the bed. Elizabeth stood in the doorway, and told her that the soldiers had gone. Mrs. Miller pounded the bed with her fist, and then she sat up. She had thrown the pillow against the wall, and said that if she could cry, she would feel better, but she said that she couldn't cry anymore.

Elizabeth walked over to the bed, and sat down next to her. Mrs. Miller couldn't believe the things that had been going on, not just in her life, but everywhere. She had said that her husband and son were gone, she didn't know if they were dead or alive, and that she was about to be kicked out into the streets. She had to wonder if anything else could possibly go wrong, if it could, she didn't know what it could be. To her, it had seemed like everything that could happen had already happened, but then she reckoned that misery had no end short of dying.

The estimated arrival time of being within the next three or four hours had gotten closer to being six hours. Although the time of arrival had been extended, the soon to be homeless felt like the clock had been set on double time—the hour of eviction had been rapidly approaching. The simple act of waiting had gotten hard to do.

Elizabeth knew that Mrs. Miller had to be about as far down in the dumps as she could go. Still, she had to ask, but it had only been intended as an expression to show concern. When she had asked Mrs. Miller if she was alright, she said that if being backed into a corner with Satan standing in front of you was alright, then she guessed that she was doing just fine—she was angry.

Elizabeth thought that they had worried about everything that they could worry about, but she had never thought about not having a place to stay. Mrs. Miller said that she would just as soon die and get it over with. Elizabeth had been sitting on the bed with her, but she had stood up. Mrs. Miller reached out and took her by the hand. She asked her if she would please sit back down next to her, because she was afraid of being left alone.

Sophia had been looking out the window, and she saw the soldiers when they arrived. She stood and watched until they had dismounted, and started walking toward the mansion. Then, she went to tell Mrs. Miller. While Sophia was talking to Mrs. Miller, they heard a knock on the door. Mrs. Miller had asked Elizabeth to help her with her appearance, so that she would be more presentable. She had told Sophia to let them in, but stall them for a while until she got there. After Sophia had left the room, Mrs. Miller said that they could wait, because she was in no hurry to see them anyway.

Before Sophia had made it to the door, there was another knock. When she opened the door, each officer removed his hat. The officer that did the talking introduced himself as General Grant. He then introduced his fellow officers as General Sherman, General Logan and General McPherson. Sophia acknowledged each as they were introduced. She then stepped aside, held the door, and invited them in. She showed them to the parlor, and she had asked them to please be seated.

After they had sat down, Sophia asked if she could get them something to drink. General Grant asked that he be excused for being so coarse, and then he asked if she would happen to have any bourbon. Sophia said that she did have bourbon. When she looked at the other three, they said that they would have the same. Sophia had gone to get their drinks while they waited in the parlor. She returned with a bottle of Mr. Miller's fine bourbon, and four crystal glasses, all presented on a piece of Mrs. Miller's finest silverware.

When Sophia walked into the room with their drinks, all four stood up immediately, each assuming a posture that was more formal than informal. She had placed the silver tray on the table, and poured each a shot of bourbon. At that moment, Mrs. Miller entered the parlor with grace and charm as if she had just walked into a ballroom. Sophia had just exited the room.

Mrs. Miller introduced herself, and General Grant apologized. He said that they had mistakenly assumed that the other young lady was the lady of the house. Mrs. Miller didn't like the idea of them thinking that Sophia owned Magnolia Manor, or that she was the lady of the house. Yet, she remained calm, chose her words carefully, and with minimal clarification. She simply said that she just works here.

Mrs. Miller had asked that they please be seated. She sat in the chair near the window, closer to General Grant than the other three. She sat closer to him, because she had correctly assumed that he was the superior officer. She looked at General Grant without speaking. She felt that since they were gathered because of him, then he should be the first to speak. After a few moments of hesitation, he did. He explained that he, and his fellow officers needed accommodations, and that they would be using the mansion as their headquarters.

Since their estimated time of arrival had been delayed by more than two hours, it had given Mrs. Miller time to think. She had put together a plan that might allow the Miller household to coexist with four Union Generals. She realized that she could probably do more with poise and politeness than she could with pride and provocation.

Mrs. Miller was very polite, and while she was talking, she focused mostly on General Grant. She said that she had children, one of which was quite young. She said that she had never had to eke out a living, but no one could blame her for that; she could be tossed out, and they could roam the streets for a while, but they wouldn't last long.

When she had first started talking, General Grant had been holding on to his glass of bourbon, but as she kept talking, he placed it on the center piece in front of him. She had told him that if he would give the order, they would leave immediately, but first, she wanted to know if they could negotiate.

General Grant told her to continue. She explained that hers was a large house with more than adequate space. If he would be so kind as to let her and her family stay in the house, she promised that they would not interfere with him or his fellow officers in any way. If he would allow himself to submit to those terms, she said that she would be most grateful.

She hoped that he would accept her proposal, because the only alternative was to vacate the premises. Even though it was war, and he held the high ground, General Grant was willing to compromise. He told Mrs. Miller that when he walked through the door, he had no intentions of negotiating. He then said that if more people would learn to meet somewhere in the middle, maybe they wouldn't have to fight. He accepted her proposal.

Elizabeth and Sophia had been standing outside the parlor. They were close enough to hear the conversation, but far enough away not to be noticed. The discussion in the parlor affected them as much as it did anyone, and they were as anxious as Mrs. Miller. Whether or not they would be able to keep a roof over their heads depended on how well Mrs. Miller could haggle with General Grant.

Their unwanted guests had left, but they said that they would be back around nightfall. After they had gone, Sophia told Mrs. Miller that she should feel proud of herself. When Mrs. Miller asked why, Sophia told her that she had just made those Union Generals back down. Mrs. Miller said that she had to be nice while she was begging, but what she really wanted to do was use a hatchet on all four of them.

Mrs. Miller felt like it was so cruel, and so belligerent that they just walk in, and present the order that they were taking possession of her house. Shortly after they had moved in, Mrs. Miller concluded that she could tolerate General Grant, General Logan and General McPherson, because they had seemed to be more considerate of her needs, even under the conditions of war.

The longer they stayed at the mansion, the more Mrs. Miller came to dislike General Sherman. After a while, her dislike for him had turned to hate. She saw him as being coldhearted, and having very little respect for anything or anybody. She had jested that the only reason he obeyed his superiors was from fear that he would be shot if he didn't.

When the war had first started, the town's population decreased significantly, because so many men had enlisted in the army and left. However, the head count didn't stay low very long. The population had grown to more than ten thousand—maybe more based on who was doing the guess work—but most of them were Union troops. The quietness that was once common had been replaced by the constant rattle of wagons, caissons, and cannons moving up and down the streets. Sometimes they could even hear the big guns roar as they discharged off in the distance. It was all more than they had ever expected. Elizabeth had said that it seemed like a bad dream, but if it was, she would like to wake up.

Mrs. Miller had designated the room assignments for their unwanted guests. They had been quartered in separate rooms, but close to each other. Elizabeth and Sophia went about doing their chores as usual. Even with the big changes that had taken place around the mansion, they still followed their normal routine.

The Generals regularly discussed military operations in the parlor. They ate with their troops, and they never put any demands on anyone in the house. The biggest problem had been just knowing that they were there, and having no idea about when they would leave.

Elizabeth and Sophia had a bit more work to do since there were four more adults in the mansion. At the end of the day, Sophia always made sure that the Generals had access to their favorite beverage which she had understood to be bourbon. Mrs. Miller felt like the stench of General Grant's cigar would be around long after he had gone—should he ever leave. She said that he had one in his mouth more often than not, and she wondered if he even removed it when he went to bed at night.

Sophia had been tidying things up in General Grant's room when he walked in on her. Her back was turned to the door, and he had startled her. When she turned around, he apologized, and said that he had returned to get some things that he needed before leaving. While searching for whatever, and probably just to make conversation, he asked Sophia if she had been frightened about having so many soldiers around. She said that it didn't bother her as long as they don't start fighting out there in the streets. He told her that she shouldn't worry too much about that, because he didn't see any reason for anything like that to happen.

As he rummaged through his belongings, he told Sophia that he had assumed that she was a white woman when they first met, and therefore, that the mansion belonged to her. Sophia looked at him, but she didn't say anything, because she didn't know what to say to a statement such as that. He was still curious. He asked if it was her father that was white or was it her mother. She said that her father was white. As he was leaving the room, he told her that it would be around sundown when they returned. As he walked away, Sophia stood and watched until he had left the mansion.

Grant, Sherman, Logan and McPherson were all still standing on the front porch when Mrs. Miller stepped outside. Directing her remarks to General Grant, she asked him if they would please dine with her at the mansion when they returned. He thanked her for the invitation, but noted that it would probably be around sundown. Mrs. Miller said that she would be expecting them.

Mrs. Miller had been wondering how long it would be before they would pack up and leave, but she dared not to ask. She had told Elizabeth that there would be four unwanted guests joining her for supper. She said that she didn't know why she had invited them, but she had. Elizabeth was sure that the invitation had been issued, because Mrs. Miller felt obliged to General Grant since he had spared them the hardship of being tossed out into the streets.

Even though he had invaded her privacy, and in effect, had taken over her home, she did still have a home. Had General Grant's attitude been more like that of General Shearman, they would have had to eat slop before Mrs. Miller would have fed them. On the other hand, Mrs. Miller knew that if General Grant's attitude had been like that of General Shearman, she would have been the one that would have had to eat slop.

Elizabeth and Sophia had both noticed that Mrs. Miller definitely had a fondness for General Grant. Even though the dining invitation had more than likely been her way of saying thank you for not throwing them out, Elizabeth wondered if it had really been necessary. Her opinion was that Mrs. Miller shouldn't have to thank anyone for letting her stay in her own home. It didn't seem right to her, but she hadn't seen much that was right in a long time.

Not a single hour passed that Mrs. Miller didn't think about her husband, but it had become evident that leaving was the right thing for him to do. Otherwise, the Generals would have taken him as their prisoner, and his mansion along with its contents would be the spoils that they would share. She had heard stories about plundering and destruction of property all around town, but so far, it hadn't happened at Magnolia Manor. In her mind, it had to be because of General Grant.

Many that had valuable items had taken the precaution of hiding them prior to the Union troops' arrival. Mrs. Miller didn't bother. She had left everything where it was before the war had started. She didn't think about silver, and crystals, and imported china. Instead, she thought about her husband, and her son—she wanted them back more than anything else.

Whenever the Generals returned to the mansion, they would always knock before entering, instead of just walking in as if the place had always belonged to them. Mrs. Miller had noticed that they had the decency to do so. Yet, she had supposed that General Sherman probably knocked on the door only because he was obeying the orders of General Grant. Had it been left up to him, she guessed that he would have blown a hole through the wall with cannon, and then walk in after the dust had settled.

When the Generals returned at the end of the day, they all arrived together. Sophia met them at the door. She told them that they would find water and fresh towels on the back porch. Sophia had gone to tell Mrs. Miller that they had returned. When she saw Elizabeth, she told her that they were washing up, and that they were a filthy looking bunch.

Unlike Mrs. Miller and Elizabeth, Sophia had found all four Generals to be interesting, and she favored the opportunity to be in their presence. Conversely, she had also noticed that the Generals didn't seem to mind when she was in their presence. She had found them to be very respectful, and even though she was a slave, it had become evident to her that they didn't treat her as one.

Although they had been corrected, Sophia wondered if they were respectful because they were still stuck on their earlier presumption that she was white, or if it was because they really were gentlemen. Whatever their reason, she loved being treated like a lady. She felt good whenever she walked into the room, and four Union Generals were quickly on their feet.

Sophia had gone to inform Mrs. Miller that her guests had arrived, and that supper would be served shortly.

They had just finished washing up, and were in the process of knocking some of the dust from their uniforms. Sophia walked out with something to wash the dust from their throat. She had placed the tray on the table, and they watched as she poured a shot of bourbon for each. When she had finished, General Sherman stepped aside and held the door for her as she went back inside.

Mrs. Miller had been in the dining room, making sure that everything was exactly as it should be. She had gotten two bottles of wine, and placed them on the dining room table. When she joined the Generals on the porch, her thoughts were the same as Sophia's. They looked as if they had been working in a flour mill all day. Beneath the dust, she could see their uniforms, but it was hard to tell if they were Union blue or Confederate gray. Yet, she knew that it was not of their choosing.

Mrs. Miller was finely attired, dressed as if her evening appointment was to be with her husband attending a formal affair at the State House. When the Generals saw her, they were awed by the stylishness of their host. At the same time, they recognized the inappropriateness of their own dress.

Politely, General Grant had acknowledged her classy presentation, and he apologized for their inability to present themselves more appropriately. She said that she understood, and then she stepped aside and held the door for them, as they made their way to the dining room.

Elizabeth and Sophia would see to the kids eating later. At the table, the Generals remained standing until Mrs. Miller had been seated, and only then did they join her. Sophia could tell that Mrs. Miller loved being treated like a lady by the Union officers, even if one of them had to be General Sherman. When dinner was over, General Grant thanked Mrs. Miller for allowing them to enjoy the evening in her presence. General Sherman, General McPherson and General Logan each expressed their appreciation.

General Grant had asked Mrs. Miller if she would join them in the parlor, and he promised not to discuss military tactics. She smiled and said that she would. When they had all been seated, Sophia placed a bottle of bourbon along with a bottle of sherry on the table in front of them. General Grant did the honor of pouring, but not before asking Mrs. Miller if she cared for anything. She declined, and said that an occasional glass of wine at dinner had always been enough for her.

While they were talking, General Grant finally got around to asking about Mr. Miller. He told Mrs. Miller that he was aware that her husband was a member of the State Legislature. Mrs. Miller had already considered that he would check around until he found out who owned the mansion that he had chosen to occupy. Since he already knew, she acknowledged that he had been correct.

General Grant had asked Mrs. Miller if her husband was a soldier. She said that his sixtieth birthday was behind him, and she imagined that he would be more of a burden than an asset as a soldier. She said that he had left town when he found out that the Union troops were headed their way; he was afraid that he might be taken prisoner. General Grant said that he had made a wise decision.

Mrs. Miller told her guests that she had a son that volunteered as soon as the war started, and she wondered if she would ever see him again. General Grant said that there were a lot of mothers wondering the same thing. He said that he would be glad when the war was over, and that he wondered how things had gotten so far out of control. They chose to avoid any further discussions regarding Mr. Miller, or the war.

Most of the talking had been an exchange between Mrs. Miller and General Grant. Sherman, Logan and McPherson spoke occasionally, but mostly, they just listened. After a while, the conversation had shifted to Sophia. General Grant said that the first time that they saw her they had presumed that she was the lady of the house. Mrs. Miller said that she was not surprised, and no harm had been done.

General Logan had said that it seemed to him like it was common for slave owners to have children by slave women. Mrs. Miller had agreed with him, but it was definitely something that she would rather not have to discuss. Nonetheless, General Logan pursued the issue even further. He had said that it must be hard for southern white women to have to deal with something like that.

After he had made the statement, Mrs. Miller looked at General Grant. However, General Grant didn't see her, because he had been looking at General Logan. Mrs. Miller had noticed that General Grant's eyes had told General Logan to discontinue with his line of talk. Since the question had already been asked, Mrs. Miller willingly agreed that he had been correct with his assessment, but she said that there wasn't much that could be done about it.

It was almost impossible for Mrs. Miller to understand General Sherman. She had told Elizabeth that he didn't seem to have any more feelings for things than a rock; he didn't talk much; she could never guess what he might be thinking; and he always seemed to be a bit edgy. It was her opinion that he didn't care about anything but fighting.

Mrs. Miller freely engaged in casual conversation with General Grant, and with Generals Logan and McPherson. Still, she favored General Grant more than the others. As for General Sherman, she only spoke to him whenever she had to, and that was very seldom.

Each morning after they had left the mansion would be when Mrs. Miller, Elizabeth and Sophia would swap opinions about them. The opinion expressed most often had been Mrs. Miller telling about how much she hated General Sherman. She had the same wish every time he left the house—that she would never see him again. She allowed that she should probably be nicer to him, so that he wouldn't torch the place on his way out of town.

Mrs. Miller told Elizabeth about the false assumption that the Generals had when they first arrived. They had assumed that Sophia was the lady of the house. She said that they must have felt like she had been insulted over the mix-up, because General Grant had apologized again. Elizabeth had never been surprised over the mix-up, and she knew that Mrs. Miller shouldn't have been either. It hadn't been the first time that someone had knocked on the door, and assumed the same thing.

The next morning after the Generals had left the mansion, Elizabeth asked Mrs. Miller if it would be alright if she and Sophia washed their dirty clothes. Mrs. Miller conceded that they were an awful sight. She had told Elizabeth that it should be alright, and if they didn't like it, maybe they would pack up and leave.

After finishing their chores, Elizabeth and Sophia went about gathering up their guests' grubby clothes. They all had more than one uniform, but none of them were clean. Sophia felt like they must come in at the end of the day wearing a dirty outfit, and then find another dirty one to change into for the next day.

They had washed their uniforms, and had hung them out to dry. Once they were dry, Sophia used the smoothing iron to remove the wrinkles, and she had put creases where they were supposed to be. When she had finished, she folded them neatly, and placed them in the appropriate room.

The town's population seemed to keep on increasing. The increasing numbers included the arrival of more Union troops, along with a massive influx of slaves that had walked away from the plantations. Some slaves had walked away, because there was no one there to make them stay. Therefore, the door to freedom had been opened, and the only thing that they had to do was walk through. Others had left because they had no choice. Their owners had told them to leave, because they could no longer feed them.

Gins that processed the cotton for shipment had been demolished by whatever means possible. Cotton had been their main source of income, but production had declined sharply. Farm equipment had been destroyed, and most things that would burn had become ashes.

Union troops had assembled most of the slaves, or what used to be slaves, in the southwest sector of town. In the beginning, there were only a few, and the military had provided them with food. However, as the head count increased, food supplies dwindled, and the process ended. Any edible crops that remained in the fields had been harvested, and consumed by whoever got there first. The same was true for livestock. Planting anything edible was almost useless, because it would more than likely end up in someone else's stomach. After a while, it had gotten to the point where the definition of food was anything that they could get to stay down.

Eventually, there were so many used to be slaves quartered in the southwest sector that living conditions had become deplorable. The lack of adequate housing, and food supplies coupled with the lack of sanitation had resulted in rampant diseases, and death among the population.

Every person assembled there had at one time or another, dreamed of being free. After being free, they had to wonder if it might be better if they could go back to the old ways; freedom had been like stepping out of one hellhole and into a bigger one. Their dreams had turned to nightmares, because they never thought that freedom could be so painful.

They had been placed in the southwest sector of town, a place that literally became a swamp every time it rained. The drafty one room log cabin on the plantation had been given up in exchange for a lesser shanty located at the edge of a swamp on the backside of Hell. Their little isolated burrow never found a place on the map, but it had been named Frog Town—with due consideration, the name may have been applicable.

Elizabeth had relatives and friends that had been quartered on the southwest side, and it was depressing for her to think about what life had to be like for them. She had been to that part of town to see for herself, but no sooner than she had seen it, she wished that she hadn't. Almost every day, they had to take at least one to the cemetery, and then wait for a day or so to see who would be next. Even though she and Sophia had food to eat and a roof over their heads, they had nothing of their own, and therefore, nothing to give other than a show of compassion and a constant prayer.

Mrs. Miller had assumed that all of their slaves were gone, because there was nothing to keep them from leaving. However, Alfred had chosen to be there until the end. He was at the mansion every day—weather permitting—maintaining the grounds, and keeping everything as neat and as beautiful as ever. She had told him that if she could walk outside, and be blinded to everything except the yard, she would be herself again.

The children didn't seem to be bothered by the war, or what was going on around town. Charles and Richard had been relentless with their attacks, firing their make believe rifles at every Yankee that came down the street—hit and run tactics. Soldiers just looked at them and laughed—saying boo would have scared them senseless. Yet, they never surrendered, and they had made the decision to keep it up until the last Yankee soldier had left town.

It was late when General Grant and his associates returned to the mansion. Mrs. Miller was upstairs, but Sophia had heard them when they knocked on the door. She let them in, and as they stood in the entryway, she told them that since it was late, she had gone ahead and placed something for them to drink in their rooms.

The next morning, Elizabeth and Sophia were up and about as usual. The aroma of Elizabeth's fresh coffee brewing on the stove spread throughout the house. General Grant had walked into the dining area and he got their attention. General Sherman, General Logan and General McPherson walked in right behind him. The four of them were standing there in their clean, wrinkle free Union blues.

Elizabeth didn't know it, but she was looking at four of the country's top ranking military officers. She told them that she and Sophia had gotten tired of seeing them come in everyday looking like something that the dogs had dragged in. Her words may have sounded brazen coming from a slave, but they had not been perceived as such. Sophia filled their coffee cups, and they sat on the back porch. When they were ready to leave, General Grant thanked Elizabeth and Sophia. He told them that it felt good to be in clean clothes.

General Grant was about to mount up when he gave the reins to one of his aides, and walked back to the mansion. Mrs. Miller had been standing on the porch. General

Grant removed his hat, and asked her if she would do him the honor of accompanying him during the evening while he reviewed the troops. Mrs. Miller was stunned by his invitation, but at the same time, she felt honored by his courteous gesture. She didn't even know what he meant by reviewing the troops, but she had told him that she would be delighted.

Mrs. Miller had heard that the latest estimate on the number of Union troops in town was about fifteen thousand with more on the way. People in town wondered why their little spot on the map had become so important. She told Elizabeth that General Grant had invited her to accompany him while he reviewed his troops later during the day. Elizabeth wanted to know what he had said when she told him that she wouldn't do it. Mrs. Miller said that she didn't tell him that she wouldn't do it, but rather, she had accepted his invitation.

Elizabeth and Mrs. Miller started an exchange that had a little more attitude in it than usual. Elizabeth had asked Mrs. Miller what she thought it was going to look like with her riding around with a Union officer looking at his soldiers. Mrs. Miller said that it would look like she's riding around with a Union officer looking at his soldiers. Elizabeth got bold enough to tell her that she must be out of her mind, and doing something like that would just give people something to talk about. Mrs. Miller said that she didn't care much about what people talked about anymore. Besides that, she said that it was none of their business what she did.

During the afternoon, General Grant arrived back at the mansion to pick up Mrs. Miller. He was escorted by a small detachment of troops. Mrs. Miller commented on the beautiful rig that she would be riding in. The black carriage was drawn by two well matched, and handsomely harnessed steeds. Mrs. Miller told Elizabeth that it all looked so formal. Elizabeth said that he had probably stolen the carriage and the horses from somebody around town, because soldiers don't ride around in something that fancy.

Mrs. Miller was finely attired, and so was General Grant. He was wearing a clean, wrinkle free Union blue uniform, one that had creases where they were supposed to be. The beautiful carriage and horses along with their military escort had made it all appear so correct. He had stepped down from the carriage, and he had started walking toward the mansion. Mrs. Miller knew how to be formal. She remained on the porch and waited as he approached. When General Grant was close enough, he reached for her hand to assist her down the steps.

Elizabeth, Sophia, Charles and Richard had been standing on the porch watching. Looking at Charles and Richard, General Grant wondered aloud if those two young troopers would like to go along. He had noticed that they were in the yard every day attacking his troops.

As soon as he had heard the words, Charles started making his way down the steps and toward the carriage. Richard had his doubts—he didn't know if the invitation included him—he was still standing on the porch. When he looked up at Sophia, she gave him a nudge—one that had almost pushed him off the porch, but he knew what it meant. They had climbed aboard, and then left the mansion with a show of style that would surely attract attention, and that was alright with Mrs. Miller.

The troops were stationed on the outskirts of town. When General Grant arrived with his guests, all were in full military dress, and ready for inspection. Mrs.

Miller had never seen anything like it before in her life. Thousands of soldiers, lined up like statues, and in perfect military formation.

When the carriage stopped, General Grant stepped down, and after an exchange of salutes, four enlisted men walked up leading a mount, one each for General Grant, General Sherman, General Logan and one for General McPherson. The Generals mounted up, and at a walk, they rode their horses through the rank and file. Mrs. Miller and the children remained in the carriage with the driver. It had been a first for her, and it had been so impressive, and so unforgettable.

It was almost sundown when they returned to Magnolia Manor. When they arrived, Elizabeth and Sophia had supper on the table. Mrs. Miller, her Union guests and Charles and Richard all sat at the table together. Elizabeth and Sophia listened as Mrs. Miller talked about the grand ceremony that they had seen.

The next morning, Mrs. Miller told Elizabeth and Sophia about how glad she was that General Grant had invited her to accompany him. She wondered if it was something that they had to do, and he wanted her to see it, or if maybe it had been a display that was set up to try and make amends for what they had done to her. Whatever the motive, it had been very impressive.

The Union troops had built a fort less than two miles northwest of town—Mrs. Miller had noticed it. The fort was located on property owned by Austin Miller. The structure was unconventional in that it was pretty much like a big pond. Dirt from what would be the inside of the compound had been dug up, and used to build an earthen embankment that would be the wall of the fort. When it was completed, the circular earthen embankment was about twelve feet high with an inside area of about two acres.

On the south side of the fort, they had a trench that was about five feet deep, and referred to as the rifle pit. Soldiers could stand in the pit and fire at the approaching enemy. The trench extended to a stream that was located about three hundred yards downhill from the fort. If under fire, and if it became necessary, soldiers could travel back and forth to the stream to get water without being seen or shot.

Mrs. Miller had the masterminds behind all of the military activity in her house. She had asked General Grant if he was about to turn their town into a battlefield. He assured her that it would not be a battlefield, and that all of the activity was more of a precautionary measure than anything. In addition, he said that it was a good location for deploying troops and supplies.

Mrs. Miller and her guests were in the parlor. She had told General Grant that the fort located northwest of town was on land that belonged to her and her husband. He said that he didn't know that, but that it had been built as a deterrent—more or less for just in case. Still, he apologized for having placed the fort on their property. He explained that the site had been selected because of its strategic location, but that the fort did nothing to devalue the property.

Mrs. Miller knew that General Grant was not going to remove the fort, and she figured that he probably knew who the property belonged to. She had confronted him just to let him know that she hadn't been kept completely in the dark. As far as the town becoming a battlefield, she didn't think that southern troops would engage the enemy within the confines of their own town. She even told General Grant that it would be ridiculous. Yet, every now and then, she seemed to relish the idea of hounding her guests for a while.

It had been raining all night, still General Grant and his team left the mansion early the next morning. When they returned at the end of the day, they were covered with mud. Mrs. Miller asked whether or not they had eaten and they said yes. She didn't have a storehouse full of foodstuffs like in the past, but before retiring for the evening, Mrs. Miller extended an invitation for the Generals to have breakfast with her the following morning.

Sophia had already placed a bottle of bourbon and some glasses in the parlor for them. She always knew the routine. They would walk in, spend a few minutes talking with Mrs. Miller, and then sit in the parlor, undoubtedly discussing the war. However, before going to the parlor, they changed their muddy clothes to keep from turning the mansion into a pig sty. After they had gone to the parlor, Elizabeth and Sophia washed their uniforms, and hung them near the cook stove to dry.

Sophia had been downstairs checking on the blue uniforms that she had drying near the stove. While she was there, she stopped by the parlor. It wasn't necessary, but she stopped anyway. She realized that Mrs. Miller had gone to bed, and she knew that Elizabeth was in her room.

Sophia entered the parlor, but not slowly as if she might be apologizing for interrupting. She entered in a flash that created a breeze in her wake. She did it with flair and confidence as if Magnolia Manor did belong to her. Maybe not, but chances are that she had been flirting.

When Sophia walked into the room, Generals Grant, Sherman, Logan, and McPherson all stood up, and it was exactly what she had hoped that they would do. They had stood up simply because she had entered the room. Since the first day of their arrival—when they thought that she was the lady of the house—she had been treated with respect. She stood there commanding the attention of four Union Generals, and she was in love with the feeling. She had put on an impeccable performance, and she didn't miss a cue, because it was she that had choreographed the scene.

She didn't ask if they needed anything before she went to bed. Instead, she took center stage and asked will the Generals require anything before she retired for the evening. General Grant said that they seemed to have everything that they needed, but he thanked her for being so thoughtful. When she had said goodnight and walked away, they remained standing, and didn't move until she was out of sight. She knew that they didn't move, because while walking away, she could see them from the corner of her eye. They just stood there, and they kept watching.

It had gotten late when Sophia finished ironing out the wrinkles on their almost dry uniforms. She was the only one in the mansion that hadn't gone to bed. She folded their clothes and she had placed them on the floor just outside the door to each one's room without disturbing them.

Mrs. Miller was up early the next morning, because of her breakfast engagement. When her guests entered the dining room, they were sharply attired in their Union blues and they got Mrs. Miller's attention. She told them that they looked a lot better than they did the first time that they had dined together. General Grant said that it was all because of Elizabeth and Sophia.

It had become obvious, not only to Mrs. Miller, but to her guests as well, that the food supplies at Magnolia Manor had gotten low. Still, Mrs. Miller saw to it that they had access to the best that she could offer. No one had ever complained, and no apologizes had been necessary.

While sitting at the table, General Grant informed Mrs. Miller that they would be leaving town after breakfast, and therefore, they would be giving back her home. Even under the prevailing conditions, and like always, General Grant remembered to be courteous. He admitted that they had forced their way in, and infringed on their privacy. Yet, he told Mrs. Miller that she had been a most gracious host in spite of their unwanted presence. Mrs. Miller was glad that they were finally leaving, but she realized that having them there had been nothing like what she had expected.

After gathering their belongings, General Grant and the others exited the mansion. A trooper held their mounts as each one threw their satchel across their horse's back, and then mounted up. Mrs. Miller, Elizabeth and Sophia stood on the porch, and watched as each officer gave them an informal salute, and then rode away.

A long column of troops had already started moving down the street. With General Grant leading the way, they made their horses strike a gallop as they headed toward the front of the column. The line of soldiers seemed endless as they rode out of town.

Troops were still moving passed when one of the supply wagons pulled in at the mansion—as close to the porch as possible. Curiosity had Mrs. Miller, Elizabeth and Sophia standing on the porch watching. Two troopers climbed down from the wagon. One of them told Mrs. Miller that General Grant had left orders for them to leave their cargo at the mansion. They unloaded a large quantity of food supplies from the wagon, placed them on the front porch, and then drove away. Among the hoard were two cases of bourbon whiskey—the same brand that had been dispensed at Magnolia Manor. When Mrs. Miller noticed it, she said that they had thought of everything.

After they had gone, Mrs. Miller said that their guests were better men than perhaps she had realized. Elizabeth agreed, she said that they had left a lot of food, and they could certainly use it. Mrs. Miller knew that their food supplies had to be getting low, but she didn't know how low. Elizabeth had been telling her that they had more than they really had just so that she would have one less thing to worry about.

At last, Mrs. Miller had her house back. She and Elizabeth sat on the porch just to while away the time. She admitted that she was glad that they were gone, but if she had to share her house with someone, she was glad that it had been General Grant rather than some of the other no accounts in uniform.

They had been sitting on the porch for a long time as soldiers, supply wagons, cannons and caissons kept moving past the mansion. Elizabeth wondered how far back it was to the end of the line. Mrs. Miller said that they would find out, because for the rest of the day they were going to sit back, watch them go by, and do nothing.

Elizabeth knew that Mrs. Miller was glad that General Grant and the others had finally left her house. Elizabeth's attitude regarding their guests had been about the same as that of Mrs. Miller. Even though they had all been respectful enough, she was just glad that they had packed up and were finally gone.

Sophia's attitude had not only different, it was completely opposite of that of Elizabeth and Mrs. Miller. Sophia didn't mind having them at the mansion, because they were polite and courteous, and she didn't think that they had been any trouble at all. Elizabeth had said that they were nothing but trouble, but she wasn't biased with her opinion. She had blamed both the Union and the Confederacy for the big mess that was going on. She said that the black people that were stuck on the southwest side of town, and starving to death were there because of them.

Elizabeth felt like Mrs. Miller was about to lose her mind when they had first been told that General Grant and the others were taking her house. After a while, she had a change of heart, and she had decided that maybe they weren't so bad after all. Elizabeth told Sophia that it was a good thing that she had settled down and taken on a different mindset. If she hadn't, she said that they would have had to lock her up somewhere.

In the end, when they had a chance to think about it, they decided that they were definitely better off with them staying at the mansion than not having them. They hadn't been bothered by thieves or troublemakers. Their presence had made them feel completely safe, and they hoped that General Grant had threatened somebody should any harm come to the residence of Magnolia Manor.

Fifteen

The town was in a mess, but the grounds around Magnolia Manor had stayed well-manicured, thanks to Alfred. He had been busy for several weeks trying to cut enough wood to carry them through the winter. Mrs. Miller told him that she would pay a fair wage if he could find someone to help with the work. Getting someone to help wouldn't be a problem. The town had a lot of hungry people around—white and black—looking for something to do to earn a dollar, or for that matter, willing to just work for food.

Back when Mrs. Miller had first started having trouble with depression, Elizabeth made it a point to be close by. Then, however, she got to where sometimes Elizabeth had to be with her out of necessity. They would sit on the back porch, and lose themselves in talking about what used to be. Yet, they always had to come back to today, because all of the yesterdays had gone, and the todays were so ugly that they couldn't be ignored. Mrs. Miller wondered if her life had been such that she was then paying for the things that she had done.

Elizabeth was a stronger woman than Mrs. Miller, undoubtedly due to their different backgrounds. Elizabeth had been hardened, simply because, she had always been a slave. She could take what she had, and make the most of it. Mrs. Miller had never known what it was like to want for something, and not be able to have it. She didn't care for the less expensive, and she had always opted for the best that money could buy. On the other hand, Elizabeth had never had much of anything, and the things that she wanted were not even for sale, things like freedom, peace of mind, equality ... just basic human rights.

Elizabeth had been bothered by the chaotic goings on just like Mrs. Miller, but even with the chaos, Elizabeth's life had been pretty much the same, even with the war. She didn't have much to lose, and she wouldn't let herself be disappointed by making wishes that wouldn't come true. She just tried to make it through each day, and then take the wait and see attitude for the next—it hadn't been much different from what her entire life had been like.

Constantly, Mrs. Miller worried about her husband and her son, Albert. Every once in a while, she would get a letter, or a message by word of mouth that Albert was alright, but never anything regarding her husband. He had headed south when he left town with the Confederate troops. She knew that he couldn't keep up with soldiers that were on the move day in and day out. He had the foresight to take some money with him when he left, but she doubted that he had any left. She had considered that he may have even left the country, maybe for South America, or maybe one of the islands off the coast. She wondered if perhaps he might have changed his name, and then blended in as being just another old man feeling the effects of hard times.

Too often, townspeople had to listen to the sound of gun shots as fighting took place not so far away. Thousands of troops had been mobilized in the Savannah, Tennessee area—blue and gray just waiting for the order to charge.

Two days, Mrs. Miller, Elizabeth and Sophia sat on the porch and listened to the continuous roar of cannons—rumbling like thunder—over at Shiloh. Mrs. Miller—rattled and worn—wondered if Albert was still on his feet, because she had gotten word that he was there. She hoped that those at home—the noncombatants like herself, Elizabeth, Sophia and all of the others—had not accustomed themselves to the sights and sounds of war, so that they looked and listened just to be entertained.

When it started, it was impossible for anyone to believe that the war would last so long. It seemed like they had been fighting everywhere, and it looked like they had as well. In the beginning, the South felt like they had the greater advantage by fighting in their own arena, and on their own turf; they felt like the balance of victory had been tilted in their direction from the very start. They would quickly thrash the enemy into submission, and then dictate the articles of surrender.

For a long time, fighting in their own arena had given them the advantage. As the war progressed, the Union army kept them in their arena. After years of fighting, the South had used up everything that they had to fight with. In the end, their arena had crumbled, and caved in around them. The South had collapsed, and what used to be was no more. Everything lay in ruins. Their only recourse was to put down their weapons, and go home—they couldn't fight anymore, because they had so little to fight with.

When peace had been declared, families waited for their loved ones to return, knowing all the time that some wouldn't, but always hoping that theirs would. Months after the war had ended, men still wandered in, because they had to travel so far, and most of the time on foot. Some had been hindered, because of what the war had done to them, and therefore, unable to travel but a few miles each day. Yet slowly, and with many on makeshift crutches, they followed the road that led to home.

Wives and mothers, and old men and children sat on the porch, and looked down the road, each hoping and praying that the next person that they saw rounding that curve would be him coming home. When it had been long enough for them to realize that he had probably been one of the unfortunate casualties of war, they kept waiting and watching.

Some returned home, and when they walked into the house, they were barely recognizable, because they had been forever changed. Scarred, crippled and short of mind, they realized that it would have been better to settle their differences at the conference table, but then, it was the wisdom of hindsight.

Many had been teenage boys when they left home, and their fighting had been limited to subtle licks passed back and forth with their brother. When they returned home, they were hard to the core, but with ghastly memories that had made them grow up too soon; the ugliness of war had been scored in their minds like ruts from a steel wheeled wagon going down a muddy road—there to haunt them forever.

Albert, had distinguished himself at the battle of Shiloh, and he had earned the rank of Captain. He returned home within a few days after the war had ended. When he walked up to the door of the mansion, he didn't bother to knock; he just opened the door and walked in.

He had his back turned while closing the door. When he had turned round, Charles and Richard were looking at him as he stood there in his Confederate grays. The boys had no idea as to who he was—his facial features had been disguised by a stubby beard, because he hadn't shaved in so long. To them, he was just another soldier, but he was one that they had seen many times—he just looked different.

Albert didn't say anything, nor did the boys. They just stood there staring at each other. Albert knew that one had to be his brother, and the other had to be Richard, but he didn't know which was which. Instead of trying to figure it out, he knelt down, and put his arms around both of them.

Albert was squatting down talking to Charles and Richard when Mrs. Miller walked into the room. When he saw her he stood up, and she hurried to him. She had put her arms around him, and said that she was afraid that she wouldn't see him again.

Elizabeth and Sophia could hear them talking, and they had gone to see who it was. When she had recognized Albert, Elizabeth hugged him first, and then she gave him to Sophia. When Albert took his arms from around Sophia, he said that he had been trying to identify Charles and Richard. Placing her hand on their heads, Sophia told him which was which.

After a while, Richard and Charles remembered Albert, but his memory was vague to both of them.

Charles had said that when he and Richard saw Albert, they thought that the soldiers had come back. Albert asked what soldiers they were talking about, but Mrs. Miller said that they could talk about that some other time.

Albert had looked around, but he hadn't seen Mr. Miller. When he had asked about him, Mrs. Miller said that she didn't know where he was. She explained why he had left town, and that she hadn't heard from him since the day that he left. Albert was sure that it wouldn't be long before he made it back, getting around was just slow. Like his mother, he had no idea as to where Mr. Miller had gone, or if he was even still alive. He had been telling her things to help keep her hopes up, and his as well.

Later that day, Sophia told Elizabeth that it was a good thing that none of Mrs. Miller's friends were in the house to see Albert's confusion over Charles and Richard. As it was, it didn't bother Mrs. Miller, and she understood why Albert didn't know one from the other. Whenever they were off at a distance, she had the same problem, and she had been seeing them every day.

Albert had been off to war, and he knew what it was like. Many times he had wondered if he would make it home, but every soldier that had ever gone into battle had probably wondered the same thing. When the war had ended, he was part of a group that had been plodding along in the direction of home. During the journey, one of his friends had separated from the group, and he had headed off in another direction all by himself.

Thinking that his friend may not have been paying attention, or was perhaps confused, Albert caught up with him, and told him that he had been going in the wrong direction. His friend said that he wasn't going home; he was going somewhere else, so that he could live alone. Albert asked why, and he said that every time that they had engaged the enemy, he had always asked God to keep him alive. With his face permanently disfigured, he said that God had always answered his prayers, and kept him alive. Yet, he wasn't going home, because his wife and children wouldn't be able to sit across the table from him and eat without getting sick at the stomach when they looked at him.

In every battle that they had fought, he said that he had always been upfront, willing to kill, and hoping that he wouldn't be; then, however, he would like to die, but he was afraid to pull the trigger on himself. He had asked Albert to tell his family that he had been killed in battle. Then he handed his saber over to him, and asked if he would present it to his wife. Just before they parted ways, he said that if he had it to do again, he wouldn't ask God to keep him alive—it would be easier to die on the battlefield.

Day after day, Mrs. Miller fretted about her husband. She felt like it had been long enough for him to make it back home. She worried about him while the war had been going on, but when it had ended, she worried even more. She worried more, because her thoughts were no longer about him hiding out from Union troops. Instead, she had started thinking that he was no longer alive. Whenever she didn't have anything to do, which was quite often, she sat on the porch and kept watch. Anyone headed in the direction of Magnolia Manor, and bearing the slightest resemblance to her husband would get her attention. Yet, it would always be the wrong man.

Mrs. Miller had sent Alfred into town with the horse and buggy to pick up some supplies. Stores had a few things, but not much. She told him to get what he could find. She had gone back to doing what occupied most of her time, looking down the street with the hope of seeing her husband. After a while, she saw Alfred returning to the mansion. He was a good distance away, but she had recognized the rig.

She had gone to her bedroom to be alone, and she stood near the window looking outside. Minutes later when she heard footsteps, she turned around, and standing in the doorway was her husband. He had caught a ride home in the buggy with Alfred. When she saw him, she didn't say a single word, and she didn't rush over to put her arms around him. Instead, she kept standing near the window, looking at him and crying out loud. Elizabeth and Sophia stood in the doorway behind Mr. Miller and watched.

Mr. Miller had walked over and put his arms around her. They held each other, and the only sound in the room was that coming from Mrs. Miller—she couldn't stop crying. He kept on holding her, and he let her cry. After she had taken her arms from around him, he turned around, and looked at Elizabeth. She had been standing in the doorway, wiping the tears from her own eyes—she was glad that he had come home.

Alfred had sent Charles and Richard inside, and they were holding on to Sophia when they saw Mr. Miller. The man that they were looking at seemed almost like a stranger to them, but they soon figured out that he was their father. However, Mr. Miller had been puzzled, and he stood there looking at them. He was just like Albert, he didn't know which was which, but he did know that both were his.

He had sat down on the side of the bed, and Sophia pushed both boys closer to him. He leaned over, and held them close to his chest, and kissed the top of their heads. He still didn't know one from the other, but he didn't care, he was just glad to have them next to him. He had asked about Albert, and the other kids. Mrs. Miller told him that Albert was fine, and that they had all gone into town.

Mr. Miller had stood up to give Elizabeth a hug. He then looked at Sophia, but he didn't know if he should or shouldn't. Since he couldn't make up his mind, Sophia stepped forward, and put her arms around him. In spite of everything, she too was glad that he had come home.

Sophia had told Elizabeth that when she was pregnant with Richard, Mrs. Miller told her that they might someday get over what Mr. Miller had done to them. She guessed that maybe that day had come. Elizabeth said that Mrs. Miller was happy that the family was back together, even if it was a little mixed up.

Elizabeth was glad that Mr. Miller had returned, because it would rid her of the mental overload that had been hers to bear. With him back at home, she wouldn't have to pass her burden on to him. Instead, she could simply cast it aside, and let it fly away to go somewhere and disappear. She had supposed that maybe things would get back to normal. As soon as she had thought about things getting back to normal, she wondered if things would ever get back to the way they had once been. At that moment, things were in a big mess. Every time she looked outside, she was reminded of the ugliness that had swept across the country, and left the dead and dying in its wake.

Mr. and Mrs. Miller had been sitting out back, partly because the view from the back porch was better than the view from the front—the town was too ugly to look at and kick back. While he had been gone, he said that he had been able to get bits and pieces of information from time to time about what had been going on back at home. It was like a jigsaw puzzle, but he could put most of it together, and then imagine the rest. Whenever he got news of things, it was old, but still it was news.

He had already assumed that his plantations and other properties had all been destroyed. He was surprised when Alfred picked him up in town, and told him that the mansion was still standing. He had imagined that it would have been the first target for someone's torch, and he had expected it to be nothing more than a pile of ashes.

He told Mrs. Miller that his constant worry had been for the well-being of her and the children. He knew that she had a defiant temperament, and that she wouldn't hesitate to go up against any would be intruders—even those dressed in blue. He had imagined that if Magnolia Manor had been put to ashes, it would have been because of Yankee troops taking revenge, because of a run-in with her.

When the war started, he had been hesitant about leaving town to avoid the possibility of being arrested for treason. He had been reluctant, because his wife knew nothing about survival if things got bad. She didn't know, because from birth, she had had the proverbial silver spoon in her mouth, and she had never been without it. For her, a challenge meant making sure that she didn't omit any of the town's upper crust from her guest list. Struggles and hardships, she had never experienced—there had always been someone else to deal with adversity.

He said that he had often wondered if Elizabeth and Sophia would still be at the mansion—he had hoped that they would be. He knew well that when and if it came down to eking out a living, Elizabeth could do it as well as anyone. He had seen how other slaves had walked away, and he thought that Elizabeth and Sophia may have done the same thing.

The town didn't look anything like it did when he left. Mrs. Miller told him about how the Yankees had set fire to it when they were leaving. The only reason why the mansion didn't go up in smoke had been because the wind blew the fire in the direction away from their place.

When she had started telling him about General Grant and the others taking over the mansion, Mr. Miller became alarmed. She told him that they had forced their way in, but they conducted themselves as gentlemen, and that they had even left a large stock of supplies when they left. That indicated to him that their presence had probably been more of a nuisance, or an inconvenience for her than anything else. She also told him that he had a fort located on his property. Even though it was there, they never did have to use it for fighting, because the closest fighting around had been about eight miles or so away.

The town had been put to shambles mostly because someone just wanted to see it burn while looking back as they rode away. Mrs. Miller said that the torch wasn't lit by the troops under General Grant's command. He had kept things pretty much under control, except for some plundering. She was sure that Grant's presence had been the reason why their house had not been ransacked.

Mr. Miller supposed that they should all be thankful that General Grant had chosen Magnolia Manor as his temporary headquarters. Mrs. Miller said that they had gone through a lot of bourbon during their stay, but they even replaced it on their way out of town. He had told her that she was a stronger woman than he had ever imagined. She told him that the only thing that she had done was worried; she didn't know what she would have done had it not been for Elizabeth, Alfred and Sophia.

When Mr. Miller left town, he had intended to stay with the Confederate troops, but he quickly found out that he couldn't keep up. He had traveled with them for a while, but then, he had to go off on his own. Most of his time had been spent in some out of the way place that had been pretty much forgotten about. After a while, he was sure that he looked as much like nobody as anybody, and that he had blended in with the locals.

He had seen some awful sights on his way home. During his trek, he realized that it would be a long time before the South would have any semblance of what it used to be. Human casualties and physical destruction had been such that seeing was the only way of believing.

On his way into Bolivar, he had seen all of the former slaves living in shanties on the southwest side of town. He had not been surprised, because he had seen many, and they were all alike. Not so long ago, he had lots of slaves, but he had already come to the conclusion that neither he, nor anyone else in the country would ever own slaves again. It was an era that had ended, and it would force the South to adapt to a new way of doing business.

Although slavery had ended, Mr. Miller knew that farming would continue just from necessity. There were thousands of former slaves that needed a way of providing for their families, and working on shares would become the new way—sharecropping. The landowner would provide the resources, and share the profits with those that provided the labor. For many, however, sharecropping would be nothing more that slavery by another name.

He had already seen what was left of most plantations, and it wasn't much. Places that at one time had been majestic scenes on the landscape had been put to the torch, and the only asset left being the soil itself. It had held on simply because it wouldn't burn, and couldn't be smashed to smithereens.

Mr. Miller had been thinking about Alfred, Elizabeth and Sophia. That day when he had returned home, Magnolia Manor looked as if it had been off limits to the forces of war. It looked the same as it did on the day that he had left. No one had suffered from the lack of warmth during the cold days of winter, and although it had taken its' toll, mental anguish had been their hardest enemy. They had helped take care of his family while he was gone, and he had to let them know that he owed them more than what he had given, which was not much.

Mr. Miller had asked Mrs. Miller to go with him to his study. He told her that he had been thinking about Elizabeth, Sophia and Alfred. They were still there at the mansion, going about their daily routines as if nothing had changed. He said that people don't have slaves anymore, but Elizabeth, Sophia and Alfred made it seem like they hadn't heard the news.

Mr. Miller had said that they needed to talk to them to see if they would be staying or moving on. Mrs. Miller felt like it was obvious that they had planned on staying, because they hadn't left. She wondered if they had stayed on, because being there was better than being anywhere else. He said that they couldn't expect them to keep doing what they had been doing without being paid.

He said that before the war, he had been thinking about giving Elizabeth, Sophia and Alfred their freedom, but he had waited too long. Abraham Lincoln had done that for him. Although it was something that he had thought about, he had never mentioned it to anyone, not even his wife. Since they were free, he wanted her to know that it was something that he would have definitely done if it hadn't been for the war.

When the war started, all of his slaves could have walked away at any time, but Elizabeth, Sophia and Alfred had chosen not to. Although his wife had undoubtedly experienced the most turbulent years of her life, her hardships had been lessened, because of them. When he had the thought of giving them their freedom, he said that he couldn't say that it would be because he owed them something, because he owed something to every slave that he had ever owned. He explained that his initial thoughts about giving them their freedom had been due to the fact that he had a more personal relationship with them than with any of his other slaves.

Mrs. Miller listened as he told her about thoughts that she had never considered him having. He never flinched when he told her that his situation had been compounded by the fact that he had a child by Sophia, and that being the case, it had put him in a more than awkward position. He said that he had a black son, and even though he was black, he couldn't have stood by and let him grow up as a slave. Since his son was no longer a slave, he said that he wouldn't sit around and watch while he scrounged around trying to eke out a living.

He had told her things that she had never imagined that he would say. He explained that he had never said anything about it before, because he didn't want her to get angry, but it had become something that he had to talk about. He said that Richard had been born a slave, but to him, he was like Charles—both were his sons. He had tried, but he couldn't put one before the other.

Mrs. Miller had asked why he found it necessary to tell her all of those things when he could have easily kept them to himself. When she asked the question, he said that while he had been gone, he had lots of time to think about things, and he had decided that his wife had the right to know. He had asked her if she was angry, and she told him no. She said that she had always been aware of his feelings for Richard. She said that for a long time, she was sure that she would never feel the way that he did about him, but anymore, she said that he's just Richard— he's in the family.

He had started talking about Alfred and Elizabeth. He said that he had known for a long time that they loved each other. He felt like they should have been given their freedom a long time ago. Instead, they were slaves right up to the end. He insisted that he should have given them their freedom rather than being forced to do it; he had his chances, but he didn't do anything.

Before leaving his study, Mrs. Miller told him that she was glad that he had told her how he felt about Richard. Even though she had guessed that he loved him, she didn't know for sure. She did ask why he had waited so long to tell her. However, before he could say anything, she told him to forget it. She said that she already knew the answer to the question.

It was Saturday morning, and Mr. Miller had gotten back used to the morning signal that had gotten him out of bed for so many years, the smell of Elizabeth's freshly brewed coffee. He had gotten dressed, and then he made his way to the kitchen. He didn't wait for Elizabeth to do it for him; instead, he poured himself a cup of coffee. Elizabeth told him that she could have done that for him, but he said that he didn't mind.

Elizabeth had known him for a long time, and when he sat down, she could sense that he was in a different mood. He had been independent enough to pour his own cup of coffee, and then he sat at the table just to while away the time with her. He didn't even have his newspaper.

Elizabeth had really been surprised when Mrs. Miller showed up—bright and early. Elizabeth poured her a cup of coffee, and then she sat down at the table and started talking. Elizabeth didn't mind, but she had started to wonder if perhaps something was brewing other than the coffee pot. It was very unusual for Mrs. Miller to be up so early, and feeling good about it.

Sophia had gotten out of bed, but she was upstairs. She didn't expect anyone else, especially Mrs. Miller, to be up and about so soon. Elizabeth placed their breakfast on the table, and she liked watching them go through the motions of enjoying whatever it was that had them feeling so up-beat.

The Millers had made a decision on how to settle with Elizabeth, Sophia and Alfred. After breakfast, Mr. Miller decided that it was time to get it done. He could see

Alfred working outside in the yard. He had gone out onto the porch to get his attention. Mrs. Miller had Elizabeth and Sophia on the porch when Alfred got there. By then, they all had suspicious minds, and they had all started to wonder what could be going on. When they had all gathered on the porch, Mr. Miller invited them to have a seat. Then, Elizabeth, Sophia and Alfred had all become very uneasy, because they had never been asked to have a seat anywhere other than at the bush harbor.

Like most politicians, Mr. Miller felt like he had to set things up with a few well-chosen words before getting to the heart of things. He started out by telling them about how long they had been working for him, how loyal they had been through the years, and how they had taken care of his family during the war—just going on and on. Finally, Mrs. Miller had heard enough, and she told him to cut through all of that stuff, and get on with it. Elizabeth, Sophia and Alfred had all been sitting and listening, but after Mrs. Miller had told him to get on with it, they started wondering what was it that she wanted him to get on with.

Seeing the tension build, Mr. Miller decided that his wife was right. He should forget the speech, and get to the point. He started out by telling his used to be slaves the same thing that he had told Mrs. Miller. He said that slavery had ended because of the war, but if there had never been a war, he said that he would have given them their freedom anyway. Suddenly, the tension lessened, yet they could sense that there was more to come.

He said that there was no way that he could make up for what they had done for him and his family. He hoped that they would accept a partial payment with the idea that it would be better than no payment at all.

He couldn't afford a settlement that would be completely equitable, but he had one that he hoped would be received as reasonable. By his own admission, he had found it embarrassing to try and pay someone that had spent a lifetime being a slave.

He told Elizabeth and Alfred that he had known for a long time that they would like to get married, and that he would like to be the one to perform the ceremony. Then he told them about the house that he would deed over to them. It was in need of repair, but he would pay for the materials if Alfred would do the work. The furniture that they had used before Mrs. Miller refurbished Magnolia Manor would be theirs. It had been placed in storage.

When Mr. Miller had paused long enough for him to say something, Alfred wanted to know when he would be able to say the words so that they would be married. However, Elizabeth answered Alfred's question. She said that nobody would be getting married until the house had been repaired, and it was ready for them to move into.

At last, he got around to Sophia. He looked at her with a hard stare. Then, as if he had been waiting for his mind to assimilate the right words, he started to talk. There in front of Mrs. Miller, he said to Sophia that she was the mother of one of his children, and that he loved him. When he said it, Elizabeth thought that he had put an end to one of the best feelings that she had ever had. At that moment, she was sure that he shouldn't have said what he had said.

Having not lost her nonchalant style, and maybe feeling like she had freed herself long ago, Sophia stared back at Mr. Miller in the same way that he had been staring at her. Cautiously, Elizabeth and Alfred had glanced at Mrs. Miller, but the expression on her face had never changed. He never had before, but there in front of everybody, Mr. Miller apologized to Mrs. Miller for his infidelity. All while he had been talking, Mrs. Miller had remained calm and unscathed about everything that he had said. However, when he apologized to her, she cried, but not because she was angry.

He didn't apologize to Sophia for what he had done to her, but he said that he would see to it that she and Richard had a home of their own. He said that it might take a while, but when he found the right one for sale, he would get it. Mr. and Mrs. Miller had gone back inside, and they left the others on the porch to think about their new life.

In the beginning, Elizabeth, Sophia and Alfred had absolutely no idea as to why they had all been assembled on the porch, and asked to have a seat. However, what they had heard was what they had always wished for, and then their wish had suddenly been granted. It was the next best thing that could happen after being told that they were no longer slaves.

They had all made the decision that they would keep working at the mansion. Elizabeth had started tending the chores with a smile on her face. The job didn't seem to be so tedious anymore. She told Sophia and Alfred that it seemed like somebody had been holding on to all of the good things that were theirs, and then they gave them up—life had become worth living.

Mrs. Miller had said it before, but she said it again. She told her husband that he had been very generous—not from the standpoint that he had given them too much, but from the standpoint of just being fair. No sooner than she had told him, he reminded her that he had not been generous at all. If he were to be truly fair, he would have to give his former slaves almost everything that they owned. He had only given them enough to move some things a little closer to being right.

Mrs. Miller wondered aloud if they really understood how much their lives had changed and what it meant. They had been standing at the window looking out into the yard. He told her to listen for a moment, and then tell him what she had heard. After listening, she said that the only thing that she could hear was Alfred singing. Then he asked her if she had ever heard him sing before. She had said no. He said that he hadn't either.

Sophia had been keeping an eye on the kids out back, while Mr. and Mrs. Miller sat and watched. As always, Mrs. Miller just couldn't believe the affection that her children had for Sophia. Charles and Richard had made their way onto the porch. Charles had walked over and leaned against his father's leg, and Richard did the same, but on the other side. They had been talking to him, and both referring to him as daddy. Mrs. Miller looked at them, but it didn't seem to bother her like it once had. Sophia had gone over to get the kids, but Mr. Miller said that she could just leave them alone.

Sophia had walked back out into the yard. She was alone, so she strolled around and looked at the flowers. She stopped at Amanda's rose bush, and looked at it for a while. It was obvious that Alfred had always given it a little more attention than any of the other plants.

Mrs. Miller said that she was glad that Elizabeth had decided to keep working at the mansion, so that she could do the cooking. She could do it once in a while, but she didn't want to depend on Sophia's culinary skills every day. Mr. Miller agreed that Elizabeth was by far the better cook, but he felt like Sophia would get better with time. Mrs. Miller said that she would have to get better, because she couldn't get any worse.

Elizabeth had said to Alfred that it was strange how they had been waiting for so long to get married, and when the time had finally come when they could, they had decided to put it on hold. Alfred said that he had thought about the same thing, and that's why he had been working like a slave to hurry and get the house finished.

Elizabeth and Sophia had told Mrs. Miller that they were going to walk to the store in town—things had really changed, they didn't ask if they could go, they said that they were going. They hadn't planned on being gone long, and they wouldn't be shopping for anything special. They were mostly interested in just seeing the town. Sophia had lived most of her life just down the street from the courthouse, but after all those years, neither she nor Elizabeth had ever walked down the streets of the town where they lived.

Sophia had bought a few things just so that she could say that she had gone shopping. It was new to her, and she loved looking at all of the beautiful things that were for sale. They knew the owner of the store that they had gone into, and he knew them. He had been a longtime friend to Mr. and Mrs. Miller, and he lived near Magnolia Manor.

Sophia paid for the few items that she had, and they had left the store. They walked down the street on their way back to the mansion. It was Saturday, and there had been lots of people in town, a few that Elizabeth and Sophia had been knowing, but a lot more that they didn't know.

They were about to turn the corner when they met a man that they would rather have not seen. It was evident that he had been drinking, because he had gotten close enough for them to smell it on his breath. He had started making sexually offensive remarks to Sophia. Whenever they tried to move on down the street, he would step in front so that they couldn't go past.

Elizabeth and Sophia were about a half block down the street from Austin Miller's law office. He had spent a few hours working, and was just locking the door to go home. He walked down the street in the direction toward Elizabeth and Sophia. As he got closer, he recognized them, and he also recognized that they were being harassed. Elizabeth and Sophia had their attention focused on the man that had been giving them a hard time. Therefore, they didn't see Mr. Miller until he was standing there with them.

Mr. Miller had gotten to be in his mid-sixties, but still rather capable—at least, he thought so. He had walked around Elizabeth and Sophia, and he approached the man from the rear. He was still hassling Sophia. Mr. Miller had taken hold of the man's collar from behind, and he pulled him backwards. Being caught off guard, the man's feet got tangled, and he had fallen down.

He laid sprawled on his back, and looking up at the three people that were looking down at him. Mr. Miller told him that he had let too much whiskey cause him to make a big mistake. He had put his hand into his leather satchel, and pulled out an old pistol, one that probably hadn't been fired in years. When he had pulled the hammer back and had it cocked, Elizabeth and Sophia thought that he was ready to find out if it would still shoot. Instead of pulling the trigger, he bent over, and let the tip of the gun barrel rest between the man's eyes. He told him that if he ever did that again, drunk or sober, he would kill him.

Sophia had been impressed. She told Mr. Miller that the South might have won the war if he had volunteered. He didn't know the man's name, but he said that he was just some of the trash around town that they could do without.

Elizabeth was glad that he had come along when he did. However, she told him that he could have been hurt, and that he was crazy to do something like that at his age. He said that he had his pistol. Elizabeth told him that he didn't know if that old gun would even shoot. He said that if he had pulled the trigger and it misfired, then he would have used it to pistol whip him.

Mr. Miller, Elizabeth and Sophia walked on down the street. He still had the pistol in his hand—he kept it handy for just in case. He put it away only after he had looked back, and saw that the drunk had walked away in the opposite direction.

A couple of months had passed since Mr. Miller had told his house staff about being homeowners and earning a salary, but Elizabeth and Alfred still hadn't married. It was no one's fault; it was just that repairing the house had taken a while. Alfred worked on it part time, because he had been working for Mr. Miller to earn a salary. They had kept things on hold, but Alfred finally got it finished.

The Millers had more furniture in storage than Alfred and Elizabeth needed. Therefore, they picked through and took what they wanted. Since the house was ready, Alfred told Elizabeth that he was ready.

Sophia was glad that her mother would soon have a husband, and she was glad that it would be Alfred. Sophia liked Alfred. Since she had never had anyone that was really a father, Alfred fit that description for her more than anyone else.

Elizabeth had told Sophia that she would speak to the Millers about setting a date for their marriage. Sophia had asked why was it necessary to set a date when she could just walk in, and say that they were ready to get married. Elizabeth told her to just leave that up to her, and she would take care of it. Sophia said that Alfred was ready to get married, and she asked Elizabeth why wasn't she ready. Elizabeth said that she was ready, and then she told Sophia to go wash the dishes. Sophia said the dishes had all been washed. Elizabeth told her to go and wash them again, and that she could take care of her own marriage.

Mrs. Miller and Elizabeth had agreed that Sunday after church would be a good time for the marriage. She and Elizabeth had started making plans—brief as they were. Mrs. Miller said that they would have the ceremony in the parlor. All of the kids would have on their Sunday clothes, and they could take part in the wedding. Mrs. Miller said that she would tell Mr. Miller, and there shouldn't be anything else to do.

The following Sunday, Mr. and Mrs. Miller attended church as usual. They took the two oldest kids with them and left the others at home. Sophia and Elizabeth had gotten the younger kids dressed, and then they donned their finest. They wanted everything to be ready when Mr. and Mrs. Miller returned home. Alfred had arrived, all gussied up and looking good in a suit of clothes that he had borrowed from somebody. They all sat around on the back porch and waited for the Millers to return. When they did, Mrs. Miller told Alfred that she hardly recognized him.

They all stood around and watched as Mr. Miller performed the ceremony. He had read a few verses from the Bible. When he had gotten to the part about the ring, he asked if there was a ring, but he was pretty sure that there wasn't. However, they had all been surprised, including Elizabeth, when Alfred put his hand in his pocket and came out with one. He had purchased it with money that he had earned working as a handyman.

When instructed by Mr. Miller, Alfred slipped the ring onto Elizabeth's finger. Mr. Miller had pronounced them man and wife, but Alfred said that there's one more thing that they needed to do. With no explanation, Sophia placed a broom on the floor. Elizabeth and Alfred held hands, walked up, and jumped the broom. Mr. Miller said that jumping the broom had made it official. Everybody laughed except the kids. They just watched. As far as they knew, jumping the broom was just part of the ceremony.

Everybody stood on the porch and watched as Alfred and Elizabeth rode away in the buggy. Elizabeth still worked at the mansion during the day, but no more on weekends. She and Alfred had been married, and the remainder of their nights and weekends would be spent together in their own home.

Sophia helped the kids change clothes so that they could go outside. After being outside for a couple of hours, she decided that it was time to get started on cooking supper. Mr. and Mrs. Miller had been sitting on the porch enjoying the beautiful afternoon. He felt good about Alfred and Elizabeth. They had been in love with each other for a long time, and for a long time they had to wait. He had asked Mrs. Miller how long she had known that they were in love. She said that she never had been sure until after the war had started, but she had suspected that they might be before then.

Sophia let the kids help with cooking supper. It was something that Elizabeth didn't do—she would tell them to scat in a minute. With Sophia in charge, they could help if they wanted to.

Cooking had taken a lot longer than usual, but they got it done. Sophia had told Mary to tell Mr. and Mrs. Miller that dinner is now being served. Mary informed them using the same formality with which she had been instructed. She said, "Mr. and Mrs. Miller, dinner is now being served." They had been so surprised by Mary's announcement. When they walked into the dining room, all of the kids had been seated at the table, and waiting very attentively. The kids had told Mrs. Miller that Sophia had let them help with the cooking, and she could see the proud look on their faces.

When Sophia removed the lids to expose the contents of each dish, the chicken, potatoes and peas all looked like Elizabeth had prepared them herself. Mr. Miller looked at Mrs. Miller with an expression indicating that Sophia had finally learned how to cook—he had always said that she would catch on; it was just a matter of time. Sophia placed food on the kids' plates while Mr. and Mrs. Miller waited and watched.

Mrs. Miller had been paying attention to the graceful style that Sophia had in the dining room. Everything seemed so formal. The kids had started eating, and they thought that the food was great. Mr. Miller couldn't wait to dig in, because he loved fried chicken. He had taken a bite from the drumstick that he was holding, and when he took it down from his mouth, he looked at it. The drumstick had been cooked to a golden brown with just a slight crunch on the outside, just the way that he liked it. On the inside, he didn't know whether to call it rare or raw, but whatever it was, he couldn't eat it.

Sophia had gone back to the kitchen to get the dessert. Mrs. Miller never bit into her chicken after she saw what Mr. Miller had. Instead, she had decided to just spread a pat of butter on a biscuit, and take it from there. The biscuits looked good, but they were rather hard and crusty. However, she did manage to get one open. The kids were still eating and enjoying every bite. It was good to them, probably because they had a hand in its preparation.

Mr. Miller had seen Mrs. Miller wrestling with her biscuit, so he decided to make do with peas and potatoes. He had tried them and they were good enough. Mrs. Miller decided that if he could stomach the peas and potatoes, then she could do the same. Mr. Miller had placed the bone from the drumstick back on his plate. Mrs. Miller could easily get by with eating a small amount, and not drawing any attention to herself, because she never ate much anyway.

Sophia had placed a beautiful cake on the table, one that was covered with white frosting. When it was time for her to serve dessert, the kids tore into it first. Mr. and Mrs. Miller figured that it must be alright. In fact, they had concluded that Elizabeth had baked the cake, because it looked like one of hers. They each had a slice, and they had taken a bite. Just when they wanted to leave it alone, Mary said that Sophia had let them cook the cake, and that they had made it special for them. That's when they both knew that they had to eat it, whether they liked it or not.

Mr. Miller had forced his dessert down—hoping that it would stay down—and then he declared that he was about to burst from eating so much. Mrs. Miller said that she wasn't very hungry, but that it really was delicious. The kids were all proud, because they had helped cook their first meal, and they had watched it be enjoyed by their parents. Sophia had been a bit nervous at first about cooking, but she and the kids had put it together, and it seemed like everything had turned out just fine.

Mr. Miller left the table, and he had gone out onto the porch. He couldn't leave the drumstick that he had bitten into on his plate without having to explain why. However, he had left the bone on the plate, but he had removed the meat, wrapped it in his handkerchief, and stuck it in his pocket. Standing on the porch, he tossed it as far away as he could, but he had held on to the handkerchief.

Monday morning, Elizabeth was back at the mansion. It was a big change from what it had once been. Mr. Miller knew that she was back, because he could smell the coffee pot. After he had gotten dressed, he went to the kitchen. She had his breakfast ready and waiting along with a cup of coffee. He sat at the table, and ate everything that was on his plate. Seeing that he had a good appetite, and was eating had made Elizabeth feel good—she hated to cook, and then see him stand there and nibble on stuff. After he had finished, he got his satchel and left.

Elizabeth had wondered what could be wrong with Mrs. Miller. Mr. Miller had just left, yet she was up and about—much too early for her. Mrs. Miller said that she was about to starve. Elizabeth told her to sit down while she fixed something for her to eat. Meanwhile, Elizabeth poured her a cup of coffee. While filling her cup, Elizabeth said that Mr. Miller had eaten like he was a field hand. Mrs. Miller told her that Sophia and the kids had cooked supper, and she didn't know what they had put in it, but it was awful.

Elizabeth had put a plate of bacon and eggs in front of her. Mrs. Miller ate while Elizabeth fiddled around. Everybody in the house, except the kids, knew that Sophia wasn't much of a cook, because cooking had always been left up to Elizabeth. Sophia helped sometimes, but she usually had her hands full just taking care of the children.

Elizabeth had gone to Sophia's room. She and Richard were still asleep. Elizabeth gave her a gentle nudge, and told her that it was time to get up. Sophia sat up and said that it seemed like they had just gone to bed. Elizabeth said that, it's still time to get up, because there's work to do.

Elizabeth could see her husband working outside every now and then when she walked past the window. It was a happy morning for her, and she felt so blessed that she was alive to enjoy the day. Everything seemed so different, and the morning had been so beautiful—her life had become such that she could see the sun on the horizon in the same way as Mr. Miller.

Mr. Miller had told Alfred that he could make more money as a carpenter than he could by taking care of his yard, and working as a handyman around town. Alfred was curious about who would take care of the yard work. Mr. Miller said that he would get someone else to take care of it.

Mr. Miller didn't know how quickly a yard could get out of hand. About a week after Alfred had started working as a carpenter, the yard had started looking rough. Mr. Miller had asked Alfred if he could recommend someone to take care of the yard. He recommended

Jacob. Mr. Miller said that he didn't know Jacob. Alfred told him that Jacob had helped with the cleanup around the house back when they had that storm. Then Mr. Miller remembered.

Mr. Miller talked to Jacob, and he was glad to have a job, any job. Jacob didn't have a family, at least no one that he knew about. He had been sold years ago, and he had no idea as to where his family might be, or if they were even still alive. He was getting along in years, but he could still get around well enough. He was glad to have the job as caretaker of the yard, because it was something that he could do, and do well.

Sophia's rose bush, the one that Mr. Miller had given her to plant in remembrance of her friend Amanda, still looked good. The first day that Jacob worked at the mansion, Sophia went out and told him about it. Jacob promised that he would keep it looking beautiful for her, and for Miss Amanda.

It was Sunday morning. Those that favored it had gone to the fancy church in town—some that didn't had been dragged along anyway. The others had chosen the bush harbor and they rode with Alfred. He had a recently acquired used carriage that he had bargained for. His wife sat next to him. It was a two seater with plenty of space.

As soon as they had arrived, Alfred stood and shouted so that everybody could hear him when he announced that he and Elizabeth had gotten married. Then he told them about their new house, the one located on the north edge of town. They had indeed stepped up a few rungs on the ladder. However, there were many at the bush harbor that were happy about the changes that had taken place in their lives as well. Things for them had shifted, and had gotten on the plus side.

The town had been made ugly by the fire that swept through during the war. There were hellacious reminders of unwanted memories all around. Yet, for those that had decided to always call it home, they were sure that things would get better. They just need some time.

At one time, it had been speculated that the town would become one of the major cities in the State, but those thoughts had gone. There were some that had simply gotten fed up with the looks of things; it would take too many tomorrows for them to get back to where they were before the war. Desperately in need of a better place to call home, many had packed up, and moved away.

Mrs. Miller was disgusted with where she was. Living in a magnificent mansion, but in a town that seemed to her like it had died. The finer things of life that she had enjoyed before the war had all but disappeared. As much as she loved entertaining guests, and living high, then was not the time to flaunt their social standing or economic status. It was simply not the right time because too many people had to work too hard just to make it from one day to the next. During the good times, she didn't mind showing off her elite lifestyle, but then, even she knew that it was time to pull back on the reins, and be careful not to run anyone down.

SIXTEEN

Albert was away in college studying law. He frequently wrote letters to his mother, otherwise, she would worry too much about him. Mrs. Miller's daughter, Mary spent lots of time at her uncle's house across town, and in a year or so, Charles and Richard would be teenagers. Charles had been going to school for several years, but Richard started after the war had ended. Mrs. Miller wondered where the years had all gone. Then, there were some that she hoped would not only be gone, but also forgotten.

It had been a while since Sophia had received a letter from Emily or Caroline, and she wondered about them. When she had found the time and was alone, she wrote a letter to both. She told them about what Mr. and Mrs. Miller had done for them, giving them a house, and then working for them and getting paid; she was glad that she was no longer a slave. In the letter, she said that when they were teenagers, they lived near each other, but they couldn't visit much because she was a slave; since she was no longer a slave, they couldn't visit at all, because they lived too far apart.

Since the war, Mr. Miller had noticed that his wife and Sophia seemed to have let bygones be bygones. If not, they had at least mellowed out some. He didn't know what had happened that caused them to settle down. He had supposed that it may have had something to do with the war—having to work together to survive ... he wasn't sure.

Mr. Miller had come home from work, but it was sooner than usual. As soon as he walked in, he told Sophia that he had found a house for her and Richard. He had told her where it was located, but she didn't know exactly where it was—the town was still a bit foreign to her. He had said that they could ride down, and have a look at when Alfred stopped by to pick up Elizabeth.

When Alfred showed up, he took them to see the house. Mr. Miller, Sophia, Elizabeth, Charles and Richard had all climbed aboard. The carriage had been a little overcrowded, but they managed to squeeze in. It wasn't far from the mansion, and when Sophia saw the house she loved it. They had all gone inside to see what it was like. It had even been furnished. The only thing that Sophia and Richard would have to do would be to get their personal belongings and walk in.

Later during the evening, Mr. and Mrs. Miller were talking about the house. Mrs. Miller felt like Sophia would probably want to move in as soon as possible. That being the case, they would have to hire someone to be at the mansion during nighttime and on weekends.

Sophia had been walking around, knocking the dust off of this and that, and she heard them talking—she hadn't been eavesdropping; they didn't do much of that anymore. She interrupted their conversation. She said that she had been thinking about the problem of not having someone at the mansion at night. She asked if it would be alright if she kept on working, and staying at the mansion like always.

Mr. Miller had asked if there was something about her house that she didn't like. When they had looked at, he had the impression that it was just what she wanted, and therefore, that she would be anxious to move in. Sophia said the she would like to work, and keep staying at the mansion. That way, she could rent her house to somebody and make more money.

Mr. and Mrs. Miller had been surprised by Sophia's offer, but they liked the idea of her staying on at the mansion. Sophia had never been the best housekeeper in town, but they had gotten used to her. She and Mrs. Miller didn't kick up the dust anymore, and it would be a good arrangement for everybody—things would stay pretty much as they had always been.

Later, Mrs. Miller said that Sophia had come up with a good idea. Mr. Miller agreed. He said that she could earn more money, and it would keep them from having to find someone else to replace her. Charles and Richard liked the idea. Even though Sophia's house wasn't far away, they preferred being under the same roof, because they were running buddies, and they didn't want to be separated.

The days of the bush harbor had come to an end. An old rundown building, one that had been refurbished and given another chance at life, had become their new church. Members of the congregation, including Elizabeth and Sophia, stood and watched as the bush harbor was brought to the ground. It had never been much to look at, but they still hated to see it be knocked down, and then become firewood.

When it fell, Elizabeth said that a lot of memories had fallen with it. Sophia agreed, and said that some had been good memories and some not so good. Elizabeth didn't respond to her comment. She knew that Sophia's words about some of the memories not being so good had been made in reference to Daniel.

Austin Miller was sixty eight years old, and he had as many irons in the fire as ever. It was January, and he had to go to Memphis—something to do with the railroad company that he had been representing. The morning that he left was cold and rainy, but that wouldn't be much of a problem, because he wasn't far from the train station. He was up early, got dressed, and went to the kitchen for his morning cup of coffee.

No one was up with him except Sophia. Elizabeth had not yet arrived. Sophia had his breakfast ready, but like always, he ate a little while reading the newspaper, and sipping on his coffee. He usually nibbled at breakfast when Elizabeth cooked—he nibbled less after Sophia had started.

He was still sitting at the table when Elizabeth walked in. When he saw her, he knew that Alfred was waiting outside, because he had said that he would give him a ride to the train station. He had gulped down the remainder of his second cup of coffee, and then said that he should be going. He had to leave a little early, because he needed to make a stop at his office in town.

He had gone to the bedroom to tell Mrs. Miller goodbye, but as usual, she was still asleep. When he had opened the door, he noticed the light from outside coming through the curtains on the window. He eased over and pulled them closer together to keep the room dark. Hoping not to disturb her, he kissed her on the cheek, and then pulled the door shut on his way out. He had gotten his belongings and headed for the front door. Elizabeth and Sophia walked with him just to say goodbye since no one else was up to see him off. He had reminded them that he would be back in just a few days.

A couple of hours had passed before Mrs. Miller had gotten out of bed. When she sat down at the table, she asked how long Austin had been gone. When Elizabeth told her, she said that he's always on the run, and she wished that he would stop and spend more time at home. Elizabeth said that he had been at it for so long that she didn't think that he would have it any other way. Mrs. Miller supposed that she was right.

Mr. Miller's original plan had been to take care of his business in Memphis, and then return home. He had finished with his business in Memphis, but since he was already in Memphis, it would be a relatively short ride down the Mississippi by steamboat to his plantation in Mississippi.

It had been raining and sleeting before the steamboat left Memphis. Still, he had decided to make the trip anyway. When the steamboat arrived at the landing in Austin, Mississippi, several inches of slush had already accumulated on the ground when he stepped off the boat.

The trip to his Mississippi plantation had been a last minute decision. Therefore, no one expected him, and consequently, there was no one at the landing to give him a ride to the plantation. In spite of the weather conditions, he got his luggage, and decided that he would make the trek on foot. He felt like he was in good enough shape, and the one and a half mile walk wouldn't be a problem—he could be there in less than an hour. He had made the trek, but when he arrived at his plantation house, he was completely numbed by the cold wet conditions that he had chosen to tackle.

Upon arriving at the plantation house, he made a fire in the fireplace and then changed into some dry clothes. He sat by the fire until he was warm, and then he went to bed.

During the night, he would get up whenever the room got too cold and put more wood on the fire.

The next morning, Isaac had noticed smoke coming from the chimney and he had become curious. Since the house was supposed to be unoccupied, he walked over to see who was inside. When he walked in, he saw the wet clothes on the floor, and Mr. Miller was in bed, but he was awake.

Mr. Miller explained what had happened, and admitted that he had made a dumb decision. Isaac had put more wood on the fire to warm the room. He then told Mr. Miller that he would go and get Jenny—his housekeeper whenever he was at the plantation. She had made a pot of coffee to help him warm up. He spent most of the day in bed with Isaac and Jenny in the house with him.

The next morning, Jenny noticed that Mr. Miller had a fever—she and Isaac had stayed with him all night. She had started treating him with some of her home remedies. Even though she had lots of faith in her medicinal potions and her ability to ply them, they didn't do what they were supposed to do.

Jenny then sent Isaac into town to fetch the doctor. He had made a much quicker trip than usual, and the doctor rode back to the plantation with him. When they arrived, Mr. Miller was still in bed. After examining him, the doctor concluded that he had pneumonia. After doing what he could, the doctor decided that he should stay with him for a few hours to see how he progressed. Several hours had passed, but Mr. Miller's condition had not improved, in fact, it had seemed to worsen.

The doctor spent the night in the plantation house along with Jenny and Isaac. The next day, Mr. Miller was no better than he had been the day before. By then, the doctor had done everything that he could do, but he had chosen to stay with him. Word had already spread that he was sick, and several of his friends had arrived—friends from Mississippi, and some had come down from Memphis. Three days had passed, and the doctor had stayed with him the entire time. On the fourth day after his arrival, Austin Miller died at his beloved Mississippi plantation.

A telegram had been sent to his home town of Bolivar to let the people know of his death. When the telegram had been received, the telegrapher was shocked, because he had seen him only a few days ago, and he had been in good spirits. The telegrapher walked down the street with the message in hand, and he entered the store of George Newbern. George Newbern had been Austin Miller's good friend and neighbor. The telegrapher showed him the message, and after he had read it, he sat down. Then he said that he would tell his wife.

They had been good friends, but then, it had become incumbent on George Newbern to deliver the worst of news. It was cold and dreary outside, yet he had chosen to walk. Slowly, he made his way to Magnolia Manor—unconscious of the freezing temperature and the north wind in his face. Even so, he had been in no hurry, because he wanted to give Mary Jane just a few more minutes to assume that she was still married to Austin Miller.

He had walked up to the door, but he hesitated before knocking. When he did, Elizabeth opened the door and invited him in. He had asked to see Mrs. Miller. Sophia had heard his request, and she said that she would get her. Elizabeth showed him to the parlor. When Mrs. Miller walked into the parlor, Elizabeth and Sophia had turned to walk away.

Mr. Newbern had stood up, and he spoke before Mrs. Miller had the chance to welcome him to her home. He had told Elizabeth and Sophia that they should hear what he had to say. Then, Mr. Newbern asked Mrs. Miller to please sit down. Suddenly, everyone had become quiet—no longer anticipating, but quite sure of what was to follow. Mr. Newbern didn't use a lot of words. He simply said that a telegram had been sent, and that Austin was dead.

Mrs. Miller didn't say anything. She kept sitting on the sofa, staring at George Newbern, and then at Elizabeth and Sophia. Elizabeth had walked over to the sofa, and sat down next to her, but neither of them spoke, they just sat there. Finally, it was Sophia that asked what had happened. Mr. Newbern told them that he had gone to the plantation in Mississippi, and had to walk from the boat landing to his house in the rain and sleet. He had gotten wet and caught pneumonia. When Mr. Newbern had asked Mrs. Miller if there was anything that he could do, she simply said no. Sophia then showed him to the door.

Mrs. Miller kept sitting on the sofa—surprised, shocked, dazed, distraught, speechless, everything—she didn't know what to do. Elizabeth had asked her if she wanted to lie down, but she said that it wouldn't do any good. She said that she would have to tell the children.

Sophia said that she would get them. When the children were gathered around her, she told them that their father had died. Charles and Richard were not at home when she told them, but they returned shortly afterwards. Both boys were teenagers. Even though they had been in town, they hadn't heard about the death of their father.

When Charles and Richard entered the mansion, they had been laughing and joking with each other about something. When they saw everybody together in the parlor, they stopped. They could see the expressions on their faces, expressions of sorrow. Mrs. Miller told them about their father. Briefly, the two of them stood in the entryway—they didn't know what to do, or what to say. Then Richard went outside. No one said anything to him, they just let him go.

As soon as he had found out, Mrs. Miller's uncle, Ezekiel, visited her at Magnolia Manor. He had told her that her husband's body was in route via train—the same train that had shuttled him back and forth to Memphis so many times would be bringing him home, but that time, it would be to stay. He said that he would relieve her of the burden of having to make funeral arrangements. He would take care of it himself.

When Austin Miller left home, he was alone. However, when his body was returned, it was in the company of many friends. Some had boarded the steamer when it left the town of Austin, Mississippi with his remains. People in Memphis had heard about his death before the steamboat arrived. When his body had been transferred to the train, many Memphians climbed aboard to be with him on his last trip home. They swapped stories about the man that they had referred to as a benefactor, and an asset to so many, and for so long.

In Bolivar when the train had first come into view, onlookers could see that it had already slowed down to a crawl. It crept to the station as if heavily laden and on an uphill climb. On that day, the whistle was silent. The people had lined up along the streets when the hearse pulled up near the car carrying his remains. Mrs. Miller was not amongst them. For those that had chosen to be there, it was a day that they would remember.

Mrs. Miller had asked Charles if he would go out and find Richard. He had been gone for a long time, and it took Charles a long time to find him. When Charles found him, they were both somewhat stoic, each trying to hide their emotions from the other. Charles told Richard that his mother wanted him to come home.

When he and Charles returned, Mrs. Miller asked Richard if he was alright. He said that he was. Elizabeth could see that neither Richard nor Charles was alright. She had told Sophia that both of them wanted to cry, but they had been holding it back.

At last, Elizabeth had seen Mrs. Miller as a mentally strong woman. She had maintained her composure better than most would have under the circumstances—she had not shed a single tear. At the same time, Elizabeth knew that she probably felt like she wanted to die herself. Mrs. Miller had asked Elizabeth and Sophia if they wanted to attend the funeral. Elizabeth had looked at Sophia, but for a short while, neither of them said anything. Finally, Sophia said that if any of them were to go, it would only give people something to talk about. They decided to stay at home.

Mrs. Miller had asked if they thought that Richard might want to go. While they were talking, Richard walked walked in. Then, Mrs. Miller posed the question to Richard. He said that he didn't know, because he hadn't thought about it. Richard asked Sophia if she was going. When she said no, Richard said that he wouldn't either.

A lot of people had gathered at the train station when they brought him home, but many more had gathered for the funeral. The church was full, and more were standing outside than there were inside. The funeral lasted a long time, because so many people felt the need to stand, and express their sentiments. Most of them had told similar stories. They talked about the good deeds that he had done along the way—blinded by on which rung of the ladder a person might stand, and willing to dig into his own pockets to do a favor when asked.

Mrs. Miller had lost her husband. She told Elizabeth that she felt like a heavy weight had been pressing down on her, and that she didn't know what to do. She remembered the morning when he left town. He had closed the curtains to block the sunlight from shining into her bedroom. She had been about half awake and about half way asleep. She remembered him saying goodbye, but not with words. He had kissed her on the cheek before leaving the room, and she wanted to always remember—he had said the perfect goodbye.

Mr. and Mrs. Miller's daughter, Annie, had been attending school in Middle Tennessee. When she received word of her father's death, she left school and headed home immediately. She attended the funeral, and soon afterwards, she became ill. Her doctor said that he had never seen anything like it before. The only thing that he could attribute her illness to was grief for her father. Mrs. Miller buried her daughter two weeks after burying her husband.

Elizabeth had been with Mrs. Miller every day, and Sophia was there both day and night. It was obvious to her doctor, and to everyone in the mansion that Mrs. Miller was standing at the edge. Another step and she would go over the side. Her uncle Ezekiel had visited her every day. He would sit and talk with her, and he had spent hours at her side. She had been depressed, and she had every reason to be.

During her entire life, she had always preferred to socialize with the elite class, and she didn't care for being around the underprivileged. Then, the very people that she had once shunned, simply because they had been less fortunate, had become the people that knocked on the door at Magnolia Manor just to say that they were sorry. Too much, too close together had been put on her, and they wanted her to know that they cared—they wanted to share the burden so that it wouldn't be so heavy on her.

She often sat in the parlor, and talked with people whom she had never spoken to before. They were people that she had to have passed on the street at some time or another, but she had looked the other way. Even though they had been strangers, then they were welcomed inside, because she needed them. Elizabeth and Sophia were both surprised by what she had been doing, opening her door to those that were down and out, because in the past it had never happened.

Mrs. Miller's uncle, Ezekiel, had started managing her farming enterprise, along with several other business ventures that she had. It had been a big relief for her when he agreed to take over the responsibility, because she knew absolutely nothing about what to do with the assets that she had inherited. She told Elizabeth that

Austin had always taken care of everything, and she didn't even know exactly what they had.

Mrs. Miller saw Richard sitting out back, and she had gone out and sat down with him. Since his father had died, she had noticed that he was far from being the Richard that she had been accustomed to seeing. She had asked him if he missed his father. He told her that he did, and that he also missed his sister, Annie.

Richard started telling Mrs. Miller something that his mother had told him. He had referred to his mother as Sophia, but he corrected himself, and said that he meant mama. He said that she had told him that sometimes it takes a long time to get used to not having people around when they've always been around you. Mrs. Miller said that she was right. She said that she would always miss having Austin around, and that she would always miss having Annie, but they had to get used to it. She told him that they should never forget them, but they had to get used to the fact that they're gone.

It had gotten to be early spring. Mrs. Miller had been in the yard, just walking around to while away the time. Elizabeth saw her from the window, and she had gone out to where she was. Then, they walked around together. Mrs. Miller asked Elizabeth if she remembered how angry she had been at Austin when she found out that he had gotten Sophia pregnant. Elizabeth said that she did remember. Mrs. Miller supposed that time and events had changed things. She said that she was glad that her husband didn't die back then when she had been angry at him.

She recalled the day when her husband said that he loved Richard the same as he did Charles. Although she had figured as much, she said that she had been so surprised when he said it, but then she guessed that the same thing had happened to her. They walked upon Jacob. He had been on his knees scratching around in the flowers, removing the few weeds that had been trying to take hold.

Jacob had stopped what he was doing, and was laboring to get on his feet. He was a little slow, because the years had started taking a toll on him, and the rheumatism didn't help any. Jacob had asked Mrs. Miller how she was doing, and she said that she was doing fine. She told him that she had Elizabeth and Sophia to look after her. Jacob laughed, and said that Elizabeth would do a good job, but he didn't know about Sophia. He had made Mrs. Miller laugh—something that she needed to do.

Mrs. Miller had noticed two other rose bushes planted near the one that Sophia had planted in memory of her friend, Amanda. She had asked Jacob who it was that had planted them. He said that it was Richard. They looked at them, but they didn't say anything—since Richard had planted them, they knew why. She reminded Jacob not to overdo it with that rheumatism.

Mrs. Miller had gotten used to sitting in what used to be her husband's study. She would sit at his walnut desk and in his high back leather chair when writing a letter, reading the mail, or when she just wanted to be alone. She had told Elizabeth that sitting at his desk and in his chair seemed to put her closer to him, like he was there with her. Sophia walked in while she was sitting at the desk. She asked Mrs. Miller if she could talk to her for a few minutes.

Time had toned down their attitudes, and ridded their minds of some of the run-ins of the past. Things that couldn't be erased had become less potent. The hostile attitudes and snide remarks were no longer part of their repertoire. Mrs. Miller told her to sit down, and tell her what was on her mind.

Sophia asked her if it would be alright if she moved into her own house. Mrs. Miller thought that her reason for wanting to move had been because of a problem at the mansion. Sophia assured her that it wasn't. She said that she just felt like she wanted to be in her own house. Mrs. Miller said that she didn't mind, but she asked Sophia if she would find someone to take her place.

Sophia was a step ahead. She told Mrs. Miller that she had already spoken to someone, because she had been thinking about moving for quite some time. Mrs. Miller asked who it was that she had talked with. Sophia said that it was Fanny. Mrs. Miller knew Fanny after Sophia explained that Mr. Miller had helped take care of her and her children after the war ended. Fanny had been one of Mr. Miller's slaves. When the war over, she had been left alone, and with no means of providing for herself and her children. Sophia knew that Fanny's personality was such that she and Mrs. Miller could get along together.

When Sophia was ready to move, she didn't have much, only her clothing, and a few keepsakes that she had accumulated, and held onto through the years. Elizabeth had been helping her pack the few things that she had when Mrs. Miller called for Sophia. She needed to speak to her in the study. Elizabeth kept on looking around to make sure that they had packed everything. Sophia didn't know what Mrs. Miller had to say, nor had she given it any thought.

After Sophia had sat down, Mrs. Miller told her that she hoped that she could forget about some of the things that had happened way back when. She didn't know why her attitude had been such that it was, maybe because of jealousy—jealousy due to what, she didn't say. She supposed that she had made life miserable for her husband with some of her overzealous tirades around the house when he was alive.

While Mrs. Miller talked, Sophia listened. Mrs. Miller hadn't said anything that required a response, and there had been very little dialogue. However, Sophia knew exactly what she had been talking about. In essence, she had pretty much said that she would like to forget the past, and start anew.

Sophia's thoughts had been about the same as Mrs. Miller's, and she felt the need to let her know that she had already let go of the past. When she was ready to leave, Sophia had asked Mrs. Miller if she could give her a hug. Mrs. Miller said that she would be very disappointed if she didn't. Elizabeth had an arm full of bags—stuff that belonged to Sophia. When she walked past the study, she saw Sophia and Mrs. Miller hugging each other. She never slowed down. Instead, she walked on past, so that she wouldn't be noticed. After going at it for almost twenty years, Elizabeth reckoned that they had decided to call it quits.

Mrs. Miller asked Sophia if she would stop by sometime and visit, and she promised that she would. They both had gotten up from their seat, and Sophia was about to leave when Mrs. Miller stopped her. She gave Sophia an envelope that had been sealed. She said that it was from Austin. He wanted her to have it when she decided to move into her own home. Sophia asked Mrs. Miller if she wanted her to open the envelope right away. Mrs.

Miller told her that it belonged to her, and she could open it whenever she wanted to.

They walked together out to the carriage where Alfred and Elizabeth had been waiting. Alfred helped his stepdaughter on board. Mrs. Miller and Elizabeth stood and watched as they rode away. Mrs. Miller said that they had made it seem like she was moving out of town when it's just down the street. Elizabeth agreed, but she added that it's the first time that they had ever been apart. When Alfred pulled in at Sophia's house, she told him to place her things on the porch, and that she could take them inside.

Richard and Charles had been at school all day. They were both surprised when they found out that Sophia had quit working at the mansion. Sophia and Richard's new residence had become the house that Austin Miller had purchased for them. Neither Richard nor Charles liked the idea of living apart. They would rather that things remained the way they had always been, but they didn't have any say so in the matter. Finding out that he no longer lived at Magnolia Manor, Richard had to walk down the street to his hew home.

Mr. Miller had given Sophia her house shortly after the war had ended. However, Sophia and Richard had stayed on at the mansion, and she had been renting her house out in order to make extra money. She had rented the house to a white man from France named John Umhaw. John owned the Tempest Saloon that was located in town, an establishment that had been touted by some as being the best damned saloon in the state.

Back when Sophia had made the decision that she was going to move into her own home, she told John of her intentions so that he could find another place to rent. The day that Sophia had chosen to move into her house had been based on a promise from John that he and his belongings would be out by that time.

As soon as Sophia opened the door and walked in, it was obvious that John had not moved out. She could see that his personal belongings were still in the house. When John had gotten home after closing down the Tempest, he walked in as usual. When he saw Sophia, he told her that she had frightened him, because he thought that a burglar was in the house. She told him that he shouldn't have been surprised, because they had both agreed on the date that he was supposed to be out, and she could move in. John said that he had forgotten the date.

John explained that he had been having trouble finding a place to rent. Sophia told him that he should have let her know, and they could have extended the rental agreement. The house had an extra bedroom, and Sophia had let John talk her into letting him stay there with her and Richard, until he could find another place.

Sophia told John that the bedroom that he had been sleeping in was hers, and that he would have to move to another bedroom. Sophia had already picked out Richard's room, and he was in it. The house had only one other bedroom, but John still had two choices. He could move into the smaller bedroom, or he could move out. He had decided to take the smaller room.

The house was quiet. Sophia still hadn't opened the envelope that Mrs. Miller had given to her. When she found it amongst her things, she assumed that it was something that Mr. Miller had to say to her; maybe something that he wanted her to know, but didn't want to say it when he could have done it face to face.

While opening the envelope, she had noticed that her fingers had become a bit unsteady, simply because she was anxious, and unsure about what he had written. Sitting near the oil lamp, she read the letter. He started by telling her that he loved his son Richard. That didn't surprise her, because she had heard him say it before. As she continued reading, she became very surprised. Austin Miller had deposited five thousand dollars in an account in her name at the bank. Sophia knew that it was a lot of money, and far more than she had ever expected to have in a lifetime.

After she had read the letter, she thought about her son, and how much she loved him. Then she thought about the fact that she wouldn't have a son if Austin Miller hadn't raped her. She had forgiven him, but she wondered if a person could ever completely forgive someone for doing what he had done to her.

After thinking about it, her thoughts became tangled. She had a son that she loved, she had a house, and she had five thousand dollars, none of which she would have had if she had not been raped. Then she had a question that made her head ache. Was she supposed to be happy? She had decided to leave it alone, because she realized that it was something that she could think about forever, and she would still be confused.

Sophia had walked to Magnolia Manor, but for no particular reason other than a social call. When she walked in, the place was completely quiet, nothing like it used to be. When she saw Mrs. Miller, she asked the whereabouts of Elizabeth. Mrs. Miller said that she had taken the day off to visit a friend of hers that had taken ill.

Sophia told Mrs. Miller that she had read the letter that Mr. Miller wanted her to have, and she told her about the money that he had deposited in the bank. Mrs. Miller said that she knew about the money, and that Austin wanted to make sure that Richard and his mother had a fair chance in life. Sophia then wondered if that might have been his way of apologizing. If it was, then was it supposed to make things alright—she didn't know. The only thing that she did know was that she had lots questions, and all of the answers were nothing but best guesses.

Several weeks had past, and John was still renting a room from Sophia. Meanwhile, John needed someone to help with the work around his business establishment, namely, the Tempest Saloon. He had asked Sophia if that someone could be Richard. Sophia didn't like the idea of her son working in a saloon. However, John had assured her that the place was a very respectable establishment, but to Sophia, it was still a saloon. He said that he just needed someone to help keep the place clean and neat. He had promised to keep an eye on him, and since school was out for the summer, he could earn some money. Finally, Sophia agreed. Richard had his first job, working in a saloon.

Since school was out, Charles didn't have much to do because Richard had moved. He thought that Richard would have been back visiting at the mansion, but he hadn't. Since Richard hadn't been by the mansion, Charles decided that he would go and visit Richard. He knew where Richard lived, and it was only a few minutes away. When he arrived, he knocked on the door and Sophia let him in.

He had sat down while talking to Sophia, expecting that Richard would walk in shortly. When he didn't, he asked Sophia where he was. Sophia told him that he had a job working in town. Charles asked where he was working, and Sophia told him that he had gotten a job at the Tempest Saloon. It didn't bother Charles that he was working at the saloon, but he was disappointed, because he and Richard had always spent their free time together.

Charles sat there for a while talking to Sophia. He really didn't have much else to say, but he didn't want to appear rude by leaving too soon. After all, he was in the presence of the woman that had spent more time with him than anyone, even his own parents. When he felt like he had been there long enough, so that leaving wouldn't appear impolite, he said that he should be getting home. Sophia had walked him to the door, and they said goodbye after hugging each other.

Charles had gone home. Mrs. Miller had seen him sitting out back, looking as if he might be lonely. When she asked him what was wrong, he said that there was nothing to do. She suggested that he go and visit Richard, and maybe the two of them could do something together. Charles said that he had just left their house, but Richard wasn't at home.

Mrs. Miller asked him where was Sophia. Charles told her that she was at home, but Richard was at work. Mrs. Miller hadn't seen Sophia in several days, but she had talked with Elizabeth every day when she came to work at the mansion. Yet, she said that Elizabeth hadn't said anything to her about Richard having a job. Charles told her that he worked at the Tempest Saloon. Then, Mrs. Miller knew that Elizabeth had been kept in the dark as much as she had, and she knew why.

Mrs. Miller was as outraged as she would have been if Richard had been her own son. Elizabeth had been inside, knocking the dust off of some things. When Mrs. Miller found her, she said that you'll never guess where Richard is working. Elizabeth said that she didn't know that he had a job. Mrs. Miller said that she didn't either. Before Elizabeth could ask where, Mrs. Miller told her that he had a job at the Tempest Saloon. Elizabeth felt just like Mrs. Miller. They had decided that when Alfred showed up, they would get him to take them to Sophia's house.

Alfred arrived at the mansion at the usual time to pick up Elizabeth. When he pulled into the yard with the carriage, Elizabeth and Mrs. Miller both went out to where Alfred had parked. As usual, Alfred had climbed down, so that he could help Elizabeth up to her seat. All the time, he had been wondering why Mrs. Miller had walked out with her. Neither Elizabeth, nor Mrs. Miller had said anything. When Alfred made it to the other side of the carriage to help Elizabeth, she had already climbed up and was seated, and Mrs. Miller was about to sit down next to her.

Every time before when they traveled in the carriage, someone always had to extend a helping hand to assist them with getting on board. That time, however, they climbed aboard without any assistance, and they had been quick about it. Alfred just looked at them, because he didn't know what was going on. When they were both seated, Alfred was still standing on the ground looking at them and baffled, because he didn't know what was going on. Elizabeth looked at him and told him to take them to Sophia's house.

Alfred climbed up to the driver's seat, and headed off toward Sophia's house. Unable to tolerate the suspense any longer, Alfred had to ask why they were going to

Sophia's house. Mrs. Miller told him that Richard had a job working in town at the saloon, and they were going to see if Sophia had lost her mind. Alfred didn't say anything else. Both of his passengers were angry, and he figured that the best thing for him to do was to be quiet, and keep moving.

Alfred pulled in at Sophia's house, and Mrs. Miller and Elizabeth both climbed down the same way that they had climbed aboard, unassisted. When they had made it to the front door, neither of them knocked, they just opened the door and walked in. Elizabeth was in front. Alfred had decided that they didn't need him. Whatever it was that they had planned to do or say to Sophia, they could do it without his help.

Sophia had been in the back room, but she heard them when they opened the door and walked in. When the three of them met in the front room, Elizabeth asked Sophia if she had lost her mind. Sophia didn't know what Elizabeth was talking about, and she was about to ask what was wrong. Before she could ask, Elizabeth told her that Richard had no business working in a saloon.

Again, Sophia tried to say something, but Mrs. Miller had cut in. She told Sophia that she was surprised at her for letting Richard work in a place like that. She said that he was too young to be around a bunch of drunks, and that if Austin was alive, there's no telling what he would do. Alfred couldn't see them from where he was, but he had no trouble hearing them.

When Sophia had the chance to speak, she explained that Richard's job was to just keep the floor clean, wash the glasses, and stuff like that. Thinking that it might be enough to satisfy them, she said that he was not the bartender. Elizabeth said that she didn't care what his job was, she didn't like it, and she wasn't going to stand for it. Mrs. Miller told Sophia that when he gets home, tell him that today was his last day of working at that place; if he wants a job, he could find one someplace else.

Elizabeth and Mrs. Miller didn't wait around to see if Sophia had anything else to say, they walked out of the house as quickly as they had entered. They both walked over to the carriage, and stopped. Elizabeth had looked up at Alfred. When Alfred didn't move, she asked him if he intended to just sit there, or could he be nice enough to help them to their seat. Alfred apologized, and quickly climbed down to offer his assistance. When Mrs. Miller saw Charles, she told him that his brother Richard had quit working at the saloon. Charles asked why, and Mrs. Miller said that he just quit.

Sophia told John that Richard was through working at his saloon. When she told him why, he understood the concern of Elizabeth and Mrs. Miller, but he had thought that cleaning up, and washing glasses would be alright. Sophia said that it was not alright with her mom and Mrs. Miller, and that he would have to find somebody else.

John was supposed to have been finding himself someplace else to live, but he was still in the house with Sophia and Richard. After a while, John had become very fond of Richard, and the feeling was mutual. Meanwhile, Sophia had come to the conclusion that John hadn't been trying to find another place to rent. Consequently, he kept renting a room from Sophia, and he had been there with her and Richard for almost a year.

Sophia and John were both about the same age. He had been renting a room from her for a long time—not just renting a room, but living in the house with her. That being the case, they had spent lots of time together. It could have been due to the closeness, or it could have been due to the birds and bees doing their thing. Whatever the reason might have been, the landlord and her tenant had fallen in love.

The war had been over about five years, but the heart-aches and pains that had come with it were still there, along with the sore eye from being hit so hard. Yet, with the right attitude, and a discerning eye, it was possible to believe that things might be on the mend. On the down-side, racial hatred had mushroomed like a plague.

In the midst of the racial conflict were Sophia Miller, herself a former slave, and John Umhaw, a white man from France. The two of them living together as lovers in a place where white and black didn't mix—not out in the open. The affair between them had been strange from the beginning. It had been strange from the standpoint that a white man lived in the house with a former slave woman, and no one seemed to care.

Elizabeth and Mrs. Miller had always been aware of Sophia and John's living arrangement. Not only were they aware, the whole damned town was aware. Mrs. Miller had told Elizabeth that she should try and talk some sense into Sophia before it got too late. Elizabeth said that she had talked to her several times, but it hadn't done any good.

Sophia and John kept on living together, and they were the subject of a lot of talk, but all of the talk had seemed to be from Elizabeth and Mrs. Miller. If anyone else cared, they didn't talk about it. John had become a well-liked businessman around town. He had been very generous when it came to helping those in need. Whenever someone fell on hard times, which anymore was far too often, he had always been willing to help.

Nonetheless, John and Sophia were doing the unthinkable. Maybe they got away with it, because of John's business stature, and his humanitarian acts in the community. Whatever the reason, nobody bothered them, and they kept on doing what they had been doing.

Elizabeth and Mrs. Miller had kept their gossip going, but they kept it confined within the walls of Magnolia Manor. They had looked at it from all angles, but they couldn't come up with anything that sounded reasonable enough to justify what Sophia and John had managed to pull off. Mrs. Miller suggested that maybe they should just leave it alone since that's what everybody else had done. Elizabeth agreed with her, but she said that it was still mind boggling, and she was afraid for both Sophia and John.

They had decided that they would leave it alone, but regardless of what they started out talking about, they would end up talking about Sophia and John. Theirs had been a very legitimate concern. It wouldn't have been far-fetched at all for some of the local citizens to take it upon themselves to rid the town of both Sophia and John.

Richard didn't care that Sophia and John had become lovers. In fact, he was pleased with the arrangement. He certainly didn't care about their racial differences. After all, he had been the product of a not so different arrangement, and he had lived his entire life in a similar environment.

SEVENTEEN

S hortly after the war had started, Mrs. Miller and Elizabeth started spending more time together. Eventually, it had gotten to the point where Elizabeth seemed to spend more time with Mrs. Miller than she did taking care of the chores around the mansion. When the weather was nice, they usually sat on the porch. They had been talking about General Grant. Mrs. Miller had said that back during the war, they had no idea that they were hosting the future President of the United States.

Elizabeth had asked Mrs. Miller if she thought that he was a good choice. Mrs. Miller said that he would probably be alright. She said that the biggest problem with men is that they always want to fight if they can't agree on something.

As soon as she had said that men always want to fight, Mrs. Miller thought about her husband getting into a fight on the floor of the State Legislature. Her thought had caused Elizabeth to remember him pulling his old pistol out of his satchel, and had her thinking that he was going to shoot the man in town. It had gotten to the point where they could remember him and laugh, rather than missing him and feeling sad.

Sophia saw Elizabeth at church every Sunday, and every Sunday, she had to stand and listen, while Elizabeth told her what she thought about her living with John. Yet, Sophia didn't seem to let it bother her. She listened to Elizabeth, and at the same time ignored whatever she wanted to ignore. Alfred never said anything about their relationship. He had told Elizabeth that it was none of his business.

Sophia's live in lover was up and at the saloon early every morning. The saloon didn't have any customers at that time of day to warrant opening the doors so soon, other than maybe two or three souse heads that couldn't wait. Sophia usually spent most of her time at home. She had become a seamstress, she was good at it, and it was profitable for her. She had her bank account that Mr. Miller had left for her, and instead of spending that money, she had been adding to it.

Lucy Pimberton lived down the street from Sophia, and they had known each other since right after the war. Although they knew each other, Sophia never considered that she and Lucy were close friends, just more or less, acquaintances. However, when Lucy needed to borrow money, she had always gone to Sophia. She had borrowed small amounts on several occasions, and she had never failed on her commitment to repay.

Lucy had found it necessary to borrow money again. Unlike in the past, she needed a more substantial amount. Sophia had the money. Yet, she wondered how Lucy could even imagine that she was able to let her borrow such a large sum. Although she didn't want to do it, she did it anyway.

The loan was large enough that Sophia had legal papers drawn up to secure the transaction. The lien was against property that Lucy owned in town. After Sophia had loaned the money to her, Lucy faltered on her promise to repay, and Sophia wanted her money back.

Meanwhile, Lucy had left town without letting Sophia know where she had gone. However, she still owned the property in town that had been used to secure the loan. Sophia was not about to write it off as a loss, instead she had initiated legal proceedings against Lucy.

No one seemed to know where Lucy had gone to, and no one knew whether or not she had ever been made aware of the impending legal proceedings against her. Eventually, she returned home, but her property had been sold, and her legal obligations to Sophia had been met. Mrs. Miller and Elizabeth knew that Sophia had gotten her money back, because they remembered the day when Lucy's property was auctioned off to the highest bidder.

Richard had gotten old enough to get his job back working for John at the saloon. Elizabeth and Mrs. Miller didn't like it, but they had decided to go along with it. John and Richard were both at the saloon every day.

Sophia had been straightening things up around the house when she heard a knock at the door. When she had opened it, she couldn't speak. She just stood there staring at the man in front of her, and he stared back. It was Daniel, the first boy that she had ever loved. It had been a long time, but she didn't have to tax her memory to know who he was. She had never expected to see him again, but she was glad that she had.

Sophia told him about how she felt the day that she found out that he had been sold. Daniel told her that he was sold to a family that lived in Mississippi. He didn't know what had bothered him the most, being sold and separated from his family, or being sold and separated from her. He said that it was the worst feeling of his life. Sophia told him that he didn't have to tell her about how he felt, because she had the same feeling. After the war had ended, he said that he found his parents.

Daniel had told Sophia that she was beautiful back then, but she had become even more beautiful. She remembered how shy he had always been. She told him that he had learned how to smooth talk a woman.

He said that he had married, had a family, and that he worked for the railroad. Since they had been working in the area, he wanted to see her. He had talked to Elizabeth, because he had stopped at Magnolia Manor— not knowing if Elizabeth or Sophia would still be there. He had asked Sophia if she was married. She said no, but that she had a son, and that she was living with a man that she loved.

After talking for a while, Daniel said that he had to leave. Standing near the door, he apologized for just showing up like a ghost, but he said that he had to see her one more time, so that he could stop wondering about her.

Sophia was glad that he had stopped by, and she needed to see him again for the same reason that he needed to see her—so that she could stop wondering. Just for a few seconds, Daniel held her in his arms, and then they kissed. After he had left the house, she stood on the porch and watched. When he was about to turn the corner, he looked back, and they waved at each other. When he was out of sight, she kept looking, and she knew that she had seen him for the last time.

Although brief, Sophia and Daniel had shared a passionate moment, yet he was married, and she was in love with John. However, they didn't think of it as cheating, or as being unfaithful to their new love. Instead, it had been viewed more as an opportunity—born of necessity—to close the door to their hearts, the door that had been left open too long.

It was a beautiful day, the sun was shining, the weather was warm, and it was a good day to be outside. Sophia decided to walk to Magnolia Manor, and visit Elizabeth and Mrs. Miller. On the way, she had prepared herself for the verbal thrashing that she had become accustom to getting whenever she was around them. She didn't expect that anything had changed. When she arrived, she hugged Elizabeth, and then she walked over to where Mrs. Miller had been seated and hugged her.

Elizabeth had asked where Richard was. Sophia said that he had gotten off from work, and that he had gone for a walk. Mrs. Miller said that he and Charles were probably together, because Charles had been gone for a while. Sophia, Elizabeth and Mrs. Miller all sat on the back porch together. Sophia had been waiting for them to start in on her regarding her love life, but they never brought it up.

Mrs. Miller said that Charles would be leaving home pretty soon to attend college. Elizabeth wondered aloud what Richard would do every day when Charles was gone. Nobody tried to answer her question, they just let it pass.

Elizabeth had asked Sophia if Daniel found her. She said that he did and that they had talked for a long time. Mrs. Miller said that she still remembered the day when Sophia found out that he had been sold. Elizabeth said that it would be a day that none of them would ever forget. Sophia had told them that Daniel was married and had a family. Mrs. Miller and Elizabeth had been thinking, or maybe hoping, that Sophia and Daniel would pick up where they had left off—it would be a good way to get rid of John. After finding out that Daniel had married, Mrs. Miller looked at Elizabeth and said there goes that idea. Sophia asked what idea, but Mrs. Miller said never mind.

Sophia had gotten up from her seat, and she had gone out into the backyard. Slowly she walked around looking at things. Mrs. Miller had asked her what it was that she was thinking about, but she didn't say anything; she kept staring around in the yard. Finally, she said that it seemed so lifeless and lonely out there. Elizabeth said lonely out where; Sophia said in the backyard. Mrs. Miller said that it was different for sure. Then they remembered how the kids used to romp around, and sometimes chased after Sophia—things had changed a lot.

Mrs. Miller had let her mind drift way back. She admitted that it had become a lonesome place. She missed the commotion, and then she said that she missed Austin even more. Elizabeth changed the tone a little hoping to keep Mrs. Miller from becoming depressed. She told about how he used to eat breakfast. He would walk through, and pick something up from his plate; stick it in his mouth, and keep on walking. Then Mrs. Miller laughed, and said that she had hardly ever seen him eat breakfast, because she would still be in bed.

Sophia wasn't talking much, but she had been listening to Elizabeth and Mrs. Miller. She had told them that they seemed to spend a lot of time sitting around talking. Elizabeth said that she was right about that. They talked about the good times, and every once in a while she said that they talked about the not so good times.

Eighteen

M ost of the customers at the Tempest had gotten to know Richard. They knew that his father was Austin Miller, and that Sophia was his mother. It was no secret that Richard, Sophia and John lived together. In spite of the well mixed ethnic backgrounds and social arrangement at Sophia's house, Richard had become a likable citizen around town.

John and Sophia were able to spend more time together since Richard could take care of the saloon. Sophia had once told John that the only time she had ever been anywhere was when they moved from North Carolina to Tennessee. Since it had been such a long time ago, and since she was so young at the time, that memory had become bits and pieces.

John told Sophia that Richard had been doing a good job of managing the saloon. He had told her that so that he could tell her that he had made plans to take her to New York City. She had never been anywhere. Then, when she had the chance, she had become hesitant, but only because the thought of being so far from home was somewhat frightening. She and John had talked about it, and finally she had given in, without a lot of arm twisting.

Sophia told Elizabeth and Mrs. Miller that she and John were going on a trip. Elizabeth didn't like it when Sophia had told her where they had planned on going. Elizabeth didn't know where New York City was, but wherever it was, it sounded like it was too far away to be traveling. Sophia said that she wanted to see what other places were like, because she had never been anywhere.

Mrs. Miller had supposed that John would close down the saloon while they were gone. Sophia said that Richard knew enough about the business, and that he could keep it operating while they were away. Mrs. Miller and Elizabeth looked at each other, both with a snide expression on their face. Although they had looked at each other, their cynical look had been intended for Sophia. They just didn't want her to see it.

Sophia could tell that they didn't approve of Richard being in charge of the saloon. The reality was that they didn't want Richard to have anything to do with the saloon. Yet, they had decided that they wouldn't get involved in something that was none of their business. They would just sit on the side and watch.

After Sophia had left, Mrs. Miller supposed that John Umhaw must really care a lot about her. She said that a trip like that costs a lot of money. Elizabeth granted that they had made up their minds, and that there was no way that they could put a stop to it. Mrs. Miller said that he had the money so let him spend it on her. When Mrs. Miller made that statement, it reminded Elizabeth of how she used to be with Mr. Miller's money.

John filled Richard in on all of the dos and don'ts for the saloon, not that he had to, but just as a reminder. Sophia had made arrangements with Alfred to take them to the train station. When they left town, it was the first time that Sophia had ever been on a train. She was excited, and she was surprised at how fast it traveled—zipping along at a speed of twenty five to thirty miles per hour.

The train had made several stops along the way. When they had made it to the first town that seemed like a big town to Sophia, she thought that they had arrived in New York City. John explained that there would be many stops along the way. He told her that they would even have to change trains several times; the train that they had left home on didn't go straight through.

Sophia remembered Elizabeth saying that New York City had to be a long ways to go just to be traveling, but she didn't care, she just wanted to go somewhere, anywhere, distance didn't matter. The thrill of riding on a train, seeing places and things that she had never seen before, she loved being where she was, and she loved being there with John.

They had been traveling for what seemed like a distance that should have put them in another world, but the next stop would be the end of the line for them. The train had slowed down for the approach into the city, and Sophia couldn't believe the sight. She didn't know that there was a city anywhere that could be so large. However, she was where she wanted to be; she had made it all the way to New York City.

They had found hotel accommodations, one of the finest in the city according to John. She had seen the hotel back at home, but it was nothing like the one where they would be staying. John had asked if she was having fun. She said that it didn't seem real, and that she could live the rest of her life in New York City. John was familiar with the city, because he had lived there for a while when he first arrived from France.

They had been shown to their room, and Sophia stood at the window looking at all of the people as they shuffled around in the streets below. John watched as she studied the metropolis, eyeballing it as if she had been trying to get it all fixed in her mind so that she wouldn't forget. He had said that he was taking her to dinner, and that would be another first. She told him how happy he had made her, but he said that he was the one that had been made happy, simply because she was happy.

It was an upscale restaurant. The maître d' held the chair as Sophia sat down. She noticed that the table had been set with beautiful silverware and crystals. She had recognized it because she had seen the same thing back at Magnolia Manor. She was good at plying proper etiquette and charisma—she had learned from watching Mrs. Miller—and like Mrs. Miller, she loved doing it.

When they had decided on what to order, John asked if he could order for her, and she told him that he could. Since the maître d' was of French descent, John spoke to him in his native language. When he had finished, Sophia said that she had no idea as to what they had said, but she loved listening to the two of them speaking French.

She told John that she had been impressed by the big city, the ritzy hotel, and by the classy restaurant. Yet, the thing that had impressed her most was the handsome gentleman that had been letting her experience the most eloquent evening of her life. John had lifted his glass of wine, and Sophia had lifted hers. After their glasses had kissed, he said, "I love you."

The next morning, John and Sophia toured the city by carriage. They had their own chauffeur, and they had ridden around for hours, shopping and sightseeing. Sophia said that she had been doing what Mrs. Miller used to do when she went on trips with Mr. Miller. It had all been such an unreal experience. Even though it had been happening to her, it was hard to believe that she was not dreaming.

Sophia had known for a long time that John had friends and relatives living in New York City. He wanted her to meet them, but he had said that they would do that the next day. He wanted their first full day in the city to be hers.

She had been somewhat apprehensive about meeting John's family. She wondered if they might have any objections about him being with her since she was a former slave. He had told her that his family didn't care about things like that.

The next morning, their first stop was at the house of John's uncle. Sophia was still apprehensive about meeting his family, but again, John told her that it wouldn't matter to them. Furthermore, he said that it wouldn't be anything that they had to even talk about; he wouldn't walk through the door, and say this is Sophia, and by the way, she used to be a slave. She had put her elbow to his ribs to let him know that she knew better.

John had knocked on the door, and then he had taken a step backwards to wait. When his uncle opened the door, he recognized him. Immediately, he put his arms around John, and lifted him up off the floor. They had started moving backward, one more step and they would have fallen off the porch. John had not introduced Sophia—he hadn't been given the opportunity—and his uncle had seemed to be blinded by the fact that she was there.

When they went inside, it was almost a repeat of what had happened on the porch. Several people were in the house, and John knew all of them. When they were through hugging and kissing, he introduced Sophia. After they had been introduced, John's uncle apologized to Sophia for his behavior—he had overlooked her standing on the porch, but it had not been intentional. He had asked Sophia to excuse his lack of manners. After a lot of talking and kidding around, Sophia had blended in like a member of the family, and she felt like she might be right where she belonged—mingling with the French in the middle of New York, City.

When they were back in the carriage, John asked Sophia if she was still nervous about his family. She said that she loved his family. She thought that they had a heavier accent than that of his. Yet, she didn't have a problem understanding them. John felt like Sophia shouldn't have expected to have a problem understanding them since she didn't have a problem understanding him. She told John that she could understand his family members better than she could understand him, because his French had gotten mixed up with the southern drawl.

Before leaving the city, John told Sophia that he wanted her to see the Atlantic Ocean, and see it from the deck of a steamboat. Sophia had never been on the water in any kind of boat—in fact, she had never even waded around in a pond. Standing at the dock, and waiting to board the steamer had been a little scary—riding on a boat and surrounded by so much water—but she did it.

They had traveled down the Hudson River. When she did see the Atlantic, she couldn't believe that there was a place with so much water, or that there was that much water in any place. Standing on the deck and looking out across the vastness of blue, John told her that France was over on the other side, but it was several thousand miles away.

Eventually, John had shown New York City to Sophia, and she had met many of his friends and relatives. He had said to her that part of what he had been doing was to just show her off. Back in their hotel room, Sophia was again standing at the window, having a last look at the nightlights of New York City.

Although it had gotten dark outside, the streetlights made it possible for her to still see the people moving about. The next day, they would be leaving for home. When she turned around, John was sitting on the side of the bed staring at her. When she asked him what it was that he had been looking at, he said that he was looking at the only woman that he had ever loved. Soon, the only light in their room were the reflections in the window from the streetlights that flickered below.

When Sophia and John returned home, the sun had gone down. They had thought that Richard might already be at home, but he came in shortly after they had arrived. Richard was glad that they were both back. He didn't like being the only one in the house. Sophia asked him if he had gotten tired of eating his own cooking. He told her that he didn't cook; he had been eating at Magnolia Manor. Richard wanted to know all about New York City. They sat up late, and Sophia told him everything ... she told him almost everything.

The next morning, Sophia walked to Magnolia Manor. She had to let Elizabeth know that she was back at home. She had the feeling that she had to let Mrs. Miller know as well. When she was telling them about the trip, Sophia described everything in detail. There had been some goings on that she had to keep to herself, simply because they had been personal.

The trip to New York City had drawn John and Sophia closer together than ever before. In part, that had been his reason for taking her there. While they were gone, they had talked about the possibility of them getting married. Sophia wanted John as her husband, but after talking about it, both had agreed that it probably wouldn't be the right thing to do in Bolivar. If they lived in New York City, yes, but not in Bolivar.

Everybody in town knew that they lived together, and no one seemed to care. They had come to the conclusion that getting married might be pushing things a little too far. They were happy living together, and they didn't want to create a situation that might put an end to what they already had. Sophia had said that if they were to get married and if the locals didn't get rid of them, her mom and Mrs. Miller may have taken it upon themselves to escort them out of town.

The trip to New York City was well behind them, but Sophia had thoughts about it almost every day. She had made frequent trips to Magnolia Manor to visit her mom and Mrs. Miller. Yet, almost two weeks had passed since her last visit, and that had been too long. Therefore, she had to stop by just to satisfy everybody's mind. As soon as Sophia walked in, Mrs. Miller asked her if she had gained weight. Sophia admitted that she had gained a few pounds.

Elizabeth told her that she looked like she was pregnant. Sophia didn't hesitate to say that she was. Mrs. Miller had supposed that it was probably by that saloon keeper. Sophia told her that it was John's baby that she was carrying. Then the atmosphere changed, no one had much to say anymore. Finally, Sophia said that she had to leave, because she had to stop by the store in town.

After Sophia had left, Mrs. Miller and Elizabeth started counting. They had estimated the number of weeks that Sophia had been pregnant, and then they correlated that with the date of the trip to New York City. Based on their calculations, the time of the pregnancy, and the date of the trip were a close match. Elizabeth said that she knew from the beginning that she shouldn't have gone on that trip; she didn't like it from the start.

Mrs. Miller said that before it's over, they wouldn't know the white side of the family from the black side. Elizabeth felt like they had already made it to that point. Mrs. Miller decided that she had enough to worry about without being worried about Sophia and that saloon keeper. Elizabeth had said that she was going outside just to walk around in the yard for a while. She needed to free up her mind. Mrs. Miller went with her. She said that hers had been bogged down as well.

Neither Mrs. Miller nor Elizabeth was excited about the fact that Sophia had gotten pregnant. Even more, they hated the fact that she had gotten pregnant, and was not married. Yet, they were all on the same page when they concluded that Sophia and John should never get married. If they wanted to live their lives together, it would be best to do it as live-in lovers rather than making it official.

Sophia had gotten well into her pregnancy. She had gotten far enough along that Richard and John had started taking turns staying at home with her. She hadn't been to Magnolia Manor in a while, but she had kept on going to church on Sunday. Elizabeth had told her that it was time for her to start staying at home, but she wouldn't.

When she went into labor, she was in the very place that Elizabeth had been telling her not to go, she had been at church. Alfred and a couple of others had helped her to the carriage. Elizabeth had already gotten aboard. Louisa had delivered one for Sophia, so she climbed on as well.

Richard had stayed at home to help John with something that he had going on. When they saw Alfred pull in with Louisa on board, they knew what it meant. About an hour after getting home, Sophia gave birth to their daughter, and Richard named her Katie.

John operated the saloon by himself for several days, and Richard stayed at home with Sophia. Elizabeth told Mrs. Miller about the new baby. She had asked if the baby looked like she was white. Elizabeth said that she was as white as a sheet. Mrs. Miller had figured as much. She told Elizabeth that she may as well plan on sending food to Sophia every day for a while, because there's no telling what Richard and John might throw together—Sophia's cooking was bad enough, but Richard and John ....

When Sophia was up and about, Richard started back opening the saloon each day. John would stay at home with Sophia for a while before going to work. Since they had a daughter, John had asked Sophia again if she would marry him. Her opinion hadn't changed. She wished that they could, but she knew that they shouldn't. Richard had even wished that they were married, but he also understood why Sophia had always said no to his proposal.

Sophia had gotten a letter from her friend, Caroline. In the letter, Caroline said that Emily was coming to visit, and she had planned on being at her house for several days. She wanted to know if the two of them could visit her when Emily arrived. Sophia wanted very much to see both of them again; it had been a long time since the three of them had been together, and there would be a lot to talk about.

Mrs. Miller hadn't seen Sophia's new baby. She didn't leave the mansion much anymore. Sophia had decided to take her baby to Magnolia Manor. She didn't know what Mrs. Miller's reaction might be, but she decided to do it anyway. Sophia and Richard walked, and Richard carried the baby. They had almost made it to the mansion when Elizabeth saw them coming down the street. When she told Mrs. Miller, they both watched them from the window. They had their eyes fixed on Sophia, and they could see that her arms were empty. Mrs. Miller wondered if she had left the baby at home. Elizabeth said that Richard had the baby in his arms.

As soon as Sophia and Richard walked in, Mrs. Miller pulled the blanket back to have a better look at the baby. Then she said white, black, French ... what's next? After she had been satisfied, she put the blanket back in place.

Mrs. Miller asked Richard if he was still working at that saloon. Richard told her that he was. He had taken a couple of hours off, so that he could carry the baby for Sophia. Elizabeth told him that she would be glad when he got a real job. Mrs. Miller told Richard that Charles had asked her to tell him hello in the letter that she had received. Richard told her that he had received a letter from him also. Then Mrs. Miller wondered why he had bothered to tell her to say hello for him.

Looking at Elizabeth, Sophia said that she had gotten a letter from Caroline, and that she and Emily had made plans to visit her during the summer. Sophia had directed her remarks to Elizabeth, simply because Mrs. Miller had never cared much for Caroline or Emily. Yet, Mrs. Miller told her to be sure to bring them by, so that she could see them.

Mrs. Miller's request surprised Sophia a little, but not much. Sophia promised that she would have them stop by the mansion. After making the promise, Sophia wondered if Caroline and Emily would be interested in visiting her. Mrs. Miller had told Richard that he could go on to that saloon, and Sophia could ride home with Alfred when he stopped by to pick up Elizabeth.

After Richard had left, Sophia asked Mrs. Miller if she thought that she might get married again. Elizabeth butted in, and told her that it was none of her business if she did or didn't. Sophia said that she didn't mean to pry, but that she had just been wondering. Mrs. Miller didn't mind that she had asked the question. She said that she didn't want another husband, and that when Austin died, it seemed like she had died with him. Then Sophia wished that she hadn't brought it up.

Elizabeth was the only employee that Mrs. Miller had for taking care of the house. Jacob still tended the yard, but Fanny no longer worked at the mansion. Mrs. Miller didn't have any little tots running around anymore, and Elizabeth could take care of things. It had gotten to the point where it was no longer necessary to have someone around both day and night.

Sophia had suggested that Mrs. Miller and Elizabeth sit on the porch and relax, while she cooked dinner for them. Mrs. Miller told her not to bother, and that Elizabeth would take care of it. Nobody had ever craved for Sophia's cooking, and they still didn't. Then Mrs. Miller told Sophia to sit down and relax. The three of them sat on the porch, sometimes they talked, and sometimes they just sat there quietly.

When it had gotten too quiet, Elizabeth said that she could remember when you couldn't hear yourself talk for all of the noise around the house, but it wasn't like that anymore. Again, it had gotten quiet. After a while, Mrs. Miller said that there was a lot more excitement around the house back when they were at each other's throat. Elizabeth said that they didn't get too excited about things anymore.

On Sunday afternoon in late summer, Caroline and Emily returned home. Sophia had been expecting them, but she didn't know the specific date on which they would arrive. They had easily found Sophia's house, because she had provided instructions when she answered Caroline's letter.

When they pulled in, Sophia ran out to meet them. They had made so much noise that Richard and John could hear them from out back, but they didn't know who they were. Sophia introduced her friends to her family; she could tell that Caroline and Emily had been surprised when they saw John. They knew about Richard, although they had never met him, in addition, there was Katie. They went inside and sat down. Sophia told them about how she and John had gotten acquainted, and she told them about their trip to New York City.

After it had become obvious to John that Caroline and Emily didn't mind that Sophia had been living with a white man, he loosened up. He told them that he had been trying to get her to marry him, but she wouldn't. Sophia explained why she had always turned him down. When she did, Caroline and Emily agreed that it might be too much for where they lived. They had been surprised by the fact that they were even able to live together without any problems. John wanted to marry Sophia, but Caroline and Emily still remembered when Mrs. Miller didn't want them to be friends with Sophia.

Emily had said that she loved John's accent. She asked Sophia if she had learned how to speak French. Sophia said that she could say a few words, but not enough to carry on a conversation. Richard was better at it than she was, but he had been trying to learn the language.

Sophia said that Mrs. Miller and Elizabeth wanted them to stop by for a visit. They had already planned on visiting Elizabeth, but they were surprised to hear that Mrs. Miller wanted to see them. In fact, they had thought that Magnolia Manor would probably still be off limits to them—when they had made the trip to visit Sophia, they had no intentions of stopping by to see Mrs. Miller.

Caroline and Emily had never talked with Mrs. Miller. That day when she had taken them on the tour of the mansion, they just trailed along behind and listened to her. It had been the only time that they wanted to hurry, and leave Mr. Miller's house. However, since they had been invited, they decided to go with Sophia to the mansion.

They were standing on the porch at Magnolia Manor. Caroline and Emily waited for Sophia to knock on the door. Instead, she just opened it, and walked in. Mrs. Miller had been in the study, and Sophia had gone to get her. When Elizabeth saw Caroline and Emily standing in the entryway, she hugged them. Her first thought took her back to the day when Caroline, Emily and Amanda wandered into Mr. Miller's yard—wanting to play with Sophia. Elizabeth remembered the day very well, but it had become a little sketchy for them—it had been a long time ago.

Even though Caroline and Emily had been reluctant to visit Mrs. Miller based on her past behavior, Sophia had been less apprehensive. When Mrs. Miller saw them, she put her arms out and welcomed them to her home. They could see that life's circumstances had not passed her by. It was obvious that some of the fire had gone from her character.

They had been sitting in the parlor—Mrs. Miller, Caroline, Emily, Sophia and Elizabeth. Way back when, it wouldn't have been like that. It appeared to Caroline and Emily that attitudes may have changed, but they weren't sure. When they said that they were planning on spending the night at the hotel in town, Mrs. Miller insisted that they stay at the mansion. They had accepted her offer, simply because they didn't want her to know that they were still not overly fond of her. They had not forgotten how things used to be, and they didn't know if the Mrs. Miller that they had been looking at and listening to was real of if it had all been a front.

When Alfred stopped by to pick up Elizabeth, he took Sophia home. He too had been a little surprised that Mrs. Miller had invited Caroline and Emily to spend the night—he remembered how she never wanted them in her house. Sophia remembered how they used to sneak, and talk to each other whenever Mrs. Miller wasn't around. Elizabeth reminded them that all of that had been a long time ago, and a lot of things had changed since then.

Mrs. Miller kept Caroline and Emily up until it was rather late. She had a lot to talk about with them. She told them about the things that had happened since they had moved away. Finally, Caroline and Emily got around to telling her that they were sorry about the death of her husband. Mrs. Miller said that the saddest part about it was that it didn't have to happen. He had left home feeling fine, and got caught out in some cold, wet weather, and ended up with a bad case of pneumonia.

Mrs. Miller loved listening to them talk about how they used to play in Mr. Miller's backyard with Sophia— back before he had married. Mrs. Miller told them that they had known her husband long before she had. They had never thought about it, but she was right. After Caroline had said that Elizabeth had done about as much to raise them as their parents had, Mrs. Miller said that she had done the same thing with her children.

Mrs. Miller couldn't forget that she had been a grouch, always standing between them and Sophia. Then she wished that she had been more like her husband. She was sure that her attitude had made her miss out on a lot of things that she would have enjoyed. She had supposed that the only thing that she could do was to say that she's sorry.

Since Mrs. Miller had guests, Elizabeth had arrived at the mansion a little earlier than usual so that she could cook breakfast. It was a beautiful morning, and although she had arrived early, she found Mrs. Miller already up and sitting on the back porch. Elizabeth asked if she felt alright. Mrs. Miller granted that it was strange to see her up so early, but she had decided to get up, and see the morning sunrise. It had been a long time since she had seen one. When the coffee had finished brewing, Elizabeth took her a cup.

Shortly after Elizabeth had started cooking breakfast, Emily walked in. She told Elizabeth that her coffee had awakened her. Elizabeth said that she had heard those same words many times from Mr. Miller. She said that's what got him out of the bed every morning. A few minutes later, Caroline walked in. They had both gotten a cup of coffee, and they sat on the porch with Mrs. Miller.

Emily had commented about how quiet it is early in the morning. Mrs. Miller said that it's not just early in the morning; she said that it's like that all the time anymore. Elizabeth told them that breakfast was ready.

While they were eating, Richard and Sophia walked in. Richard had Katie in his arms; she was asleep so he laid her in bed. There had been a lot of chatter back and forth between Sophia, Caroline and Emily. Richard had sat down near Mrs. Miller, and started eating breakfast. They had their own conversation going. As he had often done, Richard slipped-up, and referred to Mrs. Miller as mama while they were talking. Caroline heard him, but she saw that it never fazed Mrs. Miller, and they kept on talking.

Caroline and Emily had seen a Mrs. Miller that they had never seen before. It was like she had put everything in reverse, and had it moving in the opposite direction—mending things as she came to them. They still had a clear memory of her invisible line, the one that had always separated white from black. To them, it seemed like the line had been erased, or at least, it had become less visible, a lot less visible.

Emily had a flashback of what things had been like when they were teenagers, but she wondered what had happened that caused things to change so much. Whatever it had been, she thought that it was good—it had been a major turnabout. They were all sitting at the table eating breakfast together—white and black—and it was okay.

Sophia had come to the mansion early, simply because that's where Caroline and Emily were. They had finished eating, and Elizabeth had removed the dishes from the table. Except for Sophia, everyone else had remained seated. Sophia had gotten up to help Elizabeth.

Unknowing to the others, Mrs. Miller had picked up on a few subtle reactions from Caroline and Emily. Although subtle, she had interpreted them correctly. She told Caroline and Emily that they must be astounded at how things had changed at Magnolia Manor. She was talking about the social atmosphere, white people and black people living together, and not fighting anymore. She knew that they had to be surprised, because they could remember what it used to be like between her and Sophia.

Mrs. Miller didn't expect Caroline, or Emily to comment on what she had said, and no comment had been necessary. They just listened to her talk, and she kept it simple. When she had finished, she said that she didn't know why, but things had always been different at Magnolia Manor.

Before leaving, Caroline and Emily thanked Mrs. Miller for letting them spend the night. Mrs. Miller said that it was she that should thank them. She said that she felt a lot better after having the chance to talk to them again, and maybe do some patchwork. Caroline and Emily, along with Mrs. Miller and Elizabeth, found themselves feeling a little blue after saying goodbye.

Before leaving the mansion, Sophia took Caroline and Emily out into the yard to show them the rose bush that Mr. Miller had bought for her to plant in memory of Amanda. She explained that one of the other rose bushes was for Mr. Miller, and the other was for his daughter,

Annie. They shared a solemn moment together. Then they were reminded that they should go to the cemetery to visit the grave site of Amanda.

After leaving the cemetery, they went back to Sophia's house. It was hard for them to believe how much Mrs. Miller's attitude about things had changed. Emily had asked Sophia about how Mrs. Miller reacted when she found out that her husband was Richard's father. Sophia said that she was mad as hell when she first found out, but mostly, she was mad at Mr. Miller. It had been made clear to Caroline that she liked Richard, because she had heard him refer to her as mama, and it didn't bother her.

Sophia told them about how Richard had always called Mr. Miller daddy, and for a long time, he had called Mrs. Miller mama. Mrs. Miller didn't like it, and they had been able to get him to stop, but every once in a while he still called her mama.

Sophia supposed that little by little, Mrs. Miller had started to like Richard, because it's hard to hate children, especially when they call you mama. Emily said that she had always hated her, but not anymore. They were glad that they had spent the night at Magnolia Manor, and for the first time, they appreciated being around her.

Caroline and Emily had been fascinated by Sophia and John. However, they couldn't believe that they hadn't had any problems, especially with racial attitudes being the way that they were. Emily asked Sophia if she thought that she would ever change her mind and marry him. Sophia didn't think that she would. She still felt like they had probably pushed things to the limit by living together, and that getting married might be overdoing it.

With enthusiasm, Sophia had to tell about how the Yankees wanted to throw Mrs. Miller and everybody else out of the mansion during the war. She described how Mrs. Miller talked them into letting them stay. Then she got to the big news. She had said that they would never guess who it was that they had shared the mansion with during the war—General Grant. When Emily asked if she was talking about President Grant, Sophia said yes.

Sophia had to tell them about Daniel. She said that she had fallen in love with him, and then he was sold and taken to Mississippi. Yet, he had found her, and he had stopped by to see her not so long ago. As soon as she had told them, Caroline said that she was glad that slavery had ended. Emily had always been feistier than Caroline, or Amanda, and more outspoken. She said that the South had been devastated by the war, but if that's what it took to end slavery, she didn't care.

Together again, they realized that their feelings toward each other had remained unchanged. They were as close as ever, just like old times except for Amanda. The only thing that could come between them would be the miles, and the only thing that could separate them would be death. Saying goodbye had been hard to do, but they did.

NINETEEN

Now and then, Mrs. Miller would go to the cemetery to visit the graves of her first and second husband, and that of her daughter. When she did, she would be accompanied by Elizabeth, Sophia and Richard, or at least one of them. Sometimes they took freshly cut flowers, along with a single leaf from the magnolia tree. The same tree that they had planted in the front yard years ago— the magnolia leaf was for Mr. Miller.

Sophia and Katie had made another one of their visits to Magnolia Manor. Like most of the time, Elizabeth and Mrs. Miller had been sitting on the back porch. During fair weather, that had become their favorite place to be. Sophia sat on the porch with them and Elizabeth held Katie. When Elizabeth had held her long enough, she turned her loose, and let her have the backyard. Mrs. Miller sat with them for a while, and then she told Elizabeth that she was going to lie down. When she had gotten up to go inside, Elizabeth got up as well. Mrs.

Miller told her to stay with Sophia. She said that she could put herself in bed.

After Mrs. Miller had left, Elizabeth told Sophia that Mrs. Miller hadn't been feeling well. Sophia had taken it to mean that she just didn't feel well on that particular day, but she had interpreted things wrongly. Elizabeth told her that the doctor had been stopping by to see her for several days, but he didn't know for sure what was wrong with her.

After finding out about Mrs. Miller's health, Sophia started visiting her more often. Elizabeth was still working during the day, but there was no hired help at the mansion after Elizabeth went home. Sophia told Elizabeth that she could spend the night with Mrs. Miller until she was well again. Elizabeth told Mrs. Miller about Sophia's offer, but she insisted that she didn't need anyone. However, Sophia started spending nights with her anyway. Sophia had told Richard and John that they would have to take care of themselves until Mrs. Miller started feeling better.

Albert had been practicing law for a while. Charles was expected to return home within a few days from school, but just to visit. His law degree was still out there in front of him, and he had some more work to do before he could hang a shingle on the door.

John had asked Sophia to marry him more times than she could remember, but her answer was always the same. Whenever she said no to his proposals, he would tell her to at least think about it. Finally, John had come to the conclusion that Sophia would never be his wife. He had even offered to take her to France, but that offer had been turned down as well.

It had been a slow day at the Tempest Saloon, and Richard felt like John may have been depressed. Richard had been there with him all day, and he noticed that John had downed quite a few shots of liquor. That was unusual, because John was not much of a drinker. Richard had spoken to him about drinking so much, but John didn't pay any attention to him. Instead, he kept on drinking. Finally, he had found a table over in the corner, out of the way of any customers, and he sat down with a bottle of his own.

Before sundown, John had taken several bottles of liquor from behind the bar, and he had placed them in a cloth sack—he didn't let Richard see him get the liquor. He had told Richard that he could close the place down whenever he was ready. Richard told him that he would take care of things. Richard was glad that he had decided to leave. He had already had too much to drink, and he had gotten close to being drunk. On his way out, Richard had noticed the sack in his hand, but he didn't know what was in it.

At closing time, Richard locked the door to the saloon and went home. When he walked into the house, he looked for John, but John wasn't there. He didn't understand why, because he had assumed that John left the saloon so that he could go home, and sleep it off.

Richard had sat up longer than usual, hoping that John would show up. When he didn't show up, Richard went to bed. The next morning, Richard noticed that John still hadn't come home. When it was time, Richard went to town to open the saloon. He had hoped that John would show up sometime during the day. Richard hadn't seen Sophia to talk to her, because she had been staying at the mansion during the night, and he was gone to the saloon by the time she came home in the morning.

At the end of the day, Richard closed the saloon, and headed home. When he entered the house, John was not there, and it seemed obvious to him that John hadn't been there since he had left. Everything was still in the same place. Even though it had gotten a little late, Richard walked to Magnolia Manor to see if Sophia knew of his whereabouts. After explaining the situation to her, she said that she didn't know where he was, and she had gotten very concerned about him.

Mrs. Miller had just gone to her bedroom, but she overheard Sophia and Richard talking. In her nightclothes, she went to see what was wrong. They told her that John was missing. Richard explained that it had been two nights since he had last seen him. Mrs. Miller told Richard to tell the sheriff if he hadn't returned by morning.

When Richard had left, Sophia and Mrs. Miller talked about John. Mrs. Miller's thought was that some of the people may have done something to him, because he had been living with Sophia. When she said it, Sophia became frightened, and Mrs. Miller wished that she had kept her thoughts to herself. The next morning after Elizabeth had made it to the mansion, Sophia told her about John being missing. Elizabeth had the same thought about him as Mrs. Miller had had—he had fallen prey to some of the local hotheads.

John had been gone for three days. Richard had reported his disappearance to the sheriff, but no one had seen him, nor had anyone heard anything from him. The word had quickly spread that John was missing, and people had been out looking for him.

Richard stopped by the mansion on his way home at night, hoping that Sophia may have heard something, because he had heard nothing. On the fourth night when Richard had gone home, he unlocked the door and went inside. It was dark, but he had lit the lamp, so that he could find his way around. In the bedroom, he found John lying across the bed. Looking at him, Richard didn't know if he had laid down and fallen asleep, or if he had laid down and died.

Richard stood at the door for a few seconds, just looking at him and thinking the worst—could he really be dead? Then, he walked over to the bed, but not too close. He still had the same chilling thought. He had leaned forward, and extended his arm, so that he could reach John. He had given him a gentle nudged to get his attention, or hoping that he could get his attention. When he didn't move, Richard nudged him again, but he still didn't move.

Richard's worst thought had taken control of his mind, and it pushed his fear aside. He put both hands on John and shook him hard. Then he could see that he wasn't dead, because he could see him breathe, and he had moved a little on his own. John opened his eyes and looked at Richard, then he closed them as if going back to sleep. Richard kept shaking him, and finally he opened his eyes again. He had been on his back, and he looked at Richard as if he was a stranger. John didn't know where he was, or how he had gotten there.

Richard had helped him up, so that he could sit on the side of the bed. He sat there looking at Richard—holding on to the bed while watching everything go around in circles. Richard was glad that he had come home, but he was in bad shape. Richard asked him where he had been.

Before John could respond, Richard told him that every-body had been worried about him. John didn't feel like talking, but Richard insisted on knowing where he had been. Richard could see that he was in a half crazed state of mind, but that was because he had obviously been drunk for so long.

John told Richard that he had spent the last few days in an abandoned cabin down near the river. Richard asked him what for, and John said that he wanted Sophia to marry him, but she won't. He said that he didn't feel like doing anything but getting drunk, but he didn't know how long he had been drunk. He asked what day it was, and Richard told him. John said that he had come home, because he had run out of liquor, and that he had gotten hungry.

Richard helped him up off the bed and let him sit in a chair. They kept talking while Richard got some food together so that he could eat. While John ate, Richard went to Magnolia Manor to tell Sophia that he had come home. He had to tell her, because she had been so worried about him.

Richard had to knock on the door when he made it to Magnolia Manor, because it was after hours, and the doors had all been locked. Sophia let him in. She had assumed that it was just another one of his routine visits. Mrs. Miller was asleep, and Sophia and Richard sat in the parlor.

Richard told Sophia about the condition that he had found John in, and he told her his reason for doing what he had done. They talked just a few minutes and then Richard left. Sophia had gone back to be with Mrs. Miller. She sat in a rocking chair near her bedside. She had gotten used to being with her at night. She would sometimes doze off for a while, but mostly she slept during the day.

The next morning when Elizabeth arrived at the mansion, Sophia told her that John had come home. She told Elizabeth that he had been off somewhere trying to drink himself to death. Elizabeth asked why he wanted to do something like that. Sophia told her that it was because she wouldn't marry him.

After Sophia had finished talking to Elizabeth, she went home. She found John sitting on the back porch, drinking some coffee that he had made. He was suffering from a bad hangover after being drunk for four days. Sophia had made breakfast for him, hoping that something to eat would help bring him back to life, and make him want to live again.

Sophia told him that Richard had filled her in on the stupid stunt that he had pulled. John was sick, and not in much of a mood for talking, but he told Sophia that he had been in love with her for a long time, and he wanted her to be his wife. Again, Sophia explained that it would probably raise too many eyebrows if they were married; they had to leave things the way they were. Again, John said that they could move to France, and it would be different, but Sophia said no to that idea also.

While John was eating, he told Sophia that Richard had put something together for him to eat last night. He told her about how awful it was, but he had to eat it, because he had been so hungry. Sophia told him that being hungry, and suffering from a hangover served him right, and that it might teach him a lesson. She told him that he had walked off, leaving everybody wondering where he was, and some had even thought that he was dead.

He told Sophia that she was the only woman that he had ever asked to marry him. He had placed his empty plate on the floor near his chair. Sophia had made it clear that she wouldn't marry him, yet he seemed to have the idea that if he asked her enough, she might change her mind. He told her that if she wouldn't marry him, then he would never get married—he didn't want anyone else.

It had taken several days, but John had gotten himself together and he had started managing the saloon again. Charles had come home, but just for a few days. When Richard found out that he was back, he told John that he needed to go home for a while to see his brother. John said that he could take care of the saloon, and he told Richard that he could take a few days off from work until Charles had left.

Mrs. Miller had been feeling better, but still not quite up to par. Yet, she felt good enough so that Sophia didn't have to spend nights with her anymore. When Richard arrived at the mansion, he found Mrs. Miller and Charles sitting out back. As soon as Richard arrived, the conversation shifted from Charles and his mother to Charles and Richard. Mrs. Miller sat and listened, but she didn't let it sink in too much. They had started talking about things that were of little interest to her.

Although she had already been told, Mrs. Miller did pay attention when Charles told Richard that he had planned to get married as soon as he finished law school. When he told him, Richard knew that her name had to be Lizzie. Still, Charles kidded with him by saying that he had dumped Lizzie for another girl that he had found.

Charles and Richard had said that they would be back in a couple of hours, and then they left together. Elizabeth had seen them leave, and she asked Mrs. Miller if she knew where they were going. She said that they didn't tell her, and she didn't bother to ask.

Mrs. Miller had told Elizabeth that she may as well sit down, and relax for a while. They had gotten to the point where they could and would talk about just whatever. They remembered, and rehashed some of the things that had happened at the mansion. Things that at one time had been swept under the rug or kept in the closet had become fair game for conversation and even laughter— they didn't care anymore.

Mrs. Miller told Elizabeth that Richard had done more to bring peace to Magnolia Manor than anyone. She said that when Richard was just a little tot, he used to call her mama, and he called Austin daddy. She remembered how he used to crawl onto her lap, and she would rock him to sleep.

She said that back then, she didn't want Richard calling her mama, and she didn't want to hold him in her arms while he slept, because he was black. Since Richard didn't know the difference between white and black, she couldn't keep on pushing him away just because he wanted to be near her. She recalled how she and Sophia had butted heads for so long, but they didn't anymore. In her mind, she said that things had changed because of Richard.

Charles had spent only a few days at home, but that was as long as he could stay. The day before he left had been spent entirely with his mother, but also in the company of Elizabeth, Sophia and Richard. Mrs. Miller had become accustomed to taking a nap during the day, but she passed on it so that she could be with the family. When it seemed like some had gotten bored with just sitting around, Mrs. Miller suggested that they all visit the cemetery.

Richard and Charles had to walk to the south side of town where Alfred had been working. They had decided to use his carriage for transportation. While they were gone, Sophia went outside to pick some fresh flowers for the graves. Jacob had been working in the yard all day. When Sophia told him what she was doing, he went over to the magnolia tree, and plucked a single leaf from a limb along with one of its fragrant flowers.

Jacob had been around long enough to know how they did things. While he was still standing near the magnolia tree, Sophia told him to get enough for Annie's grave. When Jacob told her that her rose bush looked good, the one that she had planted for Amanda, Sophia stopped and had a look. While she was looking at it, Jacob snipped a stem from the bush, one that had several flowers on it. He gave the stem of roses to Sophia. They didn't say anything, but each knew what it was for.

At the cemetery, Mrs. Miller had mixed emotions. Some of the things that she thought about had made her smile, and some had made her want to cry, because life seemed so empty without them. Not far from each other were the graves of her daughter, her first husband, and that of her second husband. They placed a floral on each. Sophia had given the stem of roses to Mrs. Miller, so that she could place it on the grave of Austin Miller.

The next morning, Richard took Charles to the train station. He stayed with him until he had climbed aboard and left. With Charles gone, they fell back into the rut that had become theirs, and got back to their daily routine.

While Charles had been there, Mrs. Miller said that it seemed like Magnolia Manor had come back to life. She conceded that it was not to the extent that it used to be, but it was livelier than it had been.

TWENTY

Mrs. Miller had good days, and some that were not so good, but she never complained. She hadn't been away from the mansion in quite a while, because she didn't feel like going anywhere. When she felt good enough, more often than not, she would be in her favorite place—on the porch with Elizabeth at her side.

Almost two months had passed since Sophia had spent a night at the mansion. She didn't have to, because Mrs. Miller had been on the upside, and feeling good. Yet, whatever it was that had been causing her ups and downs had come back again. Sophia had started back spending nights with her. She was not back because Mrs. Miller had asked her to; she was back because Elizabeth had told her to.

Katie had gotten to where she preferred staying at the mansion with Sophia rather than staying at home with Richard and John. John wished that Sophia could be at home with him every night. To compensate for her absence, sometimes Richard would take care of things at the saloon, and John would stay at home to be with Sophia during the day.

Mrs. Miller had told Sophia that even though they were not married, she knew that neither she nor John cared for being separated from each other every night. Her empathy had been mostly for Sophia, because she still didn't care much for John. Her feelings may have been influenced by the fact that John was a white man, and she didn't like the idea of him staying with Sophia. If that was the reason, she didn't talk about it. Although she had told Sophia that she didn't have to stay with her at night, Sophia stayed anyway.

Charles felt like he had been in school forever, but he finally graduated with a degree in law. He had hung his shingle in town, and within walking distance of Magnolia Manor. When he came home, he moved back into the same bedroom that he had grown up in.

The paint on the shingle that Charles had hung outside of his law office was still wet when he married Lizzie. After they were married, they lived with Mrs. Miller. Lizzie was the only one that had to move, because Charles was already there.

Charles had been married only a few months when Richard told him that he had been thinking about getting married. Charles was surprised, because Richard had been keeping it quiet. Richard had told Sophia about Sarah, but no one else. However, Sophia had been trying to talk him out of getting married. Her concern had been whether or not Richard could support a wife, because he had always depended on her.

Sophia didn't want to be the one standing between her son and his marriage. Therefore, she told Elizabeth and Mrs. Miller about Richard's wedding plans. She had told them with the hope that they would tell him that he should delay things for a couple of years—it would get her off the hook if Mrs. Miller or Elizabeth told him that he should wait. However, her idea backfired. Elizabeth and Mrs. Miller thought that it would be alright. Mrs. Miller told Sophia that the time had come for her to let him stop holding onto her dress tail, and get out on his own. Elizabeth said that the only reason he had his hand on her dress tail was because Sophia wouldn't let him turn loose.

Sophia decided that she may as well go ahead and give Richard her approval. Mrs. Miller had already said that if you are man enough to work in a saloon, you certainly ought to be man enough to get married—he was twenty one years old. Mrs. Miller wanted Richard to get married at Magnolia Manor, because she wanted to be at the wedding—in just a few minutes, they had changed Sophia's mind, and selected the site for the wedding. The only thing left was to decide on the date, but they had supposed that they should leave that up to Richard and Sarah.

Elizabeth had gone home for the day. Charles and his wife, Lizzie, were in the parlor when Richard walked in. Lizzie and Richard had known each other before she and Charles were married, but only through Charles. They sat in the parlor and talked for a while. Lizzie told Richard that Mrs. Miller had been up all day, and that she was getting ready for bed. Richard had been on his way home, but he had stopped by mainly to see how Mrs. Miller was doing. Aside from that, Mrs. Miller had gotten to the point where she expected him to stop by on his way home. Richard stood up, and said that he should go see mama before she falls asleep.

After Richard had left, Lizzie asked Charles if Richard called Mrs. Miller mama all the time. He told her that he had gotten into the habit of calling her mama when he was a little boy. When he had gotten older, they tried to make him stop, but it didn't work.

The door to Mrs. Miller's bedroom had been left open, and Sophia was turning back the covers on her bed. Richard had stopped in the doorway. Both Sophia and Mrs. Miller had their backs turned, so Richard tapped on the opened door. When Mrs. Miller turned around, Richard said hello mama. Sophia told him to refer to her as Mrs. Miller. Calmly, Mrs. Miller told Sophia to hush, and close the door on her way out. After Sophia had left, Mrs. Miller told Richard that back in the old days, saying something like that would have been enough to cause a flare-up, but they could get away with it anymore.

After Mrs. Miller had laid down, Richard sat in the chair near her bedside. Mrs. Miller placed her hand in his, and held on to it. She told him that she had been looking forward to the wedding. Richard thanked her for allowing him to get married in the mansion. She told him that he didn't have to thank her. She said that it's like Austin used to say, "It's just the right thing to do." She asked Richard why he hadn't brought his bride by the mansion so that she could meet her. He didn't know why, but he promised that he would.

Richard had been concerned about Mrs. Miller's health. That was the reason why he had been stopping by the mansion so much. When he told her that he had been concerned, it only confirmed what she had suspected—he had been worried about her. She told him that he should stop fretting so much, and that she had been feeling a lot better. He had gotten up from his chair and pushed it aside. He then knelt down beside her bed to tell her goodnight. She had placed her arms around him, and she held him close to her chest.

Sophia had been sitting in the parlor with Charles and Lizzie. Richard had been with Mrs. Miller for about thirty minutes. Sophia had gotten up to check on them to see if they were alright. As she made her way toward the bedroom, curiosity had Charles and Lizzie following her. When Sophia opened the door to Mrs. Miller's bedroom, they saw Richard kneeling on the floor near the bed with his head resting on Mrs. Miller's chest. She still had her arms around his shoulder.

They both had ignored the opening of the door. Sophia still had her hand on the doorknob; she stepped back, and eased the door shut. Sophia, Charles and Lizzie stood outside the door for just a moment, and then they returned to the parlor. They had seen Mrs. Miller and Richard expressing their feelings to each other, and it had been a sensitive moment.

Lizzie had been surprised by the compassion that they had for each other, but not Sophia and Charles. Lizzie was surprised, because it was something that she had never seen before. On the other hand, she had never been part of a household where shades of black and white functioned the way that they did in Magnolia Manor.

Charles had excused himself, and he had gone outside. Sophia didn't know if she should or shouldn't, but she did anyway. She told Lizzie about Richard being Charles' half-brother, and how angry Mrs. Miller had been when she found out that her husband had gotten her pregnant. Lizzie knew that Richard and Charles were half-brothers, and she could easily understand the anger that Mrs. Miller had to have had toward her husband. Yet, she couldn't understand how Mrs. Miller had come to treat Richard as if he were her own son—he had been born a slave, and the product of her husband's unfaithfulness.

Charles had been waiting to talk to Richard. He had thought that he would spend a few minutes with Mrs. Miller and then say goodnight. Since Richard had been in the bedroom with her for so long, he and Lizzie went to bed. Sophia wanted Richard to leave so that she could maybe get some sleep. She didn't want to go into Mrs. Miller's bedroom and tell Richard that he should leave because it had gotten late—Mrs. Miller had already told her to leave them alone. Sophia had decided that she would lie down for a while until Richard had left.

The next morning, Elizabeth arrived at the mansion at about the same time that Sophia had gotten up. Sophia told Elizabeth that Richard had stopped by last night to see Mrs. Miller. She didn't know what time it was when he left, because she had fallen asleep and didn't wake up until morning. Elizabeth said that she would go and peek in on her. When she opened the door, Richard was sitting in the chair near her bedside, and both were sound asleep. She closed the door, and left them alone.

Sophia had sat down on the back porch. Elizabeth told her that Richard was still in the bedroom with Mrs. Miller, and that both were asleep. Elizabeth said that she felt like crying. Sophia told her that they had gone through all of that last night, and it's too early to start again.

When Elizabeth got her eyes dry, Charles and Lizzie walked out on the porch and sat down. Elizabeth said that since everybody was up so early, she had better get started on breakfast. Before she could go back inside,

Charles and Lizzie said that they didn't care for anything other than some coffee.

Charles had asked what time it was when Richard left. Sophia told him that he didn't. She said that he had spent the night in the bedroom with Mrs. Miller and that they were both asleep. That put a damper on things, and they had started to talk less. They just sat on the porch and started around out back.

Sophia had gotten up to get the coffee cups, and Elizabeth had the coffee pot. They filled the cups on the porch. After a while, they heard footsteps that got louder and louder, because they were getting closer and closer. They stared at the door to see who would open it. Richard opened the door, and then he held it for Mrs. Miller. When they could see her, they all stood, as if she was the commanding officer, and they were the rank and file.

Elizabeth had questioned whether or not she should be out of bed, but Mrs. Miller felt good. She had said that the morning was too beautiful not to get up and look at it. She said that she and Richard had a good talk last night, they had gotten plenty of sleep, and they were ready to face the day. Charles had given her his chair, and he and Richard sat on the steps. Mrs. Miller had asked Sophia if she had any more coffee. Sophia said yes ma'am, and she got a cup for her.

Everything had the makings of a beautiful day. They were feeling good, because Mrs. Miller was feeling good. Sophia had refilled their coffee cups along with one for herself. Then they sat and listened to the birds singing in the trees. The sun was just on the horizon, and it was becoming more spectacular with each passing minute. Mrs. Miller looked at it and said that if Austin could see it, he would stand there and look at it until it ended—he loved the beautiful sunrises and sunsets.

Mrs. Miller wondered aloud how many other houses in town had white people and black people sitting on the porch drinking coffee together—it had been a tongue-in-cheek remark, because the answer was none. She remembered telling Elizabeth that Magnolia Manor had two races of people, mixed to the point that you couldn't tell one from the other. She didn't think that it had ever mattered much to anyone except her, and she didn't think that it mattered much to her anymore. She had said that Richard was her half white or half black stepson—whichever way you want to look at it—they had spent the night together, they had talked a long time, and it had done more for her than all of the Sunday sermons that she had ever heard.

Springtime had been magnificent, but it had started to give way to summer. Yet, the transition from one season to the next had been as beautiful as the first welcomed blossoms of spring. All year long, the flowers and shrubbery in the yard had been at their finest—thanks to Jacob.

For a long time, Mrs. Miller had been having good days and bad days. However, somewhere between the changing of seasons, the good days had all gone away, and it had become time to let the bad ones go the way of dust in the wind. She had had enough.

Near her bedside stood her families—those that carried her heritage, and one that carried that of her husband. Then there were those that had been grandfathered in, because they had been there for so long. They were with her in her final hour, so that she wouldn't be alone.

All but Richard watched as Elizabeth slowly pulled the bed sheet up over Mrs. Miller's face. Richard had already left the mansion. Charles and Sophia had walked out to the back porch, and they could see him. Slowly, he walked down that gentle grade that at one time led to the bush harbor. Charles had asked Sophia if she thought that he should go and talk to him. She simply said, let him go.

The yard at Magnolia Manor had three rose bushes, one for Amanda, one for Annie, and one for Mr. Miller. Jacob had taken a piece of rootstock from the rose bush that had been planted for Mr. Miller, and he transplanted it next to the parent plant. Part of what had been his had become hers.

Mrs. Miller had never been a person that offered many apologies; such was not her style. Sophia remembered how she and Mrs. Miller had always butted heads—more accurately, they had hated each other—but long before she had died, ill feelings had long since ended. She supposed that Mrs. Miller had apologized many times—she had done so through Richard. Although there had been a time when they were sure that it would never happen, Sophia and Mrs. Miller had both experienced what it would feel like to put their arms around each other, and speak words of kindness.

Sophia had thought about herself. She had often told Elizabeth about how much she hated Mrs. Miller, but like Mrs. Miller, she too had never said I'm sorry. Then she hoped that Mrs. Miller had been able to interpret her requests for forgiveness by the things that she had done.

Sophia and Mrs. Miller were probably more alike than either had ever considered. Both were high-strung and strong minded with little or no constraints—Mrs.

Miller because she had been that way from day one, and Sophia no doubt due to the influence of Amanda, Caroline and Emily—Austin Miller could probably be included as well. Whatever the reason, they had both rubbed each other the wrong way for a long time, but in the end, they met in the middle, and they raise the white flag. Mrs. Miller probably had it right, "Things were just different at Magnolia Manor."

When Austin Miller died, Magnolia Manor had been weakened. When Mrs. Miller died, Magnolia Manor did too. Although having been continuously occupied, it remained empty, just a shell and a reminder of what used to be. Seemingly, having a mind of its' own, like it had been meant only for those that had lived there first, and wanting no others to follow—certainly hiding some secrets.

Today, still turning the heads of passersby, and like a slab of granite, slow to surrender to the forces of time, maybe because it had been well built, or maybe because time has been halted by the eerie powers of old ghosts that have been dead set against change. Eerie spirits whose charge has been to keep the present in the past by turning todays into yesterdays—toiling away to make it happen, but some still slipping past, because time is so relentless. They're the shadowy figures walking the line that separates reality from imagination as only they can do—not favoring either, but close enough to both to make us wonder. Could it be? Does anyone know for sure? Perhaps the answer is maybe ... just maybe.

Personal Notes From the Author

Sophia and Austin Miller were my great-grandparents. I suppose that I have reason enough to hate him, but I don't. Yet, I sometimes wonder why not.

Austin Miller raped my great-grandmother. Their son, Richard, is my grandfather. Had he not raped Sophia, then I would have never been born. Had I not been born, it couldn't matter to me, nor could it matter to anyone else, it would be impossible. Messed up as it is, and it's due to we the people, I am glad that I have experienced life on the planet earth.

When I use that rationale to justify not hating Austin Miller, then it seems like I am being selfish. It seems like I am saying that whatever he did to Sophia is alright if that's what it took to get me here. But it doesn't sound right.

Although it's over and done, and there's nothing that anyone can do to change things, I still find myself bogged down thinking about it. It's just a thought, but sometimes I feel like it's holding on to me and won't let go. It could be that it's not even worth thinking about, and it's just something that I let become an issue when I didn't have to. Maybe I should set myself free and forget it, let it fly the way of dust in the wind.

Made in the USA
San Bernardino, CA
23 August 2014